The
Administrative
State

The
Administrative
State

A Study of the Political Theory of American Public Administration

Dwight Waldo

With a new introduction by
Hugh T. Miller

Transaction Publishers
New Brunswick (U.S.A.) and London (U.K.)

Second printing 2007

New material this edition copyright © 2007 by Transaction Publishers, New Brunswick, New Jersey. Originally published in 1948 by The Ronald Press Company.

This book is printed on acid-free paper that meets the American National Standard for Permanence of Paper for Printed Library Materials.

Library of Congress Catalog Number: 2006044527
ISBN: 978-1-4128-0597-1
Printed in the United States of America

Library of Congress Cataloging-in-Publication Data
Waldo, Dwight.
  The administrative state: a study of the political theory of American public administration / Dwight Waldo; with a new introduction by Hugh T. Miller.
     p. cm.
  Originally published: New York: Ronald Press Co., [1948].
  Includes bibliographical references and index.
  ISBN 1-4128-0597-X (pbk. : alk. paper)   c,
  1. Public administration. 2. Public administration—United States.
  3. United States—Politics and government. 1. Title.

JF1351.W3   2006
351.73-dc22   2006044527

TO
MY PARENTS

CONTENTS

PART I

The Rise of Public Administration

PART II

Problems of Political Philosophy

PART III

Some Fundamental Concepts: A Critique

TRANSACTION INTRODUCTION

I. A Young Scholar from De Witt

Clifford Dwight Waldo was born in the small farming village of De Witt, Nebraska in 1913 and died in 2000 in Falls Church, Virginia.[1] In the span of those eighty-seven years he left an indelible mark on the field of public administration, as a prominent scholar at both the University of California, Berkeley, where he also served as director of the Institute of Governmental Studies, and Syracuse University until he retired in 1979. He served as editor of the *Public Administration Review* for eleven years and also served as president of the *National Association of Schools of Public Affairs and Administration.*

Waldo is widely regarded as the resident philosopher-historian of public administration.[2] His tremendous impact on the intellectual development of the field is evidenced by his many books and articles.[3] Remarkable, too, is the meaningful impact he has had on those he met along the way. After Waldo passed away in late 2000, one devotee wrote, "I wish to honor Dwight Waldo the person, and the best, perhaps the only way to do this is to describe what he has meant to me... There is little unique in such an account; what is unique is how many other persons could give similar accounts."[4] And, indeed, many have attested to Waldo's personal charm, gentleness, and nurturing encouragement over many years and in many venues.

After receiving his B.A. from Nebraska State Teacher's College, Waldo went on to earn a master's degree in political science at the University of Nebraska. With M.A. in hand, he left the Midwest for Yale University to earn his Ph.D., writing a doctoral dissertation that was, with suitable editing, to become *The Administrative State.* The original working title of that dissertation was *Ideas of Expertise in the Democratic Tradition.* Francis W. Coker, whose work had attracted Waldo to Yale in the first place, served as chair of the dissertation committee. When successfully defended in 1942, the dissertation was titled *Theoretical Aspects of the Literature of Public Administration.* In it, Waldo discerned an emerging political role for administration based on expertise not easily reconciled with the egalitarianism of democratic theory. Waldo wanted public administration to be effective and useful; at the same time he wanted to show that the literature of public administration "had a matrix of political theory."[5]

His first job out of the academy was at the Office of Price Administration in Washington, D.C. This experience in the practical affairs of government had an effect on Waldo:

> No month of my life has been as educational as my first in Washington, in which I was responsible for planning and executing the relatively small "mechanical" task of moving the Consumer Durable Goods Price Branch of O.P.A. from one building to another.... Ever since my Washington years I have regarded it as appalling that it is permitted to teach Political Science without any significant experience in public affairs...[6]

It was during that experience that Waldo developed "a very wholesome respect for the difficulties of administration."[7] In 1946, World War II was over and Waldo joined the political science faculty of the University of California, Berkeley (where he wryly recalled that he taught courses in every division of the curriculum *except* political theory). In 1948 *The Administrative State* was published. It was critically reviewed in *Public Administration Review* by Arthur Macmahon, who wrote that "Waldo's own viewpoint in developing his critique is somewhat ambiguous and his prescription a bit cloudy."[8] James Fesler, in a short review in *American Political Science Review*, extolled the challenge posed to the field of public administration by Waldo: "Premises should not go unchallenged. Professor Waldo has formulated the long-needed challenge, and the result should be a more soundly grounded literature of public administration."[9] Reflecting back on his book seventeen years later, Waldo wrote that "luck led me to a project that was 'different,' the project was executed with thoroughness, the project was one for which the time was ripe, and the impact of the book was important to the discipline."[10]

Gary Wamsley, long-time editor of *Administration & Society*, reflected the opinion of many admirers of Waldo's work when he wrote, "I am prepared to argue that his book *The Administrative State* is the most important book ever written on American public administration."[11]

II. *The Administrative State* in the Field of Public Administration

There was a style of thinking in public administration that posed obstacles to the sort of theorizing Waldo sought to nourish. Administration was thought to be the *business of government* and so the close attention to the values of scientific management distracted the imagination away from the values of political democracy. Efficiency was valued; pluralism was not. The harmony of a unified administration would accomplish more than would the discord of political contestation, according to prevailing norms. Hence, the world of task accomplishment was hard to reconcile with the world of democratic politics, but Waldo thought public administration ought to give it a try anyway, because so much is at stake.

But even in the academy, intellectuals such as Herbert Simon and Peter Drucker resisted Waldo's political theorizing. Behaviorist/positivist thinking and managerial thought were of a different mind, and these schools gained the upper hand in public administration curricula despite Waldo's efforts. The signpost of the difficulty that Waldo, and all political theorists, would have in gaining traction for theorizing democratic public administration came four years after *The Administrative State* was published.

First, an article by Waldo appeared in the *American Political Science Review* titled "Development of Theory of Democratic Administration," taking up some of the same themes of *The Administrative State*. Then, in the next issue, both Simon and Drucker responded; Waldo's rejoinder was also published.

Waldo's controversial essay expressed a point of view that democratic theorists should embrace administration, as administration is the core of modern government. The essay included a critique of past theorists, a survey of new theory that seemed to possess democratic possibilities, and one sentence about Waldo's own definition of democratic administration: "[This essay] assumes the central meaning of democracy to lie in an ethic, a set of values."[12] The values he mentioned as possible candidates—equality, liberty, and fraternity—were borrowed from the French revolution.

Simon's response set a bold and aggressive tone in behaviorism/positivism's confrontation with political theory when he wrote in the first paragraph that "the faults of Waldo's analysis are characteristic of the writing of those who call themselves 'political theorists'..."[13] The dismissiveness of not only Waldo but also political theory in general may seem narrowly simplistic in retrospect. At the time it was effective in 1) contributing to the isolation and exclusion of political-theoretical concerns in the public administration curriculum, and 2) broadening the preference among the professoriate for analytical techniques and pragmatic methodologies stylized with the look of science.

Waldo at first rejoins Simon with the same tone of voice, showing that he can dish it out, too:

> Professor Simon charges me with profaning the sacred places of Logical Positivism, and I am afraid I have. I use this figure of speech because Professor Simon seems to me that rare individual in our secular age, a man of deep faith. His convictions are monolithic and massive. His toleration of heresy and sin is nil. The Road to Salvation is straight, narrow, one-way, and privately owned. We must humbly confess our sins, accept the Word, be washed pure in the Blood of Carnap and Ayer. Then, he says, we will no longer be "enemies."[14]

Waldo seemed to enjoy the sport of it all, but he changed his tone by the end of his rejoinder. A dogmatist would not write, as Waldo did, "I don't *think* that the distinction between 'decision' and 'judgment,' however important to a logical positivist, is more than a quibble from the viewpoint of my argument. But I may be mistaken; I often am. I may change my mind; I sometimes do."[15] Waldo consistently urged that public administrationists open themselves up to the possibility of *democratic heresy* against the fictions of neutrality and administrative science. Modeling a closed mind would hardly pry open the minds of others.

What, then, could account for Simon's aggressive posture? Well, in his essay, Waldo was rather critical of the "American worship of science":

> In short, the theory and practice of private administration were shaped in a context that was in very important aspects undemocratic. The rights of property and the power of management were overwhelming... Private administration absorbed a spirit both of cold, scientific self-calculation and of condescending good will toward the employee. Both of these qualities are clearly evident at the dawn of the movement in the work of Frederick W. Taylor at Midvale Steel. It is hardly too much to say that Taylor regarded his laborers as draft animals.[16]

This science-worship ethos was thought by Waldo to be derivative of business administration where "the rights of property and the power of management were overwhelming."[17] The infusion into public administration of business values along with a particular sort of scientific stylization introduced a spirit of cold calculation as well as condescension toward employees. He was critical of Luther Gulick's hierarchical, executive-unification themes—and the efficiency value used to justify such proposals—because of their dismissal or externalization of democratic values. Gulick and other like-minded theorists "became ambivalent, schizoid, seeking ardently to advance democracy by denying its relevance to the administrative process."[18]

"Happily," declared Waldo, "various developments in recent years have cleared the ground and laid the foundation for major developments of democratic administrative theory, if we choose to push forward."[19] The demise of the politics-administration dichotomy was one such development. Another was the rejection of efficiency as the central concept of administrative study. While not as unequivocal as the rejection of the politics-administration dichotomy, Waldo noted a general trend, Simon's *Administrative Behavior* notwithstanding, to deemphasize, broaden, socialize, and even reject the concept of efficiency.

That alone might not have raised Simon's ire, but later in Waldo's essay a zinger is sent flying: "To maintain that efficiency is value-neutral and to propose at the same time that it be used as the central concept in a 'science' of administration is to commit one's self to nihilism, so long as the prescription is actually followed."[20] Then, in a footnote to this passage, he attaches this criticism to Simon by asserting that there is no realm of factual decisions from which values are excluded. Finally, Waldo speculates on how this particular roadblock to democratic administration can be removed. "Increasingly we must ask ourselves not merely, 'What is the efficiency of our means for our ends?' but, in addition, 'What are the implications of our ends for our use of means—and hence for our measurement of efficiency?' We need a fundamental reexamination of the ends-means complex, in which it is recognized that the choice and use of means has implication for the ends."[21]

The intellectual differences that Simon and Waldo expressed reverberated throughout the field of public administration and endure to this day. For Waldo, Simon symbolized but one intellectual challenge.

Drucker's response praised Waldo's article as a "tremendous contribution."[22] Drucker, too, was interested in framing the internal structure of a large organization as a field for political theory. But Drucker chides Waldo for his failure to mention trade unions, and expressed skepticism about the prospects for democracy in organizations. Waldo is accused of using a loose construction of the term democracy, "in effect nothing else than what the popular newspapers mean when they call the King of Norway 'democratic' because he rides his bicycle through the streets of Oslo... 'Participation' then becomes the *tool* of efficient administration—a psychological gadget, if not, ultimately a tool to obscure the reality of power and of decision-making."[23]

In promoting his own idea of self-governing plant communities, Drucker notes the problematic nature of employee involvement in the decision-making process. Is participation a means of obtaining consent, and therefore likely to degenerate into semantics and propaganda? Drucker writes that "Professor Waldo, in not focusing on actual decision-making, is likely to come out exactly where the social scientists, whom he rightly criticizes, come out: in a lot of talk about 'democracy' but in very little actual self-government and responsibility."[24]

Waldo responds in kind to Drucker. "To me, he says, democracy means 'participation,' which readily 'becomes the tool of efficient management—a psychological gadget.' Now that is the manner in which, I tried gently to suggest, his 'self-governing plant community' appears to me: as a psychological sop, another way of keeping employees ('subjects') happy and out of the hair of management."[25]

In the end, both Drucker and Simon earned international reputations that exceeded that of Waldo. Their messages of efficiency and managerialism better suited the worldview of twentieth-century modernity. But Waldo was a brave warrior for political theory of public administration, and an advocate for democracy as well. He expressed his ideas persuasively, in the disciplined mode of a political philosopher, which made the challenge all the more compelling in the public administration literature.

III. Waldo's Disturbing Ideas

When *The Administrative State* was reviewed in 1948, there was immediate recognition that something unsettling was taking place. First and most obvious, if the administrative state constitutes the core of modern government, as many scholars of the day were coming to believe, then questions arise as to its democratic characteristics. Waldo's courage in calling into question the self-evidence of scientific facticity was surpassed by the way he called into question democratic self-evidence. In reading the following passage from Macmahon's 1948 review, we can see that his tracking of Waldo's line of thinking leads him to an indignant defense of the legislature.

> A study like public administration is properly normative. And one of the norms it sets is to insist upon the desirability of structural and procedural arrangements which cherish both fluent politics and permanent administration and which seek to isolate major decisions for approval after discussion by the kind of organ we call legislature. Difficulties and discrepancies are not a rebuttal.[26]

Here Macmahon affirms the implications of Waldo's work for normative political theory, but proceeds to insist that status quo arrangements are the only desirable ones. That the system is not working would not count as a rebuttal, according to Macmahon. This dogmatic move highlights the problem of traveling with Waldo: In critiquing the administrative state, one must also, implicitly, critique the representative model of electoral democracy celebrated in the United States. This requires finesse, more so in 1948 than in recent years.

Eventually in public administration it became acceptable to challenge the veracity of such a claim to incorrigibility. Whether during electoral campaigns or in anticipation of the next national opinion poll, voters' wants, needs, and perceptions are manipulated. Candidates do not ordinarily compete for office on the basis of complex policy alternatives, but on the success of the *image*, as constructed by teams of campaign consultants and style coaches. In some elections, the majority of voters do not vote; those who do may be motivated by single-issue considerations. After the elections are over, the lobbyists, special interest organizations, deep-pocket corporations, and close-knit policy communities get busy generating contrived and sometimes incoherent public policy that changes the rules to favor some group or channels lucrative contracts to another. Only occasionally is the public made aware of the boondoggles—usually via screechy headlines that are quickly displaced by the next day's alarming development.

But public administration, Macmahon asserted, must insist upon the status quo institutional arrangements of representative democracy. Difficulties and discrepancies, he said, are not rebuttal. It is as though we are being asked by Waldo's critics to look the other way and not pay attention to widely acknowledged problems. Challenges to status quo structures are thus given short shrift in the public administration literature—except for those "democratic heresies" to which Waldo was drawn.

Administrative hierarchy, centralization, and rule by scientifically trained experts are self-evidently undemocratic. In his critiques of science and scientific management, Waldo managed to call into question the status of presumably neutral facts, a query that carries with it far-reaching ramifications for public sector knowledge. Though Waldo eschewed the instrumentalism of pragmatism and narrow, fact-based empiricism, he also distanced himself from the sort of one-size-fits-all public administration entailed in principles such as unity of command or span of control. The consequence was a historically informed sensitivity to the contingent. These enduring yet unsettling theoretical vectors will be considered next: first contextualism, followed by the status of a fact, and concluding with Waldo's challenge to managerialism as political theory.

1. **Contextualism.**—When Waldo complained of the inapplicability of the established techniques of science to valuing, thinking human beings, he recontextualized public administration. It does not exist in the world of objective reality, where cause-and-effect theoretical statements are verified through empirical observation; public administration is instead informed by political purposes, value pluralism, and contingent intentions. For Waldo, a mature and sophisticated public administration abandons general principles and takes into account ideas and purposes instead. Public administration is oriented to values, not facts, even when it cannot clearly see or state them. It would be a fallacy to assume that "what to do" statements can be gleaned from fact statements alone.

Before the facts come into view, human beings already have their purposes and projects. Not only observations, but abilities and intentions are entailed in contextual understanding. Humans generate history and tradition; in any present context, humans may be able to break with that tradition, may be able to criticize it, may be able to dissolve it, or may be able to remake the real according to new purposes. Tradition and society are maintained and transformed as, eventually, new purposes become enacted, reenacted, and settled into habitual practice—thereby generating a different set of worldly facts.

2. Status of a Fact.—There is no such thing as a fact apart from ideas or purposes to which that fact is attached, according to Waldo. The data never speak for themselves. There is no reality "as such." There is no fact "as such." Most importantly, there is no public administration "as such." Instead, there is a cultural context that collects, arranges, endorses, and distills the facts of public administration.

Further, modern science is more than a fact-gathering activity; it is, as Michel Foucault would claim twenty-one years later, an episteme.[27] Science is the reigning regime of discourse, the language of normalcy in modern society. Despite its claims to neutrality, it is imbued with intentions, values, and culture. There is nothing neutral about this fact.

And yet in the field of public administration a widely prevalent view is that outcomes can be measured as if the field were in possession of a mirror that accurately reflects the objective world. There is an assumption that results can be reported as if human senses, enhanced by the technologies and instruments of measurement, could leap the gap between things and the names we give them; as if performance can be assessed using variables and indicators that exactly correspond to reality. Public administration accepts narrow definitions of itself when it requires everything it does—its purposes, functions, processes, meanings, impacts, roles, relationships, and effects—to be reduced to measurable outcomes that demonstrate results. The limitations of the capacity of an indicator to measure the real have only become more clear and obvious since *The Administrative State* was first published, although this dilemma is denied or ignored today just as it was then.

Waldo's interrogation of the self-evidence of the fact was accompanied by his calling into question the democratic self-evidence of public administration.

3. Managerialism as Political Theory.—Waldo welcomed countertrends away from centralization, efficiency, scientism, and instrumental-rationalism and toward pluralism and democracy with enthusiasm and (probably unwarranted) optimism. Authoritarian ideas about human organization roused his ire. Max Weber painted a good picture of his and our own day, but the democratic theorist "must refuse to believe this is the prettiest picture of all pictures," Waldo cautioned.[28] Instead of following Weber, Waldo sought to affirm the theorists who in various ways and with varying success wrote on behalf of a democratic public administration.

Waldo's most consistent theme, then, was to theorize public administration's place in a democracy. On the face of it, the bureaucratic form does not appear to be democratic. Yet public administration, we should all agree, is done in the name of democracy. Waldo did not join the business-methods bandwagon; nor would he have endorsed an expansion of bureaucratic power without reflecting in depth about this new "ruling group." No mere tool of the legislature, the administrators who inhabit the administrative state constitute a political force in their own right. Waldo forced public administration to think of itself as a problem for political theory, but public administration did not necessarily want to be forced to look at itself this way.

To get public administration to take on these theoretical and democratic concerns, Waldo cajoled, persuaded, urged, and encouraged. On rare occasions he would go so far as to send forth a deliberate affront to his colleagues in the academy. Repeating Lane Lancaster's characterization, Waldo endorsed a sense that the public administration literature is "dull pretentious nonsense. It has a disposition toward manmade harmony. Its pretentiousness comes in getting away from cloud gazing (theory) and getting about the hard important business of how modern government does and should perform its function."[29] The public administration literature pretends it has no political theory and therefore narrows its scope overmuch, making for unnecessarily dull reading. Another way of putting it is that public administration is often not a self-aware discipline. The literature tends not to apprehend its own partiality. It does not step back from itself sufficiently to see its own perspective as a perspective. Yet, Waldo would also contend, the public administration literature does convey an important political theory, even though the authors of it are typically not consciously trying to theorize. He refused to join with any assertion of public administration's claim to neutrality. He was among those who could see quite clearly that expertise was not merely a claim of technical competence; it was a claim to power.

How much democracy should a society yield to expertise? The question for Waldo was not an either/or proposition, as both democracy and expertise deserve due consideration. The advance of specialization and the spin-off of new occupations and areas of expertise continued to grow as modern industrial society grew. Waldo wanted this issue to be faced head-on; a claim to expertise could not also be a claim to neutrality.

Yet there is no neutrality, not even for the typewriter, as Waldo amusingly demonstrated.[30] The typewriter is a thing found in western industrial culture and is something that is not found in many other cultures. It is a sign of a way of life. It uses materials such as steel, rubber, plastics, and chemicals, which are all signatures of industrial society. As someone who was keenly aware of cultural context, Waldo also noted that keys on a typewriter bear linguistic symbols for some languages and not for others. Importantly, the typewriter presupposes the presence of typists, whose expertise is not neutral in any culturally meaningful sense. All these years later, now that the typewriter has gone the way of the record player, it is easy to apprehend the cultural contingency of the typewriter, which is precisely the point that Waldo was making about all claims to neutrality.

Nor is it a neutral moment—it is a political moment—when public administration adopts business practices. Public administration is insufficiently aware of the suffusion of business values into its literature, according to Waldo, and was even less concerned with the profound effect of business on the larger culture. His criticisms did not amount to a call to action—to overthrow the bourgeoisie, for example. Rather it was a call to awareness of the link between powerful business institutions and cultural practices. To this day, public administration gobbles up business-style practices such as contracting-out, reinventing government, load-shedding, and privatization. Limited government has been the watchword of political decision-makers, and it is imbued with political signification.

Scholars in the field no longer wish to avoid political theory of public administration. Theory problems are celebrated and investigated in various venues, journals, books, and conferences as public administration theory attracts the interest and energy of scholars around the world. To many, Dwight Waldo is a pathbreaker. Hence, it would be a mistake to dismiss Waldo as a mere critic of public administration—he was a visionary philosopher of the role of public administration in politics, in society, in history, in culture, and in civilization.

Hugh T. Miller

Notes

[1] The best biography of Dwight Waldo is Brack Brown and Richard J. Stillman II, 1986, *A Search for Public Administration: The Ideas and Career of Dwight Waldo*, College Station, Texas: Texas A&M University Press.

[2] Frank Marini, 1993, "Leaders in the Field: Dwight Waldo," *Public Administration Review*, *53* (5): 409-418.

[3] Again, see Brown and Stillman. This book contains a thorough bibliography of Waldo's scholarly contributions.

[4] Gary Wamsley, 2001, "Reflections on the Passing of Dwight Waldo," *Administration & Society*, *33* (3): 247-250. Quotation is from page 247.

[5] Dwight Waldo, 1965, "The Administrative State Revisited." *Public Administration Review*, *25* (1): 5-30. Quotation is from page 6.

[6] Ibid., p. 6.

[7] Ibid.

[8] Arthur W. Macmahon, 1948, "Reviews of Books and Documents: *The Administrative State*." *Public Administrative Review*, *8* (3): 203-311. Quotation is from page 210.

[9] James W. Fesler, 1948, "Book Reviews and Notices: *The Administrative State*." *American Political Science Review*, *42* (4): 782-783. Quotation is from page 783.

[10] Waldo, "The Administrative State Revisited," p. 7.

[11] Wamsley, "Reflections on the Passing of Dwight Waldo," p. 247.

[12] Dwight Waldo, 1952, "Development of Theory of Democratic Administration," *American Political Science Review*, *46* (1): 81-103. Quotation is from page 82.

[13] Herbert A. Simon, 1952, Part I of Herbert A. Simon, Peter F. Drucker, and Dwight Waldo, "'Development of Theory of Democratic Administration' Replies and Comments." *American Political Science Review*, *46* (2): 494-503. Quotation is from page 494.

[14] Dwight Waldo, 1952, Part III of Herbert A. Simon, Peter F. Drucker, and Dwight Waldo, "'Development of Theory of Democratic Administration' Replies and Comments." *American Political Science Review*, *46* (2): 494-503. Quotation is from page 501.

[15] Ibid., p. 503.

[16] Waldo, "Development of Theory of Democratic Administration," p. 83.

[17] Ibid., p. 83.

[18] Ibid., p. 85. Even here Waldo was not totally unsympathetic, noting that in its formative years public administration was characterized by disorganization, haphazardness, amateurism, and dishonesty.

[19] Ibid., p. 87.

[20] Ibid., p. 97.

[21] Ibid., p. 99.

[22] Peter F. Drucker, 1952, Part II of Herbert A. Simon, Peter F. Drucker, and Dwight Waldo, "'Development of Theory of Democratic Administration' Replies and Comments." *American Political Science Review, 46* (2): 494-503.

[23] Ibid., p. 497.

[24] Ibid., p. 500.

[25] Waldo, Part III of Simon, Drucker, and Waldo (1952), p. 600.

[26] Macmahon, "Reviews of Books and Documents: *The Administrative State*" pp. 207-208.

[27] Michel Foucault, 1972, *The Archaeology of Knowledge and the Discourse on Language,* translated by A. M. Sheridan Smith, New York: Pantheon Books.

[28] Ibid., p. 100.

[29] Waldo, "The Administrative State Reconsidered," p. 6.

[30] Ibid., p. 15.

References

Brown, Brack and Richard J. Stillman II. 1986. *A Search for Public Administration: The Ideas and Career of Dwight Waldo.* College Station, Texas: Texas A&M University Press.

Fesler, James W. 1948. "Book Reviews and Notices: *The Administrative State.*" *American Political Science Review, 42* (4): 782-783.

Foucault, Michel. 1972. *The Archaeology of Knowledge and the Discourse on Language,* translated by A. M. Sheridan Smith. New York: Pantheon Books.

Macmahon, Arthur W. 1948. "Reviews of Books and Documents: *The Administrative State.*" *Public Administrative Review, 8* (3): 203-311.

Marini, Frank. 1993. "Leaders in the Field: Dwight Waldo." *Public Administration Review, 53* (5): 409-418.

Simon, Herbert A., Peter F. Drucker, and Dwight Waldo. 1952. "'Development of Theory of Democratic Administration' Replies and Comments." *American Political Science Review, 46* (2): 494-503.

Waldo, Dwight. 1952. "Development of Theory of Democratic Administration." *American Political Science Review, 46* (1): 81-103.

Waldo, Dwight. 1965. "The Administrative State Revisited." *Public Administration Review, 25* (1): 5-30.

Wamsley, Gary, 2001, "Reflections on the Passing of Dwight Waldo." *Administration & Society, 33* (3): 247-250.

PREFACE

This is a study of the public administration movement from the viewpoint of political theory and the history of ideas. It seeks to review and analyze the theoretical element in administrative writings and to present the development of the public administration movement as a chapter in the history of American political thought.

The objectives of this study are to assist students of administration to view their subject in historical perspective and to appraise the theoretical content of their literature. It is also hoped that this book may assist students of American culture by illuminating an important development of the last half century. It thus should serve political scientists whose interests lie in the field of public administration or in the study of bureaucracy as a political issue; the public administrator interested in the philosophic background of his service; and the historian who seeks an understanding of recent major governmental developments. The book should have value in college courses that cover these fields, and in political science, public administration, and history libraries.

There is something paradoxical in a study of the theories of a group of writers who until recently have been indifferent or hostile to "theory." These administrative writers have always supposed that they were concerned only with facts. The text nevertheless should demonstrate that they have been involved with theory in numerous and important ways. It is true that we cannot explain the beliefs and activities of these administrative students simply in terms of "currents" and "influences"; clearly, the facts to which the literature is a response are more important. But it is equally true that the literature of public administration is related to the thought of a particular time and place, has recognizable theoretical sources and tendencies, and bears the virtues and vices of the theories which it accepts as its own.

This study is based upon the various books, articles, pamphlets, reports, and documents which make up the literature of public administration. Since, however, the boundaries of "public administration" are not fixed, difficult problems of inclusion and exclusion exist. Two general rules have been followed in determining the limits of

the study: to indicate deviations from the "norms" as well as the norms, and to let the "sense of the situation" determine in cases of doubt. There is no attempt to present a history of American administrative practice; that task has been well done by Leonard D. White and others.

A word about my assumptions. Although I share with students of administration many of their beliefs, I have set myself the role of critic and have found in other doctrines what I believe are sound bases of criticism for many theories that public administration has accepted. If I seem sometimes not merely eclectic in my philosophy but opportunistic in my criticism, my defense must be Philip Guedalla's "Any stigma to beat a dogma!"

The author first undertook the study of this subject in partial fulfillment of the requirements for the degree of Doctor of Philosophy at Yale University. This volume, a somewhat condensed revision of that research, has been brought up to date by reference to much new material—for at present the horizons of public administration are broadening swiftly. In this rapid extension of the study of public administration, and of the movement itself, a great deal of importance has happened that is not yet reflected in print. Clearly aware of this condition, I regret that in this study there can be no pretense to inclusiveness beyond the published material in the field.

It is small repayment but a great pleasure to acknowledge the assistance of my friends. Among my teachers I am in the debt of Francis W. Coker, who advised and assisted at every stage of the study; of Harvey C. Mansfield, who read and criticized most of the original manuscript; and of Cecil H. Driver, who contributed much to the conceptual framework of the study. Various of my friends, particularly Harold Seidman and Hubert H. Hinshaw, aided with advice and criticism. Many prominent students of administration responded generously to my requests for information. Responsibility for the final form of the study is, of course, strictly my own.

D. W.

Berkeley, Summer, 1947.

PART I
THE RISE OF PUBLIC ADMINISTRATION

Chapter 1

THE MATERIAL AND IDEOLOGICAL
BACKGROUND

If they are to be understood, political theories must be construed
in relation to their material environment and ideological framework.
The political theories of American public administration are not
exceptions. For, despite occasional claims that public administration
is a science with principles of universal validity, American public
administration has evolved political theories unmistakably related to
unique economic, social, governmental, and ideological facts.

The Material Background

Among the factors that clearly have affected the form and content of American literature on public administration are the advent
of the Great Society, the closing of the frontier and the waste of
our natural resources, our tremendous wealth and our Business
Civilization, the "corporate revolution" and the evolution of new
corporate forms, urbanization, our peculiar constitutional and political system, the "second phase of the industrial revolution," the
increase in specialization and professionalism and the rise of American scholarship, and the Great Wars, the Great Prosperity, and the
Great Depression.[1]

The Great Society.—Whatever else it may be, "public adminis-
tion" is a response on the part of its creators to the modern world
that Graham Wallas has named the Great Society.

The text of Woodrow Wilson's early essay, "The Study of
Administration," was that "it is getting to be harder to *run* a constitution than to frame one." [2] This classic of administrative writing

---

[1] L. D. White's *Trends in Public Administration* (New York: 1933) records
the influence of some of these factors upon administrative practice (as distinguished
from writings about administration). See J. M. Gaus' *Study of Research in Public
Administration* (New York: 1930—mimeographed), ch. I; and his excellent essay
"Changes in the Setting, 1930–1944," in *Research in Public Administration* (Chicago: 1945), William Anderson and J. M. Gaus, for trends in the study of administration in relation to events and ideas.

[2] In 2 *Pol. Sci. Q.* (June, 1887), 197–222, 200. This is not the first American
work upon the subject of administration—Henry Adams' and Dorman B. **Eaton's**

3

appeared contemporaneously with the Interstate Commerce Act, and the coincidence is significant. The establishment of the Interstate Commerce Commission signalized the passage of the United States from a simple, agricultural society into a highly complex and inter-related Great Society. This new society was based upon a highly advanced division of labor and specialization of skill, a highly developed system of transportation and communication, a vast, sprawling technology—all based upon a new method of controlling environment called "scientific method."

American writers on public administration have accepted the inevitability and the desirability of the Great Society—with minor differences and with reservations as to detail. The importance of this acceptance cannot be overestimated. The most significant facts about any era to subsequent generations are likely to be precisely the ones accepted as unquestioningly as the fish accepts water. The "acceptance" of the Great Society by writers on public administration is quite as important as their various assertions—more so, since their assertions flow from this acceptance. They have not only accepted the Great Society; they have accepted the obligation to remedy its deficiencies and to make it a Good Society. This need not have been the case. Jefferson or Thoreau, William Morris or Tolstoi, presumably would not find the arguments of the administrative writers compelling.

Closing of the Frontier.—The economic and social readjustments attendant upon the closing of the frontier, and the prodigious waste of our natural resources that continued into the new period of consolidation, stimulated writing on public administration and determined its direction. The economic and political formulae of classical economics became, perhaps, a useful Myth for the period in which they were elaborated; many people found them helpful and they produced some manifest blessings. But the postulate that there is a harmony of nature, which if undisturbed would be productive of the greatest good of the greatest number, lost its appeal for many thoughtful and sensitive people with the passing of time and the altering of circumstances. The increasing ratio of population to resources, the vastness of waste and confusion, the failure of the traditional ways to produce a tolerable life for large numbers of our population even in the midst of plenty—these led an ever-

---

writings on civil service reform, for example, preceded it. Even the Founding Fathers devoted essays to administrative problems. But Wilson's essay inaugurates the period in which public administration was gradually to become conscious of itself as a distinct activity and inquiry.

increasing number of academic, literary, and civic-minded people to abandon the old faith in a natural harmony in favor of a new ideal: that of a man-made harmony. That eminent work of the Progressive period, Herbert Croly's *Promise of American Life,* may be taken as the symbol of the decision of a considerable number of citizens that we could no longer rely simply upon great natural wealth and complete individual freedom to fulfill the American dream of economic independence. The validity of the ideal of a man-made harmony, created for the most part through the instrumentality of governmental bureaucracies, has almost universally been assumed by writers on public administration—else why should they write of public administration except to damn it?

The importance of the conservation movement in hastening and confirming the adoption of this new viewpoint was apparently very great. The idea of saving natural resources soon developed into a social philosophy—saving human beings; and ultimately into the idea of a "planned" and "administered" human community. The ferment of the conservation idea is easily discernible in the early journals,[3] and while "conservation" is no longer a popular word among writers on public administration, its meaning has been absorbed into new terminology.

Our Business Civilization.—Despite increasing pressure of population on resources and continuing prodigality in the use of resources, America remained a uniquely wealthy country, and ours became characteristically a Business Civilization. This has influenced our methods of administration and our literature of public administration.[4] It has been generally "business" that has given support to the study of public administration—in research bureaus, professional associations, the colleges and universities, and regular or *ad hoc* administrative agencies. Labor, agriculture, the older professions, and "consumers" have not been as much concerned about it. Naturally, therefore, the results reflect business beliefs and practices. ("Pressures" need not be presumed.) The paternalism, the "benevolent Feudalism" of business have been reproduced in public administration. Although the *Report* of the President's Committee on Administrative Management was generally displeasing

---

[3] See, for example, "Conservation in Municipalities," by W. D. Foulke, *Proceedings of the Buffalo Conference for Good City Government* (National Municipal League), 1910, 12–21.

[4] This has received considerable attention, of course. See, for example, L. D. White, "Public Administration," in *Recent Social Trends* (New York: 1933), 1391–1429, 1426.

to the business community, future historians will record that it mirrored rather faithfully the form and spirit of current business thought on organization and management.

It is important also that the rise of public administration occurred during the golden age of private charity. In the past fifty years billions of dollars have been contributed, chiefly by the business community, to found and support dozens of activities which in other civilized countries are undertaken by the State. But for this golden flood and the opposition of the business community to the extension of governmental functions, many domains of activity would have fallen under public control much sooner than they have, or promise to be, and the problems of their administration thus posed and considered earlier. So, while business has stimulated and supported administrative study, it must be presumed that it nevertheless has reduced the amount and scope of speculation on the subject.

The Modern Corporation.—The dependence of public administration on its business background has been furthered by the influence of the "corporate revolution" and the resulting emphasis on forms of organization characteristic of business corporations. Since the appearance of Berle and Means' modern classic, *The Modern Corporation and Private Property,* we have become increasingly aware of the massive economic organizations that present the scene and even write the plot for the drama of our lives. Demonstrably, the corporation, both in its "private" and in its "public" varieties, has influenced our administrative thought, just as the institutions of the fief and the guild influenced medieval political thought.

As a device for managing municipal affairs or carrying out colonizing ventures the corporation has a long administrative history, but recent decades have witnessed the extension of its use to new fields and, to look no further than this country, a profusion of new types. Since 1900 the federal government has used the corporate form for dozens of differing activities, with the greatest variety in such matters as origin of charter, corporate powers and administrative organization; and states have pioneered in using the corporate expedient in interstate administration and in the building and management of such enterprises as toll bridges and roads. These developments have produced a considerable number of descriptive, legal, and evaluative writings.

The most interesting aspect of the influence of the corporate form lies in the fact that it has produced a literature of both centralization and decentralization. The example of private corporate practice has been one of the favorite weapons in the dialectic armory of those who have been interested in deprecating legislative or judicial influence and in aggrandizing executive power. On the other hand a number of persons have found in the practices of corporate interrelationships a hope that society can be planned and managed in the requisite degree without the disadvantages and dangers of great concentration of authority; that widespread public control and central direction can be combined with devolution in management and a democratic, "grass-roots" administration.

Coming of Urbanization.—The passing of the United States from a predominantly rural to a predominantly urban mode of life has recorded itself in the literature of public administration. This literature, in fact, is one of the forms in which the reconciliation of the old American ideal, Democracy, has been made with the new American condition, Urbanization. Democracy may not be as fervent an ideal today as it was in the Gilded Age, but the fear of great numbers of our citizens who surveyed the "City Wilderness" and were sick at heart at what was manifest from South End to Nob Hill, the fear that the destruction of democracy and its ideal was imminent, has been in considerable measure met and overcome by advances in administrative practice and by the assurances of administrative writers.[5] The American ideal has, in fact, become predominantly an urban ideal, with its emphasis upon the material and spiritual satisfactions of a city civilization. American writers on public administration have not only accepted this interpretation of the Good Life but have zealously crusaded for it.[6] To Reorganizers, those who prefer their state or county unreorganized are not only certainly mistaken and perhaps wicked: they are stupid and uncouth. Like Mill's barbarians, despotism is a legitimate mode of dealing with them until they have advanced sufficiently to profit by rational discussion!

Our Constitutional System.—Public administration has of course been conditioned in diverse ways by the peculiarities of our constitutional and political systems. For example, our unique interpretation and strong institutionalization of the theory of the separation of

---

[5] Early works on municipal government display both the fear and the hope. D. F. Wilcox' *The American City: A Problem in Democracy* (New York: 1904) is a strong statement of the necessity of reconciling urbanism with democracy.

[6] See J. B. Shannon in "County Consolidation," 207 *Annals* (January, 1940), 168–175, 168, for some interesting comments upon the urban bias of American writers on public administration.

powers, and our federal system, have created administrative problems that administrative students have sought to deal with by developing a philosophy of integration and simplification. The need for integration, in fact, has seemed so urgent that with many the "canons of integration" gained the status of universals.

It may be noted also that the separation and division of power and the lack of a strong tradition of administrative action have contributed to the proliferation of organizations of private citizens, and of public servants acting more or less in their private capacities, in order that certain functions may be performed that are carried out directly by the bureaucracies in some other highly developed nations. This "private" nature of American public administration has posed problems of the proper division of function between public and private administration and of the proper relation between autonomous or semi-autonomous organizations and the state structure.

It may also be noted that our institutional framework was partly responsible for the rise of the "spoils system," which has retarded the advance of effective administration and the rise of a tradition of government service by the "best." The fact that we have not developed a strong tradition of service by any particular intellectual, social, or educational type has invited speculative writing on the nature of administrative functions; on the problem of who should perform them, how they should be selected, and how trained—a field of much controversy.

Second Phase of the Industrial Revolution.—What has been called "the second phase of the industrial revolution" has reflected itself in American writings on public administration. Toward the close of the nineteenth century, when productive capacity began to exceed the capacity of available markets to absorb goods at productive prices, emphasis shifted from securing capital and enlarging facilities to raising profits by more effective use of productive equipment—machines and men. The chief result of this change in emphasis was the "scientific management" movement. Beginning with Frederick W. Taylor's attempt to overcome "soldiering" among laborers and his study of the variables involved in steel-cutting operations, scientific management spread upward under the spur of profit and the aegis of science, and outward under the prestige of American mass-production methods until it became an international philosophy with a vision of a New Order—one of the most interesting and distinctive social philosophies developed in modern times.[7]

---

[7] On the relationship of Taylor to the "second industrial revolution" see W. E. Atkins, "Frederick Winslow Taylor," 14 *Encyc. Soc. Sci.*, 542.

About 1910 scientific management began to be introduced into some branches of public administration, and to percolate among the students in their bureaus and schools. Today, no realm of administration has been left untouched, however lightly, by the new spirit; and some bureaus give lessons in efficiency to business. Perhaps as much as any other one thing, the "management" movement has molded the outlook of those to whom public administration is an independent inquiry or definable discipline.

Advance of Specialization.—The course which American study of public administration has taken is also a function of the very great increase in specialization which has featured our recent national life; particularly the rise of American scholarship and the growth of professional spirit and organizations. Few social and intellectual events in the history of the world have been more remarkable than the change, in the space of a generation, from the jack-of-all-trades pioneer-yeoman as a general type and ideal, to the specialist, the expert, the man who "knows his job." The typical, middle-class American in the twentieth century is not the yeoman but the professional or "skilled" man. This is the type we honor and aim to produce in our schools. Especially if a man's skill is in some way connected with "science," we accord him the deference that in some societies is accorded men of Church or State.

This change in national life has helped to force the issue of the "amateur" in government service and to blacken the reputation of the politician. The respect paid to the ideal of the expert—especially the scientist—has had as a by-product the fact that our public service is probably equal in quality to any other in these categories—and that these categories tend to dominate the service. The general movement toward specialization and professionalization has inspired much literature urging that public administration must be made a "profession"—or professions—to achieve high standards and gain prestige.

The fissiparous tendencies of specialization have made more difficult the integration of our national life and raised the question of the necessity for a new kind of "integrator"—an administrator who is a specialist in "things in general." On the other hand, some have found heterogeneity and indirection desirable, and we have had a pale image of British literature on Guild Socialism in the proposals of a few writers advocating that professional bodies be entrusted with the execution of a rather large number of "public" functions.

The rise of American scholarship, the spread of a guild spirit among scholars, and the rise of professional schools have been a part of the general movement toward specialization. The utilization of an increasing amount of our economic surplus for educational purposes; the late nineteenth-century hegira of our students to Europe, especially to German universities; the heritage of legal and philosophical interests in social studies; the founding of professional schools, particularly those in business administration; and the endowment or other provision for chairs, departments, and schools of public administration—these factors have left an indelible print in a variety of ways upon the literature of public administration since the publication of Wilson's essay.

Prosperity, Depression and Wars.—Finally, the effect of four great historical events upon administrative study must be noted: the Great Wars, the Great Prosperity, and the Great Depression. The effect of the First Great War on administrative practice and administrative writings was both bearish and bullish. Perhaps most important, the First Great War halted the sweep of Progressivism and Reform, represented on the national stage by Wilson's New Freedom. It diverted our attention from realizing the Promise of American Life to the much narrower goal of preserving America. The "New Deal" experiments in realizing the Good Life by administrative action presumably would have been made much earlier but for the intervention of the War and the Coolidge prosperity. However, the positive contributions of the War were substantial. It forced the growth of administrative organs and stimulated the evolution of new administrative devices. These developments occasioned some contemporary study and considerable subsequent examination; and the war debt undoubtedly hastened budget reform. Moreover, the War brought an enlargement of the practice and prestige of scientific management in government undertakings and government circles.

Most interesting from the standpoint of the theoretical literature of public administration was the doubt and self-examination occasioned by German successes, and the resultant emphasis upon "efficiency" as a necessary element of democracy. The unquestioned faith in democracy as a superior way of life and the boundless confidence in its ultimate triumph were shaken by the smooth precision and smashing power of Germany at war. Voices were raised and hearts were troubled, seeking an answer to the question why the unrighteous should thus flourish. The answer was "efficiency." If democracy were to survive it had somehow to add efficiency to its ideals of liberty and equality. It had to bring efficiency out of factory, school, and home, where it was already a popular ideal, and make the nation as a whole an efficient business.

But the quest eagerly begun was apparently rendered meaningless by peace. The period of more than a decade following the peace witnessed such advances as the multiplication of organizations of public servants, the extension of research in many fields, and the appearance of the first textbooks on public administration. Progressivism's spirit of high civic endeavor had all but vanished. But in breadth and depth of administrative thought the period as a whole must be characterized as stagnant in comparison with the Progressive and War periods that preceded, and the Depression period that followed. Neither the disillusionment and cynicism which followed the War nor the spirit of "get and spend" which dominated the Twenties were conducive to the spread of governmental activity or to the study of administration as a high civic endeavor.

The period of economic depression inaugurated by the market crash of 1929 affected the thinking of students of public administration in a number of ways. Perhaps most important was the change in attitude toward business. Much as American students owe to business practice and business thinking, hardly any of them are longer content with the simple objective of "more business in government." Allied to this is a general shift in sentiment toward greater government participation in economic life. The Depression's general stimulation of social conscience caused doubts to be raised as to whether "economy and efficiency" provide the ultimate criteria for judging administration, and attempts have been made either to broaden their connotations to include "social" values, or to cast them into outer darkness. Again, as in the War period, the tremendous expansion of government personnel and increase in number and variety of government administrative agencies stimulated a large amount of writing; particularly, the amount was increased and the content enriched in such categories as personnel, executive leadership and management, financial administration, and the function of the independent commission and government-owned corporation.

So far as the effect of the Second Great War can be read at this date it seems similar to that of the First Great War. There has been the same narrowing of values; this time the New Deal, not the New Freedom, was the casualty. There has been, naturally, reaffirmation of the cause of efficiency. And there has been a similar, but greater, expansion in administrative activity, providing new material for analysis and speculation.

The Ideological Framework

Up to this point we have been trying to discern the relationship between American study of public administration and its material environment—economic, institutional, "historical," and so forth. But the relationship of administrative study to the main currents of American thought during the past fifty years is equally important. In some measure the distinction between material and ideological environment is a false one. The relationship of ideas to the existential world is a matter of profound scientific and philosophical dispute; and in the above attempt to delineate the influence of "events" there has been occasional reference to ideology. However, it is assumed that ideas affect as well as reflect the course of events.

The choice of "dominant ideas" must be in some degree arbitrary, but both because of their widespread acceptance by the national community and their obvious influence upon writings on public administration the following are chosen for brief examination: the democratic ideal and related ideas such as the "mission of America," the belief in "fundamental law," the doctrine of progress and "progressivism," the gospel of efficiency, and faith in science.[8]

Democracy and the Mission of America.—Democracy has long been not only the form of government for the people of America, but a faith and an ideal, a romantic vision. This has been peculiarly our form of patriotism, our form of spiritual imperialism. The "mission of America," whether stated in religious terms or not, has been conceived as witnessing Democracy before mankind, bearing democracy's ideals of freedom and equality, and its material blessings, to the nations of the world. Belief in this mission perhaps has become less widely and intensively held during the past fifty years. Nevertheless, the romantic vision of democracy has been dimmed remarkably little by our continued experience with "realistic democracy" and *realpolitik*. Of the general influence of the democratic ideal there can be no doubt.

How have the students of public administration fared with respect to this national Ideal? Have they allowed their devotion to scientific objectivity to cut themselves off from the national com-

---

[8] On the American climate of opinion in the past century see R. H. Gabriel's *Course of American Democratic Thought* (New York: 1940); and V. L. Parrington, *Main Currents in American Thought* (New York: 1939).

munity of sentiment?[9] A few lines from one of the foremost of these students will suggest the answer: "One of the most inspiring movements in human history is now in progress. . . . A wave of organized democracy is sweeping around the world, based on a broader intelligence and a more enlightened view of civic responsibility than has ever before obtained. The theory that government exists for common welfare, that a public office is a public trust, is . . . old. . . . But responsibility for making this theory a vital principle in an empire whose sovereignty is abstractly conceived as residing in a hundred million souls and in which every officer of government is constitutionally a servant has not been considered with enough seriousness. . . ."[10] These lines do more than suggest, they epitomize the answer to the problem: our students of administration have accepted the American faith and have made an heroic effort to realize this faith by improving our institutions.

This interpretation doubtless would appear wholly in error to those who think democracy incompatible with the extension of government services and instrumentalities—to the James M. Becks, the Ludwig von Miseses, and the Lawrence Sullivans. Nevertheless, American students of administration have not loved democracy the less, but the more, because of their critical attention to its institutions and their desire to extend its services. They have not loved it the less dearly when they have insisted that it be worthy of its mission abroad by being noble at home, and when they have concluded from viewing the international scene that democracy cannot compete with ethically inferior ideals without efficiency. If "The Devil has all the best tunes," it becomes necessary to plagiarize. Early writings are full of assurances that we can adopt the administrative devices of autocracy without accepting its spirit and its ends. Beginning with Wilson's famous essay it has often been confessed, to be sure, that the forms and ethos of democracy impose limitations

---

[9] Of the Reform movement out of which public administration emerged there can be no doubt. Thus Dorman B. Eaton concludes his famous study of *Civil Service in Great Britain* (New York: 1880) with this appeal: "Thoughtful citizens . . . feel that the United States stand before the world as the original and noblest embodiment of the republican ideal in government. As the oldest and most powerful republican nation—as the example to which young republics turn for wisdom and experience—the character of public administration in the United States does not concern merely the growing millions of her own people, but the republican cause and the fate of free institutions in every quarter of the globe now and for ages to come. . . . No amount of scholarship will cover the disgrace to republican institutions of allowing the world to believe that republics must fall below monarchies in bringing high character and ability into places of public trust." 427–428.

[10] F. A. Cleveland, *Organized Democracy* (New York: 1913), 438 (by permission of Longmans, Green & Co., Inc.).

upon the administrative process which test patience and ingenuity and make efficiency very difficult. But the obligation to reconcile democracy and efficiency has ever been accepted, never rejected.

More important than the fact that this obligation has always been accepted is the fact that in the Progressive era a political theory was evolved that made a virtue of the obligation. The dilemma of democracy versus efficiency was avoided by the formula that *true* democracy and *true* efficiency are not necessarily—perhaps not possibly—incompatible. The assumptions and syllogisms of this line of thought are familiar: Democracy means an intelligent and informed citizenry organized into groups, preferably as few as possible, on the basis of issues. To realize this condition the proper institutions, such as the short ballot, a merit system, a budget system and a reporting system must function.

The imperatives of specialization of function and adequate control must be observed in the modern world; it is the citizen's proper function to learn, to judge, and to vote, while others specialize in actually running the business of government. In order for citizens to perform their functions adequately, machinery and issues must be simplified. Citizens must realize that there are two essentials in government: politics and administration, deciding and executing. When these two functions are properly separated and institutionalized it will be found that the resulting system is both democratic and efficient.

This attempt to summarize decades of political thought in a few lines may be somewhat distorting and unfair, but it is substantially correct. Until lately, administrative students have been generally concerned with excluding "democracy" from administration by making the latter unified and hierarchical, and with confining democracy to what is deemed to be its proper sphere, decision on policy.[11] It is only in more recent years that some writers have challenged the notion that politics and administration can be or should be separated and have urged that democracy is a way of life which must permeate the citizen's working as well as his leisure hours.

The Fundamental Law.—The relationship of administrative study to the notion of a "fundamental law" is as important as its

---

[11] For statements of this "orthodox" philosophy of the public administration movement see the following: F. A. Cleveland and A. E. Buck, *The Budget and Responsible Government* (New York: 1920), 15; A. R. Hatton, quoted in W. F. Willoughby, *The Movement for Budgetary Reform in the United States* (New York: 1918), 2; L. F. Schmeckebier and W. F. Willoughby, *The Government of the District of Columbia* (Washington: 1929), 26; J. M. Mathews, *Principles of American State Administration* (New York: 1917), vii.

relationship to democracy. It was widely and very firmly believed in the nineteenth century that there is a "higher law," a "fundamental moral order," upon which a firm and moral society must rest and in accordance with the rules of which it must be built. The nature and ultimate sanction of this fundamental order were differently conceived, according to the individual, but it was firm in our Christian heritage; and the "cosmic machine" of Newton and Descartes had become endowed with the moral sanctions and aura of this Christian tradition. As the century drew to a close, however, and especially as the present century has unfolded, the acids of modernity corrode this belief, and the "convention" view of law and justice has tended to come to the fore. The revival of humanism and neo-rationalism, the "socializing" of Protestant Christianity, the emergence of pragmatism, the rise of the so-called legal realists and the purging of natural law concepts from our jurisprudence, such events as these have marked our intellectual history since the Civil War.

From the beginning, students of public administration have been relatively sophisticated about higher law and the fundamentality of constitutional provisions and traditional institutions, about natural rights and the formulae of classical economics. These things they have generally rejected as the defense mechanisms of vested and antisocial interests, to be ignored or spurned. Yet it would be a serious mistake to suppose that American students have escaped the influence of the "higher law" notions widely accepted by the American community. Faith in democracy, already discussed, is just such an idea. To the extent that democracy has been thought superior and ultimate as a form of government and way of life, it has itself served as the higher law to which everything else must be referred; we have seldom permitted ourselves to doubt that democracy accords with the moral constitution of the universe. There is indeed a distinct aura of evangelical protestantism about the writings of the municipal and civil service reformers. They have always felt that moral issues are involved,[12] and until recently they have not hesitated to speak out on what they felt.

---

[12] Here is an example, chosen at random: "When I admit my belief that 'the principle of civil service reform' is one of high morality, I mean that all men who have sufficiently reflected and are sufficiently informed to entertain an intelligent opinion must and do think alike on the subject; that no one who has any claim at all to public attention really doubts that 'the principle of civil service reform' is just and beneficent; if he violates this 'principle' in official conduct, he does so, just as he may commit theft or adultery, knowing that he does wrong. I concede that there may be honest and enlightened difference of opinion as to the practical application of the principle . . . but these questions of policy have nothing to do with the *principle* of civil service reform." C. J. Bonaparte, *Proceedings of the National Civil Service Reform League*, 1889, 43–49, 43–44.

In other respects those who have produced our literature on public administration have adopted absolutist positions and insisted upon the moral imperatives of "the facts"; proposals for administrative change have too often hardened into "dogmas of administrative reform," propounded with solemnity and earnestness in the name of Science. But most important of all has been the manner in which the sanction of "principles" has been made to do duty for higher law.

Progress and Progressivism.—The past fifty years in America have been distinguished by a belief in the "doctrine of progress," so notably so that progress gave its name to an era. To be sure, the Great Wars dammed and diverted the rising stream, and most educated people now ease "progress" into their conversation in quotation marks. Still, in view of the fact that the "idea of progress" is peculiar to the modern world, the prevalence and intensity of the conviction among us has been a remarkable event in intellectual history; and it is pertinent to inquire how it has influenced administrative writers.

If the question is only: What has been the influence of the idea of progress? the answer, if not simple, must be brief. Americans, administrative students included, simply "accepted" progress—its reality and its desirability. It was a matter for apostrophe, not for argument. When in 1913 Woodrow Wilson exclaimed: "Progress! Did you ever reflect that the word is almost a new one? The modern idea is to leave the past and to press on to something new," he spoke for all the students and reformers who were writing and preparing to write on administrative subjects. His belief that man "by using his intellect can remake society, that he can become the creator of a world organized for man's advantage," has been a major premise which, though generally inarticulate, has fevered many brows and filled many pages.

But if the query is the broader one: What has been the influence of "Progressivism"? the answer is neither simple nor brief. For Progressivism was not an idea but a sheaf of ideas, old and new, and at times incompatible, held together by a buoyant faith in Progress. Progressivism found its basis in the old democratic faith, it was stimulated by the Muckrakers and the earnest efforts of Reformers, it attempted to bring ethical absolutism into the world of science, it recruited armies of Reform sworn to march in different directions into the Future, it found its highest expression in such men as Woodrow Wilson, Walter Weyl and Herbert Croly: it was a welter of ideas given a momentary unity by a common basis of optimism.

At the very heart of Progressivism was a basic conflict in social outlook. This conflict was between those whose hope for the future was primarily that of a planned and administered society, and those who, on the other hand, remained firm in the old liberal faith in an underlying harmony, which by natural and inevitable processes produces the greatest possible good if the necessary institutional and social reforms are made.

This latter group felt a resurgence of primitive democratic feeling. They knew that man is pure at heart and was but thwarted and corrupted by bad institutions, that the realization of the ideal of the free individual depended upon restricting government and maintaining the open market. These persons believed that "the cure for democracy is *more* democracy," and to that end they proposed such reforms as the initiative, the referendum, the recall, the direct election of senators, home rule, and proportional representation. They knew that the Future must well up from *below*. In opposition were those whose patience was exhausted waiting for the Promise of American Life to realize itself by natural and inevitable means, whose view of human nature was not so charitable and who had no faith in the devices of primitive democracy, who had begun to think of planning and who realized that builders need tools. These persons believed that democracy must re-think its position and re-mold its institutions; particularly it must create a strong right arm for the State in the form of an efficient bureaucracy. They knew that "the way to realize a purpose is not to leave it to chance," [13] and that the Future must be given shape from *above*.

This is oversimplification, but it is a valid and useful generalization in viewing the past half century in perspective. It is oversimplification because the two movements, the two views, have overlapped. Everyone but the rascals could agree to "turn the rascals out," and "good government" is a formula wide enough to cover a multitude of differences. It is oversimplification also because formulae were evolved to bridge the gap between the two general trends; notably formulae reconciling "true democracy" with "true efficiency" were evolved by administrative writers and were accorded wide credence. Certainly the two viewpoints can be reconciled in the

---

[13] Herbert Croly, *The Promise of American Life* (New York: 1909), 7. To convince himself of the reality of these two tendencies one need only attend a convention of the National Municipal League and go from a conference, say, on city planning, to a session of the Proportional Representation League.

realm of the ideal: an "ideal democracy" in which the citizens are all intelligent, educated, and of good will, so that very little authoritative direction is necessary, and when necessary is performed with economy and competence.[14] Some of the Progressives caught just such a vision and hence their insistence upon "citizenship" and their espousal of the ideal of "Efficient Citizenship." The Wisconsin of the elder La Follette and Charles McCarthy was a crude, earthly approximation of this *Civitas Dei*.

But although administrative students helped construct the most useful dialectic bridge between the two viewpoints, although they profess and believe in democracy, liberty and equality, they have generally accepted the alternative of a planned and managed society. This conclusion is obvious—axiomatic—but it is not so obvious as to preclude students of administration from often presuming that they labor in a sphere from which "values" have been excluded. American society is greatly in the debt of those who have given their time, energy and substance to improve administration. Still, it is in order to inquire whether, in narrowing their sphere of attention to administration only, students of administration did not also accept an unnecessary shrinking of their ideals. A society in which there are many "efficient citizens" must surely weigh heavier in the balance of American ideals than one in which there are only "trained administrators."[15] Undue attention to the "management" aspects

[14] See E. R. Lewis, *A History of American Political Thought from the Civil War to the World War* (New York: 1937), ch. 12, for a discussion of the different currents in Progressivism. Lewis says of the two broad trends I have sketched: "It might be thought that the contest was between efficiency and the democratic dogma. But I think it is fairer to say that, in a real sense, all were aspects of the same movement, all were attempts to obtain control of the political organization and make it responsive. . . ." 504–505. (By permission of The Macmillan Co., publishers.)

[15] The "efficient citizenship" movement of the Progressive era may have been futile, its ideal impossible. At any event we have been inclined in recent years to take a less generous view of the capabilities and potentialities of the "average citizen." It may be that the ideal of citizen participation through his sphere of expertise and by the medium of his professional group is all that can be salvaged from the larger ideal. But even this notion has generally remained undeveloped in favor of a vision of a trained, professional bureaucracy, ruling over a generally passive people. On the "efficient citizenship" movement see: J. D. Burks, "Efficiency Standards in Municipal Management," 1 *Nat. Mun. Rev.* (July, 1912), 364–371, 370–371; and Henry Bruere, *The New City Government* (New York: 1912), ch. 14.

The "efficient citizenship" idea is not completely dead. In the peroration of a recent address to budding administrators, M. E. Dimock allowed himself this optimistic sentiment: "Some time, perhaps, we may approach the ideal envisaged by James Bryce, when '. . . the average citizen will give close and constant attention to public affairs, . . . With such citizens as electors, the legislature will be composed of upright and capable men, single-minded in their wish to serve the nation. . . . Office will be sought only because it gives opportunities for useful public service. Power will be shared by all, and a career open to all alike.'" "Administrative Efficiency Within a Democratic Polity," *New Horizons in Public Administration* (University, Alabama: 1945), a symposium, 21–43, 43 (by permission of University of Alabama Press).

of group life in other eras has produced the not very lofty works of Machiavelli, Hobbes, and Mandeville.

The Gospel of Efficiency.—Every era, as Carl Becker has reminded us in his *Heavenly City of the Eighteenth Century Philosophers,* has a few words that epitomize its world-view and that are fixed points by which all else can be measured. In the Middle Ages they were such words as faith, grace, and God; in the eighteenth century they were such words as reason, nature, and rights; during the past fifty years in America they have been such words as cause, reaction, scientific, expert, progress—and efficient. Efficiency is a natural ideal for a relatively immature and extrovert culture, but presumably its high development and wide acceptance are due to the fact that ours has been, *par excellence,* a machine civilization. At any event, efficiency grew to be a national catchword in the Progressive era as mechanization became the rule in American life, and it frequently appears in the literature of the period entangled in mechanical metaphor.

However natural, it is yet amazing what a position of dominance "efficiency" assumed, how it waxed until it had assimilated or overshadowed other values, how men and events came to be degraded or exalted according to what was assumed to be its dictate. It became a movement, a motif of Progressivisim, a "Gospel." [16] Some of the reasons for the acceptance of efficiency as a necessary objective and a sufficient criterion for governmental reform have already been suggested: fear of exhaustion of our natural resources; the urge to make America worthy of her Mission by those who, observing the frugality and dispatch of European autocracy, blushed for democracy's slattern ways; and simple fear for the future existence of American democracy when German efficiency moved Westward in 1914.[17] More fundamental is the fact that America was attempting to adjust old conceptions and traditional institutions to the require-

---

[16] See Harrington Emerson, *Efficiency as a Basis for Operation and Wages* (New York: 1909), ch. 12, "The Gospel of Efficiency," for a remarkable apotheosis of efficiency. His remarkable credo was more extravagantly phrased, though fundamentally the same, as that of millions of his fellow citizens. See also, B. P. DeWitt, *The Progressive Movement* (New York: 1915) for an attempt at an analytical and objective statement of "The Efficiency Movement" (ch. 15) at the height of the Progressive movement.

[17] At the climax of the First Great War, M. L. Cooke wrote as follows: "It has frequently been suggested during the past decade, and especially during the past four years of the war, that democracy is undergoing the test which shall determine whether it is to sweep over the world, or stagnate and finally perish. That test is based essentially on efficiency. Democracy, if it shall flourish, must be efficient. . . ." From: *Our Cities Awake,* copyright 1918 by Doubleday & Co., Inc., 159. *Cf.* F. A. Cleveland, 2 *National Economic League Quarterly,* August, 1916, 9–16, 16.

ments of a machine technology, and efficiency came to symbolize the ideal of reconciliation. "A new era has come upon us like a sudden vision of things unprophesied, and for which no polity has been prepared," wrote Woodrow Wilson in 1901, reflecting on the confusion about him.[18] Accepting efficiency as the essential ingredient, students of administration have tried to prepare a proper polity.

Faith in Science.—His powers and comforts daily increased by the agency of Science, the average American of the past generation has felt an almost limitless confidence in whatever bears the label of Science. The change in the externals of life was so amazing, the vistas of the future presented in the Sunday supplements so astounding that anything seemed possible; a Golden Age of peace and plenty for all seemed just a short distance across the years, an age in which the living might hope to end their days among its wonders— provided that death had not by then been rendered obsolete. It was the Great Engineer Hoover who visioned the "disappearance of poverty" in our lifetime. Naturally, the uninitiated—and often the initiated—looked with awe upon this Magic (even when, in War or Depression, they have thought it Black Magic), and "scientific" became an "honorific" word—even religion and ethics found it expedient to become scientific.

The contrast between the Brave New World that seemed so near, and the alarms and excursions, the pettiness and stupidities, the confusion and force of the world-at-hand stimulated many persons to ask, "Why?" Following the lead of many of the scientists and of most of the persons whose province of study was human affairs, they frequently concluded that the New Day would not dawn until science were applied to the realm of human affairs just as it had been to the physical world, until the "power-controlling sciences" were as well developed as the "power-producing sciences." An easy and unwarranted optimism abounded that at least a technique for solving these problems of group life, if not an actual answer to the problems themselves, lay hidden within the mystery of science.

So the humanities were re-named, new terminologies invented, new buildings raised, new endowments secured. Students and reformers of all kinds fell to making human relations and governmental practices scientific: the students by engaging in a new and recondite branch of inquiry called Scientific Methodology, and the reformers either by applying current conceptions of scientific method

---

[18] "Democracy and Efficiency," 87 *Atlantic Monthly* (March, 1901), 289–299, 292.

or by the simpler method of putting a scientific wrapper on old nostrums. This faith in science and the efficacy of scientific method thoroughly permeates our literature on public administration. Science has its experts: so we must have "experts in government." Science relies upon exact measurement: so let the data of administration be measured. Science is concerned only with facts: so let the "facts" be sovereign. Science makes use of experiment: so let the mode of administrative advance be experimental.

Far from removing themselves from the realm of political theory, as many appear to believe, this devotion to a concept of reality called Science makes students of administration part of a well-known company of political theorists. Any political theory rests upon a metaphysic, a concept of the ultimate nature of reality. Students of administration, following a line of precedent which begins in the modern period with Hobbes, have simply been willing to accept the verdict of science—or more accurately, popular conceptions of the verdict of science—as to the nature of reality. It is appropriate to inquire whether these concepts of reality are consistent among themselves, whether they are valid within their proper realm, and whether, if valid, they have been extended beyond the bounds of their validity.

Chapter 2

A CLOSER VIEW: THE MOVEMENTS, THE MEN, THE MOTIFS [1]

The public administration movement is probably as well defined as was, for instance, nineteenth-century Utilitarianism, despite its want of Bentham. The movement is marked by smaller movements, separated more or less by time, circumstance, motives, and differences in personnel, and there has been fratricidal strife. Nevertheless, with the possible exception of taxpayer groups interested primarily in reduction of government expenses, there is a core of consistency, of assumptions, of motives, of logic. The movement as a whole has an ethos.

The Role of the Schools

Historically, "public administration" has grown in large part out of the wider field of inquiry, "political science." [2] The history of American political science during the past fifty years is a story much too lengthy to be told here, [3] but some important general characteristics and tendencies it has communicated to or shared with public administration must be noted.

---

[1] The role of scientific management, logically a part of this discussion, is treated in Chapter 3.

[2] Writers on public administration concede that formally and historically it is a branch of political science, but this aspect is not emphasized. See L. D. White, "Administration, Public," in 1 *Encyc. Soc. Sci.*, 440–449, 440. Cf. W. F. Willoughby, "The Science of Public Administration," in *Essays in Political Science* (Baltimore: 1937), J. M. Mathews and J. Hart, eds., 39–63, 63. Consult the bibliographical note at the end of the chapter for conscious attempts to delineate the field of "public administration."

[3] The latter chapters of Anna Haddow's *Political Science in American Colleges and Universities, 1636–1900* (New York: 1939) introduce the present era. Nothing comparable in completeness exists for the period after 1900. A survey of recent trends has been undertaken, however, in a number of essays. Cf.: W. J. Shepard, "Recent Tendencies in American Political Science," 1 *Politica* (Feb., 1934), 1–11; William Anderson, "Political Science Enters the Twentieth Century," ch. 14 in Haddow, *supra;* C. E. Merriam, "Recent Advances in Political Methods," 17 *Am. Pol. Sci. Rev.* (May, 1923), 275–295; W. F. Willoughby's Introduction to G. A. Weber's *Organized Efforts for the Improvement of Methods of Administration in the United States* (New York: 1919); L. L. Bernard, Pt. III, "The Period of Maturation and Synthesis," in "The Social Sciences as Disciplines: The United States," 1 *Encyc. Soc. Sci.*, 341–349.

The Secular Spirit.—Despite the fact that "political science" in such forms as moral philosophy and political economy had been taught in America long before the Civil War, the present curriculum, practically in its entirety, is the product of the secular, practical, empirical, and "scientific" tendencies of the past sixty or seventy years. American students—dismayed at. the inadequacies of the ethical approach in the Gilded Age, stimulated by their pilgrimage to German universities, and led by such figures as J. W. Burgess, E. J. James, A. B. Hart, A. L. Lowell, and F. J. Goodnow—have sought to recreate political science as a true science. To this end they set about observing and analyzing "actual government." At various times and according to circumstances, they have turned to public law, foreign institutions, rural, municipal, state, and federal institutions, political parties, public opinion and pressures, and to the administrative process, in the search for the "stuff" of government. They have borrowed both ideas and examples from the natural sciences and the other social disciplines. Frequently they have been inspired by a belief that a Science of Politics will emerge when enough facts of the proper kinds are accumulated and put in the proper juxtaposition, a Science that will enable man to "predict and control" his political life. So far did they advance from the old belief that the problem of good government is the problem of moral men that they arrived at the opposite position: that morality is irrelevant, that proper institutions and expert personnel are determining. The new amorality became almost a requisite for professional respect. The old curriculum of moral philosophy and allied studies became transmuted into a series of courses on the history of political theory, courses without a widely accepted rationale and tolerated only as a "cultural" gloss upon a professional education. Generally speaking, university students of public administration have been in the van of and have epitomized these tendencies.

Administrative Law and Comparative Administration.—In public administration the first major advances into realism were in the fields of public law (particularly administrative law) and comparative administration. F. J. Goodnow led these advances, although his contributions were by no means limited to his excellent legal and comparative studies; Johns Hopkins was long the recognized center for such studies. In addition to Goodnow, J. A. Fairlie and Ernst Freund were associated prominently with the development of legal and descriptive studies; but a list of those whose approach to the study of public administration has been primarily legalistic, institutional, and descriptive could be extended at length.

The New Management Movement.—The second major drive toward realism in the study of public administration was the "new management" movement. Leaders of this movement have been inclined to regard legal and descriptive study as bookish and inadequate, desirable perhaps, but only a preliminary to the really important matter of finding ways and means of managing the public's business efficiently. The sources of the New Management trend are many, including comparative studies emphasizing the role of executive leadership, the example of business, the reorganization movement, the research movement, and the scientific management movement. Since the leaders of these two latter movements were chiefly active outside the schools and since the New Management not only succeeds but overlays the legal and descriptive studies, it is not easy to suggest leaders, but no list would omit the name of W. E. Mosher, nor any study overlook the Maxwell School of Citizenship and Public Affairs.[4]

Other Academic Contributions.—The legal and comparative studies and the New Management movement may be said to constitute the main stream of academic public administration, but other formal fields of study have contributed. To the field of state government, the relationship has been very close; there also has been considerable overlapping of personnel. Municipal government likewise has been defined as chiefly a matter of "administration,"[5] and hence largely a preserve for administrative study. With the tendency to view the realm of government and politics as a realm of conflicting forces, and the role of political scientist as analogous to that of a physicist—observing, measuring, and generalizing about forces—there likewise has been a certain amount of overlapping. The "pressures" that surround the administrative process and exert "disturbing" influences upon it stimulated extensive study; in fact, administration has occasionally been envisaged as a "pressure group" itself.

On the other hand administrative students have been almost entirely indifferent to recondite studies and speculations as to the

---

[4] L. D. White has written much about the "new management" as well as contributing to its theory in his special studies. Nevertheless, I should characterize his function in and contribution to the study of public administration as "summary and synthesis at the level of common sense."

[5] See, for example, M. E. Dimock, *Modern Politics and Administration* (New York: 1937), 257.

nature of parties and other group phenomena, and have not been concerned with the abstract question of the best type of party system. This may be due to the fact that from their Reform background they received a strong feeling of revulsion toward parties and "politics," or at least the conviction that the only good party is a Reform Party. But although the prevailing attitude today is still that "politics" is a low form of activity which must be prevented from disturbing administration, beginning at least as early as Goodnow's *Politics and Administration* there has been a contrary if less potent tendency to condone parties and politics and even to praise them. Some have accepted Party as a necessary part of the democratic process and have been concerned not only to reform its operation,[6] but to inquire into its implications for the administrative process.[7] Finally, from one who came to administrative problems by way of study of political processes, we have had an extensive apologia for the American political system.[8]

Psychology.—It is the relationship of public administration to the psychological approach to the study of political science that reveals most clearly an outstanding characteristic of American administrative study—its rationalism. Some students of political processes, under the same impulse to be objective and scientific that moved students of administration, turned their attention to human nature and the formation of public opinion, and arrived at conclusions of startling import for the rationalist presumptions of the old democratic faith. For they concluded that man is in small part rational: that his mental equipment is weak and inadequate, that he is immersed in the details of his own petty concerns and moved in overwhelming measure by selfish and unlovely emotions, drives, and urges; and that public opinion is nothing but a term to denote a resultant of non-rational forces.

Public administration has been little touched by such ideas. As has been stated, there is a record of increasing sophistication.as to the part the public may be expected to play in the governmental process, and an attempt has been made to reduce and simplify the role of the citizen by such means as the short ballot and attractive, simplified governmental publicity. These conclusions, however, seem

---

[6] W. E. Mosher insisted in season and out upon a new kind of party, a new attitude toward politics. See, for example, "The Party Is the Crux," 28 *Nat. Mun. Rev.* (May, 1934), 335–340. He may be regarded as one of the few in recent years still keenly interested in the "efficient citizenship" movement. This is the more remarkable in that he was also a leader of the "new management" trend.

[7] See M. E. Dimock, *op. cit.*, 395.

[8] E. P. Herring, *The Politics of Democracy* (New York: 1940).

to be entirely on the empirical level; there are no sweeping conclusions about the irrationality of man based even at second or third hand on psychological study. What cognizance there is of psychology is chiefly of the Win-Friends-and-Influence-People school—a reflection that it is a handy tool for administrators, hence its potentialities should be exploited—and seems to have come by a process of osmosis from the literature of business administration and scientific management.[9]

On the other hand, in spite of disillusionment about the rationality of men at large, and indeed it would seem in recompense for it, there is a very firm reliance upon man's rationality when the form and interrelations of the administrative structure itself are under consideration. One gets the impression from some of the literature that organizations can be designed according to blueprints, fabricated of standardized parts, crated, shipped, and assembled on order at any time or place.[10] Administrative study is in many respects a "last stronghold" of rationalism.

The Gift of Self-Consciousness.—The conception of "public administration" as a separate entity, a definable discipline or field of study, is itself almost entirely a product of the schools; [11] the prime function of the schools has been to summarize and synthesize, to raise to self-consciousness and impose unity.[12]

---

[9] Writings which constitute possible exceptions to this generalization, such as those of Ordway Tead and C. E. Merriam, are on the periphery of the public administration movement. On present "psychological" trends cf. A. H. Leighton, *The Governing of Man: General Principles and Recommendations Based on Experience at a Japanese Relocation Camp* (Princeton: 1945); J. M. Gaus, *Reflections on Public Administration* (University, Alabama: 1947), 122, 126. The relevancy of psychoanalytic psychology for administration is being explored in some circles at long last, but I believe nothing significant on this subject has yet appeared in print, except for the pioneer writings of Harold Lasswell.

[10] See Chas. S. Ascher's whimsical essay on organization charts, "Organization (Mercator's Projection)," 3 *Pub. Adm. Rev.* (Autumn, 1943), 360–364. Cf. G. A. Graham, *Education for Public Administration* (Chicago: 1941), 4, on the rationalist presumptions of public administration.

There have been recent signs of a growing awareness of non-rational factors in administration—"I do wish that we administrative people could acquire a deeper appreciation of how serious a matter it is to dig up a flourishing tree and transplant it into someone else's back yard. It takes time to reestablish the root structure and during that time the tree withers." M. E. Dimock, "Administrative Efficiency Within a Democratic Polity," in *New Horizons in Public Administration: A Symposium* (University, Alabama: 1945), 21–43, 35 (by permission of University of Alabama Press).

[11] W. F. Willoughby constitutes a major exception—but he held a chair of political science for a long period.

[12] Beginning with Woodrow Wilson's essay "The Study of Administration," 2 *Pol. Sci. Q.* (June, 1887), 197–222. This essay has received much attention in recent years because much of it seems so modern it could have been written yesterday. It seems not to have exerted much influence, even attracted much attention, for many years. (An essay by F. P. Prichard, "The Study of the Science of Mu-

To be sure, the whole situation is still amorphous. And to the horror of academic students of public administration many persons in high administrative positions perform their duties as innocent of "public administration" as M. Jourdain of prose.[13] But academic students of public administration have attempted, and in some measure succeeded, in bringing to a focus a dozen different movements for governmental and administrative reform, using the conceptual apparatus given by the American climate of opinion and, more immediately, American political science. Moreover, to every movement, every body of techniques, every strand of thought, they have made contributions.

The Personnel Movement

A readily definable part of the literature is that inspired by and written about the personnel aspects of administration. From the time of the Civil War to the present there has been a "reform" movement and a reform literature, a movement to substitute "merit" or "training" for party allegiance as the determining factor in appointment to administrative positions. Superimposed upon this reform movement is the personnel movement. The emergence of a distinctive movement and outlook from the general reform current was due to a number of factors, but chiefly to the example afforded by the rise of "personnel administration" as a necessary ingredient of good management in business, and to the fact that, unlike most branches of political science, the study of personnel administration produces a salable skill. Recent literature on personnel is an amalgam of original reformist sentiment, ideas of personnel management derived from business administration, notions of enhanced executive power, and smaller amounts of a great variety of ideas derived from the American scene, such as equalitarianism and professionalism.

nicipal Government," 2 *Annals* (Jan., 1892), 450–457, has much the same quality of precociousness that distinguishes Wilson's essay, but it has not enjoyed even belated fame.) "Public administration" sometimes appeared as a course name or as a general designation before the end of the century (Haddow, *op. cit.,* Chs. 11 and 12, *passim*), and the legal and descriptive studies upon which later offerings were to be based were then under way; for example, a series of studies in state centralization were carried out at Columbia during the nineties. But a good case can be made for the statement that it was really not until the twenties that "public administration" reached self-consciousness—an event symbolized by the appearance of White's and Willoughby's texts. While some of the Founding Fathers of the Republic—to go back no further—wrote on public administration (See Lynton K. Caldwell's, *The Administrative Theories of Hamilton and Jefferson: Their Contributions to Thought on Public Administration.* Chicago: 1944) they did not write on "Public Administration."

[13] Academic students of public administration are in the anomalous position of posing as "practical" men among their colleagues on the faculties and being regarded as "theorists" by their colleagues in the field.

From Reform to "Management."—"It is interesting to note," writes L. D. White, "that the principal concern of the great band of original civil service reformers was not greater administrative efficiency but purified elections and a more wholesome democracy." [14] Others have noted in passing that there has been a general change from reformist and "negative" to managerial and "positive" attitudes; but the history of this shift in emphasis, showing its relationship to the course of events and ideas, has yet to be written. [15]

The Reform Movement.—Certainly the principal concern of the early civil service reformers was not greater administrative efficiency; it was the cleansing and promotion of democracy. To some extent they were interested in "greater administrative efficiency"—for part of making American republican institutions "better" was increasing their efficiency. [16] But the primary issue was moral.

There are "divine laws of social order and well-being" wrote G. L. Prentiss in an 1877 tract on *Our National Bane,* "these laws are as immutable as that of gravitation . . . Civil freedom . . . can be kept from abuse and decay only by steadfast obedience to the moral laws of the world." [17] R. Fulton Cutting reflected the still dominant sentiment in 1900 when he opined, "The real crime committed against society by the spoils system is moral, not economic. It poisons our institutions at the fountainhead, corrupting the electorate and creating a political conscience antagonistic to morals." [18]

But there was a constant secularizing tendency through all the latter part of the century, an increasing disposition to view the reform of personnel not as a high moral endeavor but as a matter of improving the quality of administration. Between Prentiss' *Bane* and Richard Henry Dana's *Merit Principle in the Selection of the Higher Municipal Officers* [19] of 1903 there is a great gulf. The former is theological, couched in oratorical language. The latter shows the effects of industrialization and urbanization, suggests

---

[14] *Introduction to the Study of Public Administration* (New York: 1939), 282.

[15] F. M. Stewart's fine history of *The National Civil Service Reform League* (Austin: 1929) is more than a chronicle of events, but does not purport to be such a history.

[16] See, for example, the final pages of D. B. Eaton's *Civil Service in Great Britain* (New York: 1880); and Carl Schurz' *The Spoils System* (Philadelphia: 1896), 6–7.

[17] New York, 2. See also, *Report,* 42nd Congress, 2nd Sess., Senate Doc. No. 10, 4.

[18] In "Public Ownership and the Social Conscience," 4 *Municipal Affairs* (Mar., 1900), 3–12, 3–4. Such quotations could be multiplied at great length. *Cf.* G. W. Curtiss, in his introduction to Eaton's study of British experience.

[19] Paper read at the Annual Meeting of the National Civil Service League, printed Cambridge, 1904.

separating policy determination from policy execution as a proper formula for reconciling old democracy and new technology, urges the necessity for expertise, and even advances to the point of distinguishing executive ability as a recognizable skill for which tests may be devised.

The Drive for "Experts."—Dana's paper may be taken as an introduction to the second recognizable stage in thinking and writing about personnel. This was the stage characterized by demand for "experts" in administration. American society was undergoing rapid changes; a new way of life and a new realm of discourse were being inaugurated. Professionalism was becoming a prominent characteristic of American life, and specialization a key to prestige. Slowly at first, then with overwhelming force, it was borne upon those interested in administrative personnel that morality in government is not enough, that no amount of simple honesty will enable a person to keep accounts, design a bridge, or manage a bureau. Not only must persons not be given positions as party plunder, not only must they be honest: they must be trained and capable. This is an essential if American government is to enlarge its purpose— even if it is to survive.

As Carl Schurz wrote in 1896, "There are certain propositions so self-evident and so easily understood that it would appear like discourtesy to argue them before persons of intelligence. Such a one it is, that as the functions of government grow in extent, importance and complexity, the necessity grows of their being administered not only with honesty, but also with trained ability and knowledge; and that in the same measure as this necessity is disregarded in a democratic government, the success and stability of democratic institutions will be impaired." [20] This growing current of thought became a part of Progressivism, and upon the advent of the First Great War, Science was a cult and Expert a fetish. The early volumes of the *National Municipal Review* are heavily salted with "scientific," "expert," and related words, documenting in unmistakable fashion the simple faith of an era.

The New Management Phase.—The third clearly distinguishable phase has been marked by borrowings from business administration, particularly scientific management, and characterized by emphasis upon personnel as an instrument for accomplishing purposes. (In the literature much depends, of course, upon the audience addressed.

---

[20] *Op. cit.,* 6–7. *Cf.* Richard Henry Dana, *op. cit.,* 3.

The crusade for merit is still the theme of literature addressed to leagues of women voters, municipal electorates, etc.) The early reformers had a general belief that business is a better and purer realm than government, hence the movement for better personnel was very susceptible to business influence. Despite the fact that Muckraking was a prelude to Progressivism, by making a distinction between bad business and good business the writers were prepared to accept almost without reservation or alteration what were thought to be better business practices. Scientific management had become widely publicized by the second decade of the century, and a considerable literature on business treatment of personnel problems was already at hand.[21] Private and public personnel administration have been very closely assimilated during the past three decades.

The Administrative Training Movement

Part of the general movement for better personnel and better management of personnel, and related to such other activities as academic study of public administration, has been the development of educational or training programs for public employees. The literature of this movement has a number of interesting theoretical aspects—for example, what it reveals of the theories of education of those interested in public administration—a type of theory which any political philosophy comprehends, expressly or by implication.

Indifference to Educational Philosophy.—It is necessary to report that this literature, with a few notable and mostly recent exceptions, is not very impressive in quality, however favorable may be the judgment on the success of the training programs themselves. The argument for and consideration of training for public administration has been largely carried on in ignorance of or indifference to the record of twenty-five centuries of thought about matters educational. Educational philosophy and political philosophy are inextricably joined, but there has been little conscious effort to consider political philosophy in relation to educational theory and procedure, nor either of them in relation to the techniques of modern society and available or potential educational equipment. There has been consequent confusion and blurring of important distinctions; as one writer has observed, it is impossible to discover from the litera-

---

[21] The record of the process of osmosis may be observed in the issues of the *Annals*. See, for example, 90 *Annals* (July, 1920), on "Industrial Stability," and 113 *Annals* (May, 1924), on "Competency and Economy in Public Expenditures," Pts. VI, VII. *Cf.* 189 *Annals* (Jan., 1937), "Improved Personnel in Government Service."

ture exactly what public administration is, who should teach it, who should learn it, and why! Happily, this situation may soon be remedied; several more recent publications, although not agreeing among themselves, have made a considerable advance in the definition of objectives, consideration of means, and appraisal of past and present accomplishments.[22]

The Setting of the Training Movement.—In fairness it should be noted that any person seeking to establish a firm rationale for a course of training has faced a very difficult problem, due to a number of facts about American life. First among such facts is the tradition of separation between the State and the educational system, the fact that our educational system has developed (following the period of religious impulse) to help individuals succeed at their own enterprises rather than to serve the public weal. Those interested in training were in a sense rootless. Not only was there no tradition of state service, there was no philosophy of state service to serve the purpose Idealism served in England, nor even the datum of a stable class system upon which their thought could build.

On the positive side, it is obvious that those who inaugurated training for administration were stimulated and influenced by industrialization, urbanization, professionalization and the general spread of scientific or "positivist" modes of thought.

Specifically, training for administration emerged out of the Efficient Citizenship movement; the New York Bureau of Municipal Research was a center of the latter [23] and formulated the first thorough program of training, a program that had much influence over subsequent developments.

The Research Movement

Another definable part of public administration is the research movement. Research is an ideal or adjunct of all conscious attention to public administration, but the research movement proper has a recognized beginning and discernible outlines. The beginning was the establishment of the New York Bureau of Municipal Research in 1906, an event of such great importance for later developments

---

[22] Notably M. B. Lambie, ed., *Training for the Public Service* (Chicago: 1935); Lewis Meriam, *Public Service and Special Training* (Chicago: 1936); G. A. Graham, *Education for Public Administration* (Chicago: 1941). See also: R. A. Walker, "Public Administration: The Universities and the Public Service," 39 *Am. Pol. Sci. Rev.* (Oct., 1945), 926–933; Egbert S. Wengert, "The Study of Public Administration," 36 *Am. Pol. Sci. Rev.* (April, 1942), 313–322.

[23] See the writings of W. H. Allen, Henry Bruere, and F. A. Cleveland, especially Allen's *Efficient Democracy* (New York: 1907). See C. E. Ridley and L. S. Moore, "Training for the Public Service," 189 *Annals* (Jan., 1937), 127–133.

that not even the briefest sketch of the history of public administration could fail to note its significance. No more revealing study of Progressivism could be made than of the activities and writings of William H. Allen, Henry Bruere, and Frederick A. Cleveland, whom Charles A. Beard has designated the "ABC powers." The philosophy and activities of others closely associated with the Bureau, for example, R. Fulton Cutting and Charles A. Beard himself, are important enough to warrant attention by students of American culture. A great number and great variety of research organizations trace their origins to the Bureau. And the importance of the Bureau's training program, which sent disciples all over the country, has just been noted.

The Bureau Movement.[24]—The spirit of the Bureau movement has deeply affected public administration. The Bureau movement was a part of Progressivism, and its leaders were leaders of Progressivism. They were tired of the simple moralism of the nineteenth century,[25] although paradoxically they were themselves fired with the moral fervor of humanitarianism and secularized Christianity. They were stirred by the revelations of the Muckrakers, but despaired of reform by spontaneous combustion.[26] They were sensitive to the appeals and promises of science, and put a simple trust in discovery of facts as the way of science and as a sufficient mode for solution of human problems. They accepted—they urged —the new positive conception of government, and verged upon the idea of a planned and managed society. They hated "bad" business, but found in business organization and procedure an acceptable prototype for public business.[27] They detested politicians and were

[24] On the history and rationale of the Bureau movement see N. N. Gill, *Municipal Research Bureaus* (Washington: 1944); J. M. Pfiffner, *Municipal Administration* (New York: 1940), ch. 4; J. M. Gaus, "The Present Status of the Study of Public Administration in the United States," 25 *Am. Pol. Sci. Rev.* (Feb., 1931), 120–134, and *A Study of Research in Public Administration* (New York: 1930—mimeographed); L. D. White, *Trends in Public Administration* (New York: 1933), ch. 22; G. A. Weber, *Organized Efforts for the Improvement of Methods of Administration in the United States* (New York: 1919); R. T. Crane, "Research Agencies and Equipment," 17 *Am. Pol. Sci. Rev.* (May, 1923), 295–303; C. E. Merriam, "The Next Step in the Organization of Municipal Research," 11 *Nat. Mun. Rev.* (Sept., 1922), 274–281; New York Bureau of Municipal Research, "A National Program to Improve Methods of Government," 71 *Municipal Research* (March, 1916), and "Citizen Agencies for Research in Government," 77 *Municipal Research* (Sept., 1916); F. A. Cleveland, *Chapters on Municipal Administration and Accounting* (New York: 1909), ch. 5. See also bibliography, Pfiffner, *op. cit.*, 81.

[25] See "The Goodness Fallacy," ch. 1 in W. H. Allen's *Efficient Democracy.*

[26] See *A National Program to Improve Methods of Government*, New York Bureau of Municipal Research, 3.

[27] Since the bureaus have been very close to the business community, the research movement naturally has been a main channel of business and scientific man-

firm in the belief that citizens by and large were fundamentally pure at heart, desirous of efficient and economical government, and potentially rational enough to "reach up" to and support a vigorous government, wide in its scope, complex in its problems, and utilizing a multitude of professional and scientific skills. They proposed to educate citizens to and assist them with this responsibility.[28] They were ardent apostles of "the efficiency idea"[29] and leaders in the movement for "useful" education. These last three notions—civic awareness and militancy, efficiency, and "useful" education—together form the core of the Efficient Citizenship movement. They caught the vision that "true democracy consists in intelligent cooperation between citizens and those elected or appointed to serve,"[30] and, while today this vision is no longer a bright and shining beacon-star, the municipal research bureaus still find in it their chief rationale.[31]

---

agement influence. (See C. A. Beard's "The Role of Administration in Government," in *The Work Unit in Federal Administration* (Chicago: 1937), 1.)

[28] "There is at present no mechanism for learning and publishing the facts of social life and public administration. Without these facts upon which to base judgment, the public cannot intelligently direct and control the administration of township, county, city, state or nation. Without intelligent control by the public, no efficient, progressive, triumphant democracy is possible." W. H. Allen, *Efficient Democracy* (New York: 1907), ix-x (by permission of Dodd, Mead & Co.). Writing of standardized and scientific accounting, personnel, and purchasing procedures H. Bruere says: "Without these devices popular rule is futile. The recall cannot be used effectively unless the public is in a position to know the facts about . . . its government." *The New City Government* (New York: 1912), 367. "Bliss was it in that dawn," etc.! Gradually, in the public administration movement as a whole, research and facts have come to be regarded less and less as devices of citizen cooperation and control and more and more as instruments of executive management.

[29] They thought of the Bureau movement as the application of the general efficiency movement to the realm of government, and hence referred to it as "the efficiency movement," "the efficiency idea," or simply "the idea."

[30] See Cleveland, *op. cit.,* 351. *Cf.* his *Organized Democracy* (New York: 1913), 439. See also the Bureau's articles of incorporation, quoted in Weber, *op. cit.,* 175.

[31] While some aspects of the bureau movement have not been altogether inoffensive, the early leaders certainly dreamed some brave dreams—a vision of man rising above and mastering his environment. This vision is best transcribed by Charles A. Beard—himself a director of the New York Bureau—"If . . . I were compelled to state in a single sentence the most significant contribution of our movement to modern civilization, I should say that it is the application of the idea of continuous and experimental research, found so effective in economic enterprise, to the business of public administration—intimately and in a deep-thrusting sense, a contribution to the processes by which modern mankind is striving with all its resources to emancipate itself from the tyranny of rules of thumb and the blind regimen of nature, becoming conscious of its destiny as an all conquering power."—Addressing the Governmental Research Conference: *Government Research: Past, Present and Future* (New York: 1926). Of course, like all people, research workers have been interested primarily in food, shelter, and clothing; and in addition they pride themselves on "hardmindedness." I have attempted to catch the movement at its highest state of self-consciousness and dedication.

The Reorganization Movement

All of these phases of administrative thought and activity—
academic study, personnel reform, administrative training, and organized research—have implied and eventuated in proposals to
"reorganize" administration. But the Reorganization movement
deserves separate consideration, for in some of its phases, particularly the movement to reorganize state governments, it has produced a characteristic and distinct literature.[32] Moreover, it seems to
be a least common denominator for a number of lesser movements,
such as budget and charter reform, that have been closely related
to the rise of public administration.

Municipal and Federal Reorganization.—In the broad view, the
Reorganization movement has had three separate aspects, united by
the enthusiasm to reorganize state government. In the first place,
as a matter of attention to levels of government, reformers and reorganizers were concerned first with municipalities and with the
federal government and later extended the rationale and formulae developed in these spheres to state government.[33]

By the end of the century the current of municipal reform which
had been growing since the Civil War had turned decisively in the
direction of centralization of administrative power, as symbolized
by the Model Charter of the National Municipal Review of 1898,
recommending the concentration of administrative power in the
mayor. By 1909, the date of the People's Power League's proposal

---

[32] On the history and rationale of Reorganization see: L. A. Blue, *The Relation
of the Governor to the Organization of Executive Power in the United States*
(Philadelphia: 1902); C. A. Beard, "Reconstructing State Government," 4 *New
Rep.* (Aug., 1915), Supp.; New York Bureau of Municipal Research, *New York
State Constitution and Government: An Appraisal* (New York: 1915), and "The
State Movement for Efficiency and Economy," 90 *Municipal Research* (Oct., 1917);
"Competency and Economy in Public Expenditures," 113 *Annals* (May, 1924),
passim, but especially W. F. Dodd, "Reorganizing State Government," (161–172)
and F. O. Lowden, "Reorganization in Illinois and Its Results" (155–160); A. E.
Buck, *Administrative Consolidation in State Governments* (New York—several
editions, beginning in 1919); G. A. Weber, *op. cit., passim;* J. M. Mathews, "State
Administrative Reorganization," 16 *Am. Pol. Sci. Rev.* (Aug., 1922), 387–398, and
"The New Role of the Governor," 6 *Am. Pol. Sci. Rev.* (May, 1912), 216–228;
J. K. Pollock, "Election or Appointment of Public Officials," 181 *Annals* (Sept.,
1935), 74–79; H. J. Ford, "The Reorganization of State Government," 3 *Proc.
Acad. Pol. Sci.* (1912–13), 78–84; H. Bruere, *A Plan of Organization for New
York City* (1917); President's Committee on Administrative Management, *Report
with Special Studies* (Wash.: 1937). This is, of course, merely suggestive, and
selected with reference to the purposes stated. See Chapter 8 for a more thorough
consideration of the literature of centralization and consolidation.

[33] This is a valid generalization despite a certain amount of centralization in
state government before the end of the century and a number of studies of these
centralizing tendencies.

to reorganize Oregon government, strong-mayor charters were already recognized as less fashionable than Commission charters,[34] and at the time of the first state reorganization in 1917 the council-manager form was fast becoming *de rigueur* among reformers.[35] On the national level, before 1910, several congressional investigations designed to improve administrative organization and procedure already had been completed.

While the influence of these activities upon reorganizers is not entirely clear, there can be no doubt that President Taft's Commission on Economy and Efficiency gave great impetus to "the budget idea" [36] and that the example of "the federal plan" of strong administrative powers in the hands of the chief executive has often been used as an argument by state reorganizers.

Comparative Government and Study of Administrative Procedure.—In the second place, broad consideration of forms of government and meticulous examination of administrative methods were gradually brought together, and both contributed to the schemes for reorganizing state government. By 1909 there already existed a long record of doubt, self-examination, and disparagement on the part of political scientists with regard to the forms of our democ-

[34] On the history and rationale of the commission movement consult: Oswald Ryan, *Municipal Freedom* (Garden City: 1915); C. R. Woodruff, *City Government by Commission* (New York: 1911); E. S. Bradford, *Commission Government in American Cities* (New York: 1911); J. J. Hamilton, *The Dethronement of the City Boss* (New York: 1910); H. Bruere, *The New City Government* (New York: 1912). See also the early volumes of the *National Municipal Review*.

[35] On the history and rationale of the city-manager movement consult: H. A. Stone, D. K. Price, and K. H. Stone, *City Manager Government in the United States* (Chicago: 1940); L. D. White, *The City Manager* (Chicago: 1927); H. A. Toulmin, *The City Manager* (New York: 1915); C. E. Ridley, "The Council Manager Plan of City Government," 1 *Local Government Administration* (Sept., 1935), 4–8.

[36] The movement for budgetary reform has been very important, but from the standpoint of its theoretical aspects it can be subsumed under the general Reorganization movement, of which it has formed a part. "It may be made one of the most potent instruments of democracy. . . . The budget provides a means through which citizens may assure themselves that their effort which has been devoted to common ends is not used for private gain, is not misused or frittered away. . . ." A. R. Hatton, quoted in L. D. Upson, "Half-Time Budget Methods," 113 *Annals* (May, 1924), 69–74. More and more the "budget" has been regarded as a device of administration, rather than an instrument of popular control.

On the history of budget thought see the various writings of F. A. Cleveland and A. E. Buck, especially, Cleveland, "Evolution of the Budget Idea in the United States," 62 *Annals* (Nov., 1915), 15–35, and Buck, "The Development of the Budget Idea in the United States," 113 *Annals* (May, 1924), 31–39. See also: 62 *Annals, passim,* and 113 *Annals, passim;* New York Bureau of Municipal Research, "Responsible Government," Number 69, ch. 4 (Jan., 1916), of *Municipal Research.* See E. A. Fitzpatrick, *Budget Making in a Democracy* (New York: 1918), and also F. P. Gruenberg, "The Executive vs. The Legislative Budget," 7 *Nat. Mun. Rev.* (Mar., 1918), 167–173 (résumé of a debate between Fitzpatrick and Cleveland) for a statement of the case of the opposition.

racy. Influenced by British experience and British writers, Woodrow Wilson, Gamaliel Bradford, and many others had contrasted our system of separation of powers unfavorably with cabinet government, and urged the need for stronger executive leadership. Students home from the Continent were anxious to find a formula that would enable democracy to secure the manifest advantages of autocracy. The traditional doctrine of separation of powers became the *bête noir* of American political science, and exaltation of the powers of the executive branch its Great White Hope. Journals, both popular and scholarly, broke out in a rash of schemes for joining more closely the legislative and executive organs, for restraining the judicial arm, and for increasing the powers and responsibilities of the chief executive. On the other hand, the Research movement (the application of the "efficiency idea" to government), which in the beginning had directed its attention primarily to matters of detail and procedure, was brought to a consideration of governmental framework and philosophy when it found its hoped for reforms balked from above. It found that "mere bookkeeping systems" [37] were not enough, that "the budget idea" was intimately related to the basic relations between the legislature and executive, and that the efficiencies and economies of business procedure require business's concentration of authority. In the state reorganization movement these two streams of thought met and mingled.

Management by the People and Management for the People.— In the third place, the state reorganization movement reflects a meeting, a conflict, and a compromise between the two great tendencies in the political thought of the Progressive era: belief in a natural social harmony and simplified and more democratic institutions, and belief in a man-created social harmony and more extensive and efficient overhead control.[38] When the reorganization movement was still inchoate the former of these tendencies was strong. The Oregon Plan was probably more concerned with direct democracy than executive management. The "reorganizations" in Wisconsin in 1911 and New Jersey in 1912 sought to secure competence, continuity, and freedom from "politics" by dispersing power among boards and commissions. To the ultimate orthodoxies, however, the centralizing and managerial tendency made the larger contribution.

---

[37] See Beard, *op. cit.*, 4–5. See also, New York Bureau, *Appraisal*, 5. *Cf.*, however, H. Bruere, *The New City Government* (New York: 1912), who subordinates "charter tinkering" to "good business management." 85 ff., ch. 13.

[38] See Beard, *op. cit.*, 3.

The year 1915 may be taken as the turning point. The *Appraisal* of the state constitution and government of New York, prepared for the constitutional convention of that year by the New York Bureau of Municipal Research, is an important document in the history of American political thought. For this "new *Federalist*" is a conscious statement of fundamental philosophy and a summary and synthesis of the political thought of the previous decades. Some of the *Appraisal* is now "dated," but for the most part American political science and public administration have since been content to work within its framework. The formulae for reconciling democracy and efficient administration have already been stated: the substitution of division of labor and specialization of functions for separation of powers; the establishment of such machinery as will simplify the voters' task and make the government immediately responsible to them; to this end and to provide leadership, the concentration of executive power and responsibility; securing for the chief executive the necessary tools for economical and efficient management; and the establishment of institutional devices, in addition to popular election, for guarding against administrative incompetence, dishonesty, and aggrandizement. The campaigns in which these principles have issued are equally familiar: the short ballot; the increase of the executive's appointing power and the abolition of overlapping terms; abolition of boards; reduction in number of departments; provision for executive leadership in forming and executing the budget; and the "merit system."

The Rationalism of Reorganization.—A characteristic, a tendency, and an unresolved conflict of the literature of Reorganization should be noted. The characteristic is its rationalism and utopianism. "Reorganizers," despite the fact that occasionally they are politically crafty in their choice of argument, exhibit as a general rule the impatience and optimism of all reformism which stems from the eighteenth century. They are convinced not only of their rightness, but that people generally prefer good government and, when the advantages of reorganization are explained, will desire as a matter of course the new and superior arrangement. There is little appreciation—in the literature—of the massive, imponderable emotional substructure of society, and scarcely a hint of a Burkian respect for the "Divine tactic" of national history. The Reorganizers stand "outside" their material, seek to impose rational principles upon it, and are inclined to believe that accomplishing their reforms will follow easily upon manipulating their concepts. The public

administration and political science fraternities were surprised at
the storm which broke around the Reorganization scheme of 1938,
were bewildered at opposition to its obvious beneficences, and an-
gered at the evil influences which balked it.

The Narrowing of Scope.—There has been, however, a tendency
on the part of the Reorganization movement to become, if not less
rationalistic, less optimistic in tone and less inclusive in its scope.
The original disposition to take Heaven by storm has disappeared.
It is no longer urged that our constitutional systems be extensively
altered.   There has been a recent disposition to accept the traditional
triadic system as an unalterable datum (or to profess belief in it
as a matter of tactics), and to secure what reform is possible within
its outlines. This together with less optimism about what may be
expected from "the public" in the way of understanding and support, has brought increasing concentration of attention upon the
administrative branch. The philosopher-king, union of all-wisdom
and all-power in one or a few as a short-cut to Utopia—there is no
more familiar pattern in the history of political theory than this.
One enlightened chief administrator with adequate power is all
that is necessary, and much easier to secure than hundreds of enlightened legislators or millions of enlightened citizens. The theory
of benevolent despotism is often rationalistic and utopian.

Confusion Regarding the Position of the Chief Executive.—
On a very important point there is considerable conflict and confusion in the literature of Reorganization, and in the literature of
public administration generally. This is the matter of the position,
qualities, duties, training, and choice of the chief executive. There
are two tendencies in American public administration (as L. D.
White has often observed): that toward the professional, nonpolitical executive (city-manager type) and that toward the non-
professional political executive (presidential type). Back of these
two tendencies is a welter of varied and conflicting ideas. It seems
clear that the generalizations that fit one of these types of executive
need not necessarily fit the other. There is patently no fixed relationship between vote-getting ability and administrative ability, and
less between vote-getting and professional training for administration. If "for representation, elect; for administration, appoint" is
a sound "principle" of public administration it is hardly consistent,
to say the least, to make of the highest elected official the chief
administrator.

Foreign Influence

Each of the movements already discussed has helped to shape the contours of the literature of public administration. Other movements, such as reporting, centralized purchasing, and planning have produced a body of writings. They are, however, subordinate in amount and in the scope of their ideological trappings to the movements already discussed, and separate discussion would be over-subtle and repetitious. But on a different level—not "movements" but "influences"—are two factors which have contributed extensively to the direction and content of the study of public administration, and which any survey of the theoretical aspects of public administration must include. They are foreign influence and business influence.[39]

"The trends of American administration," wrote L. D. White, surveying American public administration for *Recent Social Trends,* "do not seem to have been greatly influenced by foreign experience. . . ."[40] This is a valid generalization in the context in which it occurs. Still, foreign experience has patently affected American study of public administration and—unless this study has been

---

[39] Consideration of military influence comes logically at this point, but it does not seem important enough to deserve treatment in the text. At least, while it may be important, I do not find its outlines clear. Some of the more obvious points should be noted, however. First, the German army, particularly its staff organization, has stimulated writing and imitation. Elihu Root's *Annual Reports of the Secretary of War, 1894–1903,* recommended reorganization of the United States' army on the basis of Prussian experience (see especially, 62, 165, 293, 329) and reference to these reports is often made. The group that directed the New York Bureau in its early days also studied the Prussian army. *Cf.* C. A. Beard, *The Work Unit in Federal Administration,* Chicago: 1937, 2. Second, at least two important studies of administration of the United States army have been added to the literature of public administration: J. Dickinson, *The Building of an Army* (New York: 1922); and J. H. Marion, *Training and Leadership in the United States Army* (Chicago: 1939) and "Organization for Internal Control and Coordination in the United States Army," 32 *Am. Pol. Sci. Rev.* (Oct., 1938), 877–897. (Studies of military administration during the recent war are now beginning to appear. See, for example, the files of the *Public Administration Review.*) Third, military experience has obviously contributed something to thought on the subjects of staff and line, span of control, and planning. With regard to "staff and line" a great amount of confusion has obtained, which perhaps earlier or closer attention to military experience would have obviated. With regard to "span of control" its present vogue seems to come chiefly from V. A. Graicunas. (The Brownlow Committee studied military experience with a "general staff," but nothing on the subject was published.) Fourth, there are scattered references to military administration and military writings in the literature of business and public administration. See, for example, H. Pasdermadjian, "The Planning Staff in Administrative Management," 5 *Plan Age* (Mar., 1939), 84–95; and M. E. Dimock, "Executive Responsibility: The Span of Control in Federal Government," 3 *Soc. Adv. Man. Jour.* (Jan., 1938), 22–28.

[40] One-volume edition (New York: 1933), 1392. "We have no extensive groups urging guild socialism, or syndicalism, or communism, or fascism, and no one concerned as to the type of administrative reorganization appropriate to any one of these forms of state organization." *Ibid.,* 1426.

nugatory—affected administrative practice. European institutions, European-trained scholars and administrators, and European writings, have all helped to give direction and content to American administrative thought.

American Study Abroad.—A perusal of the literature of reform and Progressivism creates a strong impression that the stimulation of European example has been tremendous. Many, perhaps a majority, of the early reformers had travelled in Great Britain or on the Continent, and all of them knew at second hand of the marvels to be found there. Their writings record the initial shock and later resolves when idealistic faith in the Mission of America and observation of "realistic democracy" were brought face to face with the orderliness, decorum, and efficiency of the "monarchies" and "autocracies" that they had believed from infancy to be inferior forms of government.[41] The stimulus of example was perhaps greatest in the sphere of municipal government.[42] Conviction that European municipal government is a worthy example is writ at large in the *Proceedings of the National Conference for Good City Government* and the early volumes of the *National Municipal Review*. Glasgow and Birmingham, Paris and Marseilles, Vienna and Berlin, these were the benchmarks of the reformers. True enough, this attention to European example did not result in any extensive changes in American municipal charters; but its contribution to emotional fervor was unquestionable.

Above the municipal level, European example has contributed to the literature, if not the practice, in a number of fields.[43] Perhaps per-

[41] The question which was raised was the success, in a cosmic conflict of great Principles, of the American Experiment. "The republican theory is arraigned at the bar of public opinion. . . ." D. B. Eaton, *op. cit.*, 5. "The finger of scorn has been justly pointed at us. The European press daily mentions our unfortunate political, as well as artistic past, as ample proof of the failure of free institutions." F. S. Lamb, "Municipal Art," 1 *Municipal Affairs* (Dec., 1897), 674–688, 688. Never doubting the correctness or the ultimate victory of Freedom and Democracy, the reformers set themselves (as do Calvinists and Marxists) the arduous task of realizing Fate.

[42] See, for example, R. H. Dana, *The Merit Principle in the Selection of the Higher Municipal Officers* (Cambridge: 1904); E. M. Hartwell, "Municipal Statistical Offices in Europe," 1 *Municipal Affairs* (Sept., 1897), 525–548; W. D. Foulke, "Effective Municipal Government: A Study of the City of Frankfort-On-The-Main," 1 *Nat. Mun. Rev.* (Jan., 1912), 21–32; D. B. Eaton, *Government of Municipalities* (New York: 1899), especially chs. 12 and 13; and F. J. Goodnow, *Municipal Home Rule* (New York: 1895) and "Local Government in Prussia," 5 *Pol. Sci. Q.* (Mar., 1890), 124–192.

[43] Even the earliest statement of the very notion of a separate "science of administration" (although definitely premature) is based on European experience. By studying this science, said Eaton in his study of *Civil Service in Great Britain*, the British have purified their public life and improved their administration. "Public administration, in Great Britain, has, in fact, been reduced to something like a science. It has taken rank with legislation; having its fixed principles, its care-

sonnel is the most important. Notably, the engaging spectacle presented by the British administrative class cast a spell over all of American political science from which it is only presently emerging. We are gradually learning that administrative systems must be construed in relation to their context, both material and ideological, and that they have a syntax as well as a grammar.

The list of writers, particularly early writers, trained abroad is very impressive, both in length and in consideration of the importance of the contribution of the individuals. F. J. Goodnow, W. E. Mosher, C. A. Beard, E. J. James, H. G. James, W. B. Munro and many others spent a period at a Continental or British university. Many more recent writers have gone abroad to conduct studies of European administrative practice. Presumably—obviously—these men have been affected by their European experience, and American study of public administration has been thus affected. The recent influx of European scholars and administrators into American universities is also a factor with which to reckon. While it is too early to calculate their effects, their writings have characteristics making them easily distinguishable from American writings on administration.[44]

Types of Foreign Influence.—There are many examples of the influence of foreign writings. The Continental notion of *droit administratif* has influenced American thought and curricula. The writings of J. S. Mill, Walter Bagehot, and James Bryce enjoyed a great vogue among American political scientists and were effective in developing a critical attitude toward the separation of powers and, in the case of Bryce, toward municipal government. Foreign writings contributed to the politics-administration theory of governmental powers; at least Goodnow buttressed his argument in *Politics and Administration* by citation of Continental writers. Euro-

---

fully nurtured methods, its theory of parties, its well considered tests of capacity and character. . . ." 11c (sic). Wilson also looked across the ocean for the seeds of "The Study of Administration" (2 *Pol. Sci. Q.*, June, 1887, 197–222, 201–202) that he advocated.

[44] F. Morstein Marx, C. J. Friedrich, and Arnold Brecht come easily to mind. Their writings are distinguished by historical, philosophical, and analytical qualities almost entirely missing from American writings on administration. In *Responsible Bureaucracy* (Friedrich and Taylor Cole, Cambridge: 1932), for example, Friedrich endeavors to discover or elaborate a "systematic concept" of bureaucracy. American students have been no more interested in "systematic concepts" than in Buddist theology. (*Cf.* Philip Selznick, "An Approach to a Theory of Bureaucracy," 8 *Am. Soc. Rev.* (Feb., 1943), 47–54. But Mr. Selznick is presumably a sociologist.) These Continental-trained scholars may prove a channel for the works of Max Weber, Jan Mertl, and other recent European thinkers to exert an influence over American study.

pean writings on the budget, particularly those of René Stourm, Gaston Jeze, Maurice Block, and Emile Worms have often been cited. British official documents, such as the reports of the Machinery of Government Committee and the Committee on Ministers' Powers, have been widely read, as have the files of *Public Administration*. And recently there has been something in the nature of a "reinfection" of American administrative thought by those writers— Lyndall Urwick, Oliver Sheldon, and others—who have been more or less a part of the international scientific management movement.[45]

Business Influence

Someone has said of Utilitarianism that it crept up from the docks and markets into the chambers of state and halls of learning, that the outlook of the countinghouse became a philosophy of state and of life. Such a figure is not inapplicable to the influence that business has exercised over American study of public administration. In recent years there has been an increasing insistence that private and business administration are not or should not be identical, and there has even been self-criticism by students of public administration. But on the whole, business ideology and business procedures are still accepted, consciously or unconsciously, as desirable. Even those of the public administration fraternity who desire increasing control of business in the name of greater general welfare are generally disposed to accept the mechanisms and methods—and more of the spirit than they imagine—of the business community in which they are immersed.[46] Just as the early reformers proposed to overcome autocracy by borrowing its tools, these "New Dealers" propose to overcome business predominance by becoming more business-like—posing the old question whether means can be divorced from the ends they serve.

Reformers and "Business."—The early reformers and the pioneers in public administration accepted business example enthusiastically and practically without reservation. "The field of admin-

---

[45] "Reinfection" is a familiar theme in the history of political theory. Thus both Natural Rights and Utilitarianism were developed in France from English sources and then blown back across the channel in a much more virulent form.

[46] For example, in personnel administration—a field referred to in its early days as "the new art of handling men"—the bent is to think in terms of labor productivity rather than the satisfaction of creative effort, to compensate for work assumed to be unpleasant by more pay and shorter hours, to regard employees as means rather than as ends. In those cases in which there is a concern to "improve morale" by making workers "content" with their jobs, there is a distinctly paternalistic air. The truth of my thesis will be borne out, I think, by asking: What would William Morris or Hillaire Belloc think of administrative literature?

istration is a field of business," [47] wrote Woodrow Wilson in 1887, giving the cue to subsequent writers. During the nineties this conviction that administration is a realm of business, a realm from which "politics" should be rigorously excluded, came to be shared by practically all reformers and by educated people generally.[48]

General Acceptance of "Business."—By the first decade of this century, administration-is-business had become a creed, a shibboleth, and there was little serious criticism of the notion until the decade of the Great Depression. The business example was accepted in academic political science; and the corporate analogy was used to promote the spread of city-manager charters.[49] The desirability of business-in-government even received repeated sanction by our Presidents.

It must be recognized of course, that in some measure apparent acceptance of business, use of business analogy and dollar-and-cents arguments, must be attributed to strategic or tactical considerations. Administrative study was dependent, directly or indirectly, upon business support; and generally no plan for administrative reform could hope for a trial without the approval of the business community.[50] Moreover, the progressive and humanitarian purposes of

[47] *Op. cit.,* 209. "The officials who administer the government of a city deal with pure business questions . . . There is a close parallel between the business of a great railroad corporation and the business of a city. Both require great administrative and financial ability; skill in the selection of men, power of organization and strength of will. The ability to organize a force that will run trains for freight and passengers economically and efficiently is not in kind different from the ability to organize a force which will clean or pave streets regularly or well." Moorfield Storey, "The Government of Cities; The Need of a Divorce of Municipal Business From Politics," in *Proceedings,* National Civil Service Reform League, 1891, 47–67, 61–62.

[48] See the files of the Conference for Good City Government and the *Proceedings* of the National Civil Service Reform League. Acceptance of business values, organization, and techniques in the early period was probably not only inevitable because of the historical circumstances, and desirable because of the extreme urgency of "efficiency," but also an advance in some respects in ethical standards. Heir to the benefits of Reform, I should be ungrateful to suggest that Reform was built upon a gross error.

That the Bureau movement was particularly susceptible to business influence was noted above. *Cf.* F. A. Cleveland, *Chapters on Municipal Administration and Accounting* (New York: 1909), 357; and his "Municipal Ownership as a Form of Governmental Control," 28 *Annals* (Nov., 1906), 359–370, 363; Henry Bruere, *New City Government,* 85 ff., 365. Ch. 2 of the New York Bureau's *Appraisal* is an extended treatment of the joint stock company as a model for popular control and efficient administration.

[49] See H. G. James, "The City Manager Plan," 8 *Am. Pol. Sci. Rev.* (Nov., 1914), 602–613, 610.

[50] "The American people have a deep conviction that their business organizations and methods are uniquely successful, and they readily understand the resemblance between the city manager and the general superintendent. The council-manager plan seems to be the application of American business methods to government, a practical answer to the demand for more business in government." L. D. White,

the reformers and administrative students must not be forgotten.[51] They thought of government as an instrument for achieving community purposes, for securing more security and equality. Whether they realized it or not, this program entailed limitation upon business.

Specific Contributions of Business.—The contribution of business to the theory of public administration, in addition to its contribution to the ethos of the entire movement, has been very great, and it has already been suggested in a number of connections. Business organization, for example, particularly the corporate form, was used to justify the tenets of reorganization.[52] It was used to deprecate separation and balance of powers.[53] It was used to aggrandize the chief executive.[54] It was used to justify hierarchy,[55] to support the principle of appointment,[56] and to lend weight to the budget argument.[57]

Doubt in Depression.—Much as public administration owes to the stimulus of Progressivism and Reform, its Founding Fathers seem hardly to have been touched by the iconoclasm of the Muckrakers, nor to have travelled more than a few steps down the road that led Lincoln Steffens to indict business for the debauchery of government. It was not until the cataclysm of the Great Depres-

---

The City Manager (Chicago: 1927), 298 (by permission of the University of Chicago Press). See also, Stone, Price, and Stone, *op. cit.,* 27; Toulmin, *op. cit.,* 51; and Beard, *Reconstructing State Government,* 5.

One result of the necessity of the approval of the business community has been that reformers have often couched their arguments in dollars-and-cents terms (sometimes with tongue in cheek); and frequently have promised what could not be delivered.

[51] Beard says of Cleveland that he "escaped the illusion . . . that government is like a business organization conducted for the purpose of paying dividends to stockholders." "The Place of Administration in Government," 2 *Plan Age* (Dec., 1936), 5–10, 6. See Bruere, *New City Government,* 1–2, where under "simple prerogatives of citizenship" is blandly set forth a program well in advance of the New Deal.

[52] It is a minor irony that the author of the most trenchant criticism of "the federal plan" of reorganization (W. H. Edwards) found it to his purpose not to deny the validity of the business analogy, but to assert that the "federal" reorganizers had departed from what is in fact business practice!

[53] See E. S. Bradford, *op. cit.,* 304.

[54] See "The Story of the City Manager," 10 *Nat. Mun. Rev.* (Feb., 1921, Supp.), 20; Willoughby, *Principles,* ch. 3, "The Chief Executive as General Manager."

[55] See G. Bradford, *The Lesson of Popular Government* (New York: 1899), I, 48.

[56] See H. Hansen, *et al.,* "The Selection of City Administrative Officials," 27 *Nat. Mun. Rev.* (Nov., 1938), 536–542, 539.

[57] See Cleveland, "The Federal Budget," 3 *Proc. Acad. Pol. Sci.* (Jan., 1913), 117–131.

sion [58] and the decline of business prestige in the whole community that occasional and generally mild objections were entered to the administration-is-business dictum.[59] There have been some sharper criticisms recently,[60] but there is still hardly a suggestion as to what might replace business spirit, organization, and methods in government—except the *ancien regime*. Many students of administration are undoubtedly aware of the esthetic and ethical objections of, for example, Guild Socialism to business. But they have evidently felt such considerations too other-worldly, too far removed from the urgencies of the immediate task, to be taken seriously.

BIBLIOGRAPHICAL NOTE

Consult the following on how American writers on public administration and scientific management have defined or described such key concepts as "public administration," "administration," and "management": F. G. Bates and O. P. Field, *State Government* (New York: 1939), 257; Commission of Inquiry on Public Service Personnel, *Better Government Personnel* (New York: 1935), 34, 35; R. T. Crane, "Bureaus of Political Research," 17 *Am. Pol. Sci. Rev.* (May, 1923), 296–303, 300; M. E. Dimock, "What Is Public Administration," 15 *Pub. Man.* (Sept., 1933), 259–262, 261, 262; "The Meaning and Scope of Public Administration," in *The Frontiers of Public Administration* (Chicago: 1936), by Dimock, J. M. Gaus, and L. D. White, 1–12, *passim;* "The Study of Administration," 31 *Am. Pol. Sci. Rev.* (Feb., 1937), 28–40, 29, 31; *Modern Politics and Administration* (New York: 1937), 31, 231, 243; F. J. Goodnow, *Comparative Administrative Law* (New York: 1893), Vol. I, 1–5; *Politics and Administration* (New York: 1900), early chapters, *passim; The Principles of the Administrative Law of the United States* (New York: 1905),

---

[58] Only two exceptions have come to my attention. See H. E. Hunt, "Obstacles to Municipal Progress," 11 *Am. Pol. Sci. Rev.* (Feb., 1917), 76–87, 81; and H. L. McBain, "The Problem of Government Reorganization," 9 *Proceed. Acad. Pol. Sci.* (1920–22), 331–335, 334.

[59] *Cf.* C. A. Dykstra, "Public Administration and Private Business," 14 Pub. *Man.* (April, 1932), 117–119; and his "In Defense of Government," 189 *Annals* (Jan., 1937), 1–9, 8; H. W. Dodds, "Bureaucracy and Representative Government," 189 *Annals*, 165–172, 167, 169; Harvey Walker, *Public Administration in the United States* (New York: 1937), 9 ff.; J. M. Pfiffner, *Public Administration* (New York: 1935), 14 ff.; M. E. Dimock, "Do Business Men Want Good Government?" 20 *Nat. Mun. Rev.* (Jan., 1931), 31–37. *Cf.*, however, his *Developing America's Waterways* (Chicago: 1935).

[60] "The folklore of the business elite came by gradual transition to be the symbols of governmental reformers. Efficiency, system, orderliness, budgets, economy, saving, were all injected into the efforts of reformers who sought to remodel municipal government in terms of the great impersonality of corporate enterprise." J. B. Shannon, "County Consolidation," 207 *Annals* (Jan., 1940), 168–175, 168. See also, A. C. Millspaugh, "Democracy and Administrative Organization," in *Essays in Political Science,* J. M. Mathews and J. Hart, eds. (Baltimore: 1937), 64–73, 66.

Since his study of business administration, the attitude of M. E. Dimock is strangely ambivalent—half praise, half criticism. See, for example, his "Administrative Efficiency Within a Democratic Polity," in *New Horizons in Public Administration* (University, Alabama: 1945), a symposium.

For recent writings critical of business example and emphasizing the distinction between public and private administration, see also: E. S. Wengert, "The Study of Public Administration," 36 *Am. Pol. Sci. Rev.* (April, 1942), 313–322, 313 ff.; P. H. Appleby, *Big Democracy* (New York: 1945), *passim.*

1–13; G. A. Graham, *Education for Public Administration* (Chicago: 1941), 3–4; Luther Gulick, "Science, Values and Public Administration," in *Papers on the Science of Administration* (New York: 1937), Gulick and L. Urwick, eds., 191–195; M. V. Hayes, *Accounting for Executive Control* (New York: 1929), ch. 1, *passim;* M. B. Lambie, ed., *Training for the Public Service* (Chicago: 1935), 20, 24; J. M. Mathews, *Principles of American State Administration* (New York: 1917), 3; F. J. Miller, "Scientific Management: Nature, Achievements and Tendencies," in *Papers Presented before the International Congress of Scientific Management* (Prague: 1924), 3–8, 5; W. E. Mosher, "New Emphasis on an Old Concept," 1 *Pub. Adm. Rev.* (June, 1938—Syracuse publication), 5–6; New York Bureau of Municipal Research, *The Constitution and Government of the State of New York: An Appraisal* (New York: 1915), 89; H. S. Person, "Research and Planning as Functions of Administration and Management," 1 *Pub. Adm. Rev.* (Autumn, 1940), 65–73, 66; Kirk Porter, *State Administration* (New York: 1938), 5; President's Committee on Administrative Management, *Report* (Washington: 1937), 2; C. E. Ridley and H. A. Simon, *Measuring Municipal Activities* (Chicago: 1938), 3; W. W. Stockberger, "The Need for Career Administrators," 189 *Annals* (Jan., 1937), 91–96, 93; Ordway Tead, "Amateurs Versus Experts in Administration," 189 *Annals* (Jan., 1937), 42–47, 43; *New Adventures in Democracy* (New York: 1939), 3, 103; Harvey Walker, "An American Conception of Public Administration," 11 *Jour. Pub. Adm.* (Jan., 1933), 15–19, 15; *Public Administration in the United States* (New York: 1937), 8, 16, 61; L. D. White, *Further Contributions to the Prestige Value of Public Employment* (Chicago: 1932), 87; "Public Administration," in 1 *Encyc. of Soc. Sci.* (1933), 440; "Administration as a Profession," 189 *Annals* (Jan., 1937), 84–90, *passim; Introduction to the Study of Public Administration* (New York: 1939), 2, 4; W. F. Willoughby, "Introduction" to G. A. Weber's *Organized Efforts for the Improvement of Methods of Administration in the United States* (New York: 1919), 7, 30; "A General Survey of Research in Public Administration," 24 *Am. Pol. Sci. Rev.* (Feb., 1930, Supp.), 39–51, 39; *Principles of Public Administration* (Baltimore: 1927), 1, 7; "The Science of Public Administration," in *Essays in Political Science* (Baltimore: 1937), J. M. Mathews and J. Hart, eds., 39–63, 39, 40, 44, 62, 63; Woodrow Wilson, "The Study of Administration," 2 *Pol. Sci. Q.* (June, 1887), 197–222, 209–210.

Chapter 3

SCIENTIFIC MANAGEMENT AND PUBLIC ADMINISTRATION[1]

The scientific management movement provides enlightening perspective for the public administration movement. The two movements arose concurrently, were stimulated by much the same circumstances in their respective fields, and developed some closely similar doctrines. In some ways the more "advanced" movement, scientific management has contributed many techniques and considerable philosophy to public administration. In some areas the two movements are now overlapping or indistinguishable.

The Positivist Spirit

Scientific management and public administration are related aspects of a common phenomenon: a general movement to extend the methods and the spirit of science to an ever-widening range of man's concerns. As public administration is based in political science, which has sought to place political relationships on an objective or scientific basis, so scientific management is but a highly conscious part of a general movement to place man's economic life, particularly production, upon a scientific basis.[2] Both movements are "positivist"

---

[1] Scientific management is a system almost as elaborate as Marxism, with its central figures, its schisms, its mutations, its nuances, etc. An amateur in the field, I can hope only to have appraised correctly its main outlines.

[2] "It in no way whatsoever lessens the greatness of Taylor's contribution to suggest that his application of a scientific attack to a certain body of problems was an inevitable extension of that scientific effort and outlook which were permeating the whole intellectual life of the last quarter of the nineteenth century. The scientific approach, method, preoccupation were all in the air of 1880." Ordway Tead, "Comment," 5 *Adv. Man.* (Oct.–Dec., 1940), 145–6.

Norman M. Pearson has recently done us the service of pointing out some distinctions between "Taylorism" and "Fayolism" that are commonly overlooked. See his "Fayolism as the Necessary Complement of Taylorism," 39 *Am. Pol. Sci. Rev.* (Febr., 1945), 68–80. His thesis is that Taylorism is a system applying to the "lower," more technical and routine aspects of administration; whereas Fayolism pertains to the "higher," the "managerial" or "executive" functions of administration. Perhaps the thesis is carried too far, however; for Taylor's descendants nowadays, the world is their oyster, even though Fayol's thought and writing about the managerial or executive function were contemporaneous with and independent of Taylor's work. In any event, whether there are doctrinal differences that still divide followers of Taylor from followers of Fayol, from the viewpoint of this

47

—with striking similarities to August Comte's Positivism. They seek a growing range of indisputable fact, and an extension of the rule of law. They seek to eliminate metaphysic and to substitute measurement. And both, it is not surprising to find, profess a revised and expurgated "Religion of Humanity."

The past two centuries have witnessed many examples of positivist political thought similar to scientific management. After Comte's Positivism, perhaps the next most striking analogy is the philosophy of Saint-Simon, the French "utopian socialist." The analogy goes beyond the systems of thought. In each case there has been a band of disciples, chiefly businessmen and engineers, organized to propagate the New Way. That the Sacred College of the Apostles and the Taylor Society are of the same genus, if not the same species, there can be no doubt. Both of them are obviously related also to the "soviet of technicians" of Thorstein Veblen's *The Engineers and the Price System.* The writings of H. G. Wells—the *Modern Utopia* and *The World of William Clissold,* for example—also come to mind. The New Order to be established by Wells' scientist-businessmen would certainly pass at first glance for the New Order of scientific management. Even Technocracy may be regarded as a "sport" or "left wing" of scientific management.

Development of Scientific Management "Theory"

Scientific management began with the researches of Frederick W. Taylor and others into such matters as the variables involved in metal cutting and the most effective piece-rate system. But Taylor insisted that his method reached beyond the minutiae of manufacturing, extended his study to the production unit, and attempted to explain in speech and writing the new approach to problems of "management." [3] His followers have apologized for certain crudities in his work, and they have often admitted that scientific management has moved so far since Taylor's death in 1915 that much of his work has been invalidated. But they insist upon the genius of the man; and maintain that all of Taylorism that has been re-

study they are both aspects of a common phenomenon—an international "scientific management" movement. To one viewing from without, the question presented is similar to the question of the extent to which Marxism was produced by Engels or altered by Lenin.

[3] It is necessary to avoid, in an essay of this scope, the controversies surrounding the proper use of "scientific management" and "business administration"—whether one subsumes the other, etc. (*Cf.* Herman Feldman, "Business Administration," in 3 *Encyc. Soc. Sci.,* 87–90, 88) ; as well as any discussion whether, particularly in view of Henry R. Towne's paper "The Engineer as Economist" (1886), Taylor is really the "father" of scientific management.

jected is unessential, that all the elaborations and additions are true Taylorism because they accord with the "certain philosophy," the "mental revolution," that is the heart of the doctrine.

This is perhaps true, but if Taylor could view the literature of public administration since 1915 he would certainly be amazed. For scientific management has not always walked soberly with Science. It has been affected by the American climate of opinion; it has become Democratic, and moral in purpose. It has, both in America and abroad, become a Cause and a Philosophy of Life. It has recently been the philosophy of a "business and technical internationale," an "internationale" with its own Utopia to sell.[4]

Taylor's Philosophy.—Because he did not have the literary training or inclination to make "Taylorism" a rounded and coherent system,[5] and because his own "prejudices" did not always accord with his "system," any brief treatment of Taylor's ideas would be unsatisfactory. Let it suffice then to note that there seem to be three "levels of reality" in his system: (1) procedures or "mechanism," (2) "underlying principles," and (3) fundamental philosophy. The following quotations from Taylor illustrate each of these "levels of reality":

"MECHANISM."

The mechanism of management must not be mistaken for its essence, or underlying philosophy. . . . The same mechanism which will produce the finest results when made to serve the underlying principles of scientific management, will lead to failure and disaster if accompanied by the wrong spirit. . . . As elements of this mechanism may be cited:

Time study, with the implements and methods for properly making it.

Functional or divided foremanship and its superiority to the old-fashioned single foreman. . . .

The 'differential rate.'

Mnemonic systems. . . .

---

[4] So far as I am aware, no history of scientific management as a social and political philosophy has been published. That it deserves such a treatment I have no doubt. Yu-Tsuan Ku's thesis (see bibliographical note at end of chapter) might have served this purpose up to 1931, had it been published.

[5] *Cf.* A. H. Church, in "Has 'Scientific Management' Science?" 35 *American Machinist* (July 20, 1911), 108–112, enumerating nine different features which Taylor claimed at one time or another to be the "fundamental" or "essential" feature of his system. This article is one of the better of the many criticisms of the movement. See also: J. R. Edwards, "The Fetishism of Scientific Management," 24 *Jour. Amer. Soc. Naval Eng.* (May, 1912), 355–416; and P. Ballard, "Scientific Management and Science," 41 *Cassier's Magazine* (May, 1912), 425–430.

A routing system.

Modern cost system, etc.[6]

"UNDERLYING PRINCIPLES."

These are, however, merely the elements of details of the mechanism of management. Scientific management, in its essence, consists of a certain philosophy, which results . . . in a combination of the four great underlying principles of management:

First. The development of a true science.

Second.. The scientific selection of workmen.

Third. His scientific education and development.

Fourth. Intimate friendly cooperation between the management and the men.[7]

"FUNDAMENTAL PHILOSOPHY."

Scientific management is not any efficiency device . . . nor is it any bunch or group of efficiency devices. It is not a new system of figuring costs; it is not a new scheme of paying men . . . it is not time study; it is not motion study. . . . It is not divided foremanship or functional foremanship; it is not any of the devices. . . .

Now, in its essence, scientific management involves a complete mental revolution. . . .

The substitution of this new outlook—this new viewpoint—is of the very essence of scientific management, and scientific management exists nowhere until after this has become the central idea of both sides. . . .[8]

The Mental Revolution.—Now, the "certain philosophy," the "mental revolution," the "new viewpoint" mean the end of class conflict, but they mean more than that. They mean the inauguration of the positivist, the scientific and objective way of regarding human interrelations, in the place of either the passive acceptance of the values and institutional arrangements of one's society or the unintelligent and violent rejection of the *status quo.* They mean a change in attitude similar to that between early Italian religious painting and the meticulous naturalism of the Flemish school. One stands "outside" his material and contemplates it objectively. He discovers thus the true nature of what he regards, he discovers its laws. And he builds his system upon these laws. When this is

---

[6] *The Principles of Scientific Management* (New York: 1911), 128. (This and following citation by permission of Harper & Bros.)

[7] *Ibid.,* 130. These four "principles" are given at greater length earlier in this work (36–37).

[8] Quoted in H. S. Person's "Origin and Nature of Scientific Management," in *Scientific Management in American Industry* (New York: 1926), Person, ed., 9–10 (by permission of Harper & Bros.). *Cf.* H. H. Farquhar, "A Critical Analysis of Scientific Management," 9 *Bull. Taylor Soc.* (Feb., 1924), 16–30.

done it is not man, nor caprice, nor will, that rules: it is the System. "In the past the man has been first, in the future the system must be first." Social solidarity, absence of class conflict, is both indispensable in *achieving* the positivist goal, and a natural *result* of its achievement.

The "new outlook" begins with such matters as cutting metals. It is applied to the skills involved in trades. It is applied to the relationship between the worker and his foreman, to the relationships among workers, to the department, to the entire plant, to the series of enterprises that make up the corporate unit, to the whole industry, and finally to the entire economy.[9] The natural course of thought is "upward and outward," and finally the scientific managers achieve a vision of the entire world run on the principles of scientific management: universal peace between nations, and between social classes, the ultimate in efficiency and in material satisfactions, liberty and equality in their proper portions, general education and enlightenment. Inherent in their postulates was a tendency for Taylor and his followers to leave their low-vaulted past, to insist that not this or that specific thing is the "essence" of scientific management. Science is not Newtonian physics—if it were, it would be obsolete. It is more fundamental.

Social Solidarity.—It was the need for "solidarity" that stimulated Taylor's first researches to 'discover a "fair day's work" for a "first class man." The passages in which he recounts his discomfort at the constant warfare between himself as foreman and the laborers under his direction are very poignant. He wanted to take the matter of a fair day's work out of the realm of dispute, to make the facts sovereign. But solidarity has been more than a personal psychological drive, more than the prerequisite and the goal of a science of society. It has been the natural desire of businessmen seeking to avoid "labor trouble." No improper motives or Machiavellian maneuvers are implied. What is suggested is simply that scientific

---

[9] See M. L. Cooke and Philip Murray, *Organized Labor and Production* (New York: 1940), 82. *Cf.* "The New Challenge to Scientific Management," a symposium, 16 *Bull. Taylor Soc.* (April, 1931), 62–74. See H. S. Person, "The Development and Influence of Scientific Management," 5 *Adv. Man.* (Oct.–Dec., 1940), 187–191, 189, for a statement of the thesis that "scientific management has in it a vital element that compels extension of the area of its influence after a nucleus has been established at any point." See also his "Contribution of Scientific Management to Industrial Problems," in *Scientific Management Since Taylor* (New York: 1924), E. E. Hunt, ed.; L. Urwick, "An Industrial Esperanto," 14 *Bull. Taylor Soc.* (June, 1929), 150–153; F. E. Cardullo, "Industrial Administration and Scientific Management," in *Scientific Management* (Cambridge: 1914), C. B. Thompson, ed.

management has been developed by "business" people and that the natural desire for solidarity has driven the system forward. The idea of "the substitution of the laws of situations for individual authority, guess and whim" fits the desire for solidarity as the glove the hand.

The New World-View.—Scientific management became widely publicized just as the ideal of efficiency was reaching its crest. The Taylorists, indeed, were the high priests of the cult. They infused into "efficiency" the accumulated moral capital of centuries of Christianity and the legacy of eighteenth- and nineteenth-century reformism. They dreamed of a new world in which physical forces should be harnessed to achieve man's moral purposes, and they used "efficiency" as a convenient shorthand symbol for this ideal. "What is the aim of Scientific Management?" asked H. L. Gantt in 1912. "It is intelligently to use all the available resources and knowledge of the universe in order to realize definite ideals. . . . (The ideals of Pericles) in this generation for the first time in history can be made the heritage of all, and will be made the heritage of those who reach up their heads, their hearts and their hands, and take." [10] "In my opinion," said M. L. Cooke the following year, "we shall never realize fully either the visions of Christianity or the dreams of democracy until the principles of scientific management have permeated every nook and cranny of the working world." [11] These are statements by eminent members of the movement; the effusions of the popularizers are even more remarkable. Efficiency, expert, democracy, Christianity, conservation, productivity, freedom, equality, rule of law—scientific management has yielded to the national climate of opinion. Scientific management may rest upon science, but as a system of thought it is manifestly much more than science.

At the outbreak of the Second Great War, scientific management was an international movement and a philosophy, receiving in the various countries the impress of national character, but still one body of doctrine. [12] Taylor's principal works were translated into

---

[10] In *Addresses and Discussions at the Conference on Scientific Management,* (Hanover: 1912), 92–93. See also ch. 1, note 29.

[11] "The Spirit and Social Significance of Scientific Management," 21 *Jour. Pol. Econ.* (June, 1913), 481–493, 493.

[12] The notion of "rationalization," the management of the entire economy or large segments thereof, was first and most boldly expounded on the continent, where *laissez-faire* had never been popular. The British and Americans have laid heavy emphasis upon the ethical aspects and have talked in grave language of the Mission. In the logical atmosphere of France, rationalist qualities were emphasized; French writers have treated human relationships as though they were demonstrations in geometry.

many languages almost as soon as they were published here, and thereafter he had enthusiastic disciples in many countries. The First Great War gave impetus to his doctrine—even Comrade Lenin thought Bolshevist Russia in need of the Taylor system! After the First Great War international doctrine was followed by international organization and intercourse. The International Congresses of Scientific Management began to be held; the International Management Institute was established. A "business and technical internationale" became a reality.[13]

The Influence of Scientific Management Upon Public Administration

The theories developed by the scientific management movement have influenced the development of public administration, and some recent writings suggest an even closer union between the two in the future: the notion of a "pure theory of organization" or "Republic of Administration" leaves little barrier between them.

A number of essays have discussed the influence of scientific management.[14] Still, there is much left unexplained, much is vague. Perhaps this is true in the nature of the case; an "influence" is diffi-

---

[13] The world-view of the international scientific management movement can best be presented by means of a quotation from the records of the International Congresses for Scientific Management—to present this philosophy at second hand might excite suspicion of exaggeration:

"If we sum up the problems of scientific management, we shall find that scientific management helps to simplify the working problems, improves the standard of living, helps to abolish poverty and misery, and secures more free time for making life happier. . . . After the age of machines comes the age of scientific management, giving better opportunities to improve not only the living condition of individuals, but also of entire nations. It will teach people better understanding and co-operation, and realize a new policy, the policy of a human world. . . . A world organization of scientific management could form a right basis for the foundation of world co-operative production and organized sales, and could on a basis of social economy contribute in the highest degree towards removing the economic causes of war. . . . The new philosophy of scientific management must help to bring about the Christian philosophy of love and welfare among all nations . . . it is absolutely beyond question that a knowledge of the principles of scientific management is fundamental for the success of everybody . . . therefore . . . this discipline should be taught in all kinds of schools in every country. . . . We know that only better organization can save nations from a new Armageddon. . . ." Dr. St. Spacek, "The Development of National (sic) and International Scientific Management Movement," *Sixth International Congress* (1935), 203–208, 206. See also L. Urwick, in "General Management Section: National and Economic Significance of Scientific Management," *Seventh International Management Congress* (1938), *Proceedings*. This international discussion on the eve of the Second Great War is a fascinating pattern of hope and fear.

[14] See M. L. Cooke, "The Influence of Scientific Management Upon Government—Federal, State and Municipal," 9 *Bull. Taylor Soc.* (Feb., 1924), 31–38; and J. M. Gaus, "A Quarter Century of Public Administration," 4 *Adv. Man.* (Oct.–Dec., 1940), 177–179.

cult to determine. Nevertheless, certain facts seem clearly established, and others probable.

Advocacy by Administrative Students.—To begin with, at least two major figures in public administration have been exponents of scientific management. F. A. Cleveland, whom Charles A. Beard has acclaimed as making the greatest of all contributions to American administrative study, was an ardent advocate of the extension of scientific management to administration.[15] And W. E. Mosher from the beginning regarded his "mission" as the extension of scientific management to the public's business; his special contribution in the field of personnel administration was conceived as such an extension.[16]

Many other academic students of public administration have shown an acquaintance with the literature and practice of scientific management, and have sometimes advocated its extension, in whole or part, to government. Thus J. M. Pfiffner: "Our administrators of the future . . . must know the techniques of scientific management. Indeed, it may be that the principles of Frederick W. Taylor, adapted to social ends, will some day free the world of drudgery. . . ."[17] Thus also J. M. Gaus, who has reviewed the influence of scientific management and suggested future developments.[18] L. D. White,[19] Luther Gulick,[20] D. C. Stone and Henry Hodges have exhibited knowledge of scientific management and have shown a favorable disposition toward it. Others, A. W. Macmahon for example, evidence an acquaintance with its literature.[21]

Advocacy by "Managers."—Ever since the popularization of scientific management there has been a trickle of articles appearing in the journals of political science by "scientific managers" who want

---

[15] His address, "The Application of Scientific Management to the Activities of the State," at the Amos Tuck School Conference on Scientific Management in 1911, is very revealing of the relationship between the bureau movement and scientific management. See *Addresses and Discussions at the Conference on Scientific Management,* 313–335.

[16] Letter to the writer, December 24, 1940. *Cf.* "The Next Step in Civil Service Reform," 10 *Nat. Mun. Rev.* (July, 1921), 386–391.

[17] *Research Methods in Public Administration* (New York: 1940), 25.

[18] *Op. cit..* Also his *Study of Research in Public Administration* (New York: 1930—mimeographed), 10; and his recent *Reflections on Public Administration* (University, Alabama, 1947), 48 ff.

[19] *The City Manager* (Chicago: 1927), 257–258; "Public Administration," in *Recent Social Trends* (New York: 1933, one vol. ed.) 1391–1429, 1392.

[20] *Cf.* his contributions in *Papers on the Science of Administration* (New York: 1937), L. Gulick and L. Urwick, eds.

[21] "Departmental Management," in *Problems of Administrative Management* (Wash.: 1937).

to reform government.[22] Taylorists from the beginning have considered from time to time in their own publications the application of the new procedures and the new outlook to government,[23] and "Government" has been included by the Society for the Advancement of Management in its statement of interests. There is also a long record of appeals to engineers to become "socially conscious" in their work,[24] and an increasing disposition for students of public administration to write for engineering, business administration, and scientific management publications.

This by no means exhausts the list of obvious interrelations between scientific management and public administration. Prominent administrators, such as R. G. Valentine and M. L. Cooke, have been associated with the movement, and in the Depression there was widespread transfer of scientific managers from private to public employment, especially in public works agencies. Scientific management techniques have been widely adopted in some branches of public administration during the past thirty-five years, and—but why bludgeon the obvious till it bleeds at the nose?

Similarities between Scientific Management and Public Administration

The general resemblance in spirit and outlook between scientific management and public administration has been sufficiently observed; but the practical and professional implications of this point of view should be noted.

"Managers."—A positivist-scientific polity implies "managers." The desired conditions of coordination, harmony, efficiency, and economy, although they will rest upon natural or scientific laws, must be brought into existence and maintained in existence by human agency. Since they rest upon scientific facts and laws, only

---

[22] See the early numbers of the *National Municipal Review* for several such articles. Several issues of the *Annals* likewise offer a study in the influence of scientific management. See also, M. L. Cook, "Scientific Management of the Public Business," 9 *Am. Pol. Sci. Rev.* (Aug., 1915), 488–495; H. P. Kendall, "Business Principles Applicable to Public Management," 20 *Pub. Man.* (Oct., 1938), 300–303. These are merely illustrative. On the general subject of the influence of scientific management see C. E. Ridley and H. A. Simon, *Measuring Municipal Activities* (Chicago: 1938), 5–6.

[23] See, for example: F. W. Taylor, "Government Efficiency," 2 *Bull. Taylor Soc.* (Dec., 1916—published posthumously), 7–13; J. P. Hallihan, "Administration of the Business of Government," 2 *Soc. Adv. Man. News Bull.* (Oct., 1937), 7; and G. D. Babcock, "Scientific Management in Government Operations," 4 *Adv. Man.* (Oct.–Dec., 1940), 159–164.

[24] For example, P. A. Fellows, "Engineers in Government," 2 *Adv. Man.* (Mar., 1937), 41–43.

those trained in the scientific method of ascertaining these facts and exercising these laws can supply this human agency: they are the Managers. "Management" or "administration" thus becomes a thing-in-itself, a recognizable field of inquiry and expertise, "a function that may be observed objectively and subjected to critical analysis." It becomes a "science."

In case of both scientific management and public administration, this notion of "management, a science," is a result of the spread upward and outward of the fundamental idea of extending the objective or scientific view to environment. In both cases certain anomalies have been felt, certain difficulties experienced, in arriving at and stating the notion of "management, a science," whenever the extension had gone far enough obviously to comprehend "values." In both disciplines these anomalies and difficulties have been revealed, frequently and characteristically in discussion of the problem whether management is a "science" or an "art," and the relationship of the science and the art.

A striking feature in the upward and outward spread of the idea of applying science to organized endeavor, in the case both of public administration and scientific management, has been a disposition to draw a line between a "lower" realm to which the New Method is applicable, and a "higher" realm to which it is not. In the case of both disciplines there has been a tendency to cross the line marked out as a boundary, a disposition to extend the discipline to the whole realm of political or economic endeavor. In both disciplines the distinction has recently served the purpose of a fortified line suitable for either offensive or defensive operations, as circumstances dictate.

"A clear understanding of scientific management," writes H. S. Person, "requires that management not be confused with administration. Management characterizes the organization and procedure through which collective effort is effected; administration characterizes those considerations and decisions which establish the purposes which create the need for management and those broad governing policies under which the management proceeds . . . administration is largely a process of forming judgments, may have serious social, political and moral aspects, must be largely empirical and can utilize in but a limited way principles and laws determined by the scientific method of investigation. . . ."[25] With a few changes in

[25] Reprinted by permission from "Scientific Management: A Brief Statement of Its Nature and History," in *Scientific Management Since Taylor*, E. E. Hunt, ed., copyrighted 1924 by McGraw-Hill Book Co., Inc., pp. 5–13, 5–6.

terminology this passage, it is apparent, could be substituted for passages enunciating the same thesis respecting "administration" and "politics."

Having announced and elaborated the distinction, however, and assured us that its clear recognition is necessary to avoid "confusion and controversy," Person announces with approval a few pages further on (although in a different essay) that, "with the vision and persistence of Taylor, his managerial descendants have not hesitated to carry their principles into the field of general administration." [26] We learn also that "Taylor injected the concept that a business should exist for social service, that its purposes can be defined, its objectives planned and scheduled. . . ." [27]

This is but a striking example of a very general inconsistency. There is on the one hand a feeling that the methods of science are inapplicable when applied to "values," to decision and policy. On the other, there is an urge to extend the objective, positivist approach to an ever-enlarging complex of phenomena; indeed, having embarked upon this course, extension a further step seems always logically and practically imperative. "Managers" and "administrators" have overrun the realm of policy—as the British conquered India—not by intent and plan, but by a continuous process of "tidying up the border." The confusion that flows from adherence to both the "limited" and the "unlimited" views is an example of the general welter of thought that obtains because the realm of science and the realm of value still await a satisfactory philosophic synthesis.

Research, Facts and Measurement

In their apotheosis of "research," "facts," and "measurement," there is an extremely close parallel between the public administration and the scientific management movements, a parallel frequently resulting in closely similar literary passages.[28] Facts, research, and measurement are deemed by both disciplines to lie at the heart of science. Anything which is true—or at least significant—is a "fact."

---

[26] "The Contribution of Scientific Management to Industrial Problems," 31–36, 34.

[27] Ibid., 38.

[28] On facts, research, and measurement see: W. H. Allen, Efficient Democracy (New York: 1907), chs. 2, 3; H. Bruere, "Developing Standards in Municipal Government," 61 Annals (Sept., 1915), 199–207; Cleveland, op. cit.; A. E. Buck, "Measuring the Results of Government," 13 Nat. Mun. Rev. (Mar., 1924), 152–157; C. E. Ridley, Measuring Municipal Government (New York and Syracuse: 1927—has bibliography), and C. E. Ridley and H. A. Simon, Measuring Municipal Activities (Chicago: 1938); L. D. White, Trends in Public Administration (New York: 1933), 316–317. Cf. R. K. Gooch, "Government as an Exact Science," 9 So. Pol. Soc. Sci. Q. (Dec., 1928), 252–263.

It is the duty of scientists to discover facts. The way one discovers facts is by engaging in "research." Research, then, is the solemn obligation of a devotee of either discipline. The chief instrument or indispensable tool of research is "measurement." Measurement is in fact the criterion of genuinely scientific research. When measurement is possible, science at last has arrived; until measurement is possible research is of dubious merit and even of questionable legitimacy. Facts, research, and measurement are assumed to answer questions not only of "What is the case?" but of "What should be done?" In the spirit of the scientific maxim, "When we can measure, then we know," the assumption is made that measurement "solves problems."

From Taylor and his associates, on the one hand, and Allen, Bruere, and Cleveland, on the other, there extends a firm resolve to enlarge the domain of measurement, an unbroken missionary endeavor to extend the suzerainty of "the facts." The pioneers began with inquiries into the proper speed of cutting tools and the optimum height for garbage trucks; their followers seek to place large segments of social life—or even the whole of it—upon a scientific basis.

Planning and Principles.—Closely allied are two other notions: planning and principles. "Planning" is at once the motive for research, and the natural consequence of it.[29] It is to get away from ignorance and confusion that research is undertaken, to find a solid and unchallengeable basis for human relationships. The conquest of areas once deemed to lie necessarily in the realm of guess and drift stimulates the imagination; and the newly won areas form the basis for grander projects in extending order and control. Planning is the lacing of the stuff of Values to the frame of Science. It is the necessary link between objectives or purposes and "the facts."

Both public administration and scientific management stand midway between the eighteenth- and nineteenth-century notion of a natural harmony of nature and the "wide-open world" conceived in certain recent philosophies. There *is* a harmony of nature, but it does not bring the greatest good of the greatest number simply by not being disturbed—that is the wrong interpretation. Man must *discover* this harmony, and impose his will upon it. No, not "im-

---

[29] Scientific management is considerably the more advanced movement on the score of planning, since this was a chief concern of Taylor's, and has probably contributed to the notion in public administration. *Cf.* J. M. Gaus, *op. cit.,* 178; Cleveland, *op. cit.,* 653; M. Dimock, *Modern Politics and Administration* (New York: 1937), 376–377. Having a quarter century of background, "scientific managers" contributed some of the best literature on planning during the upsurge of interest in the subject occasioned by the Depression.

pose"; the laws of nature will suffer no interference. But by a cosmic stroke of good fortune the Laws of Nature and the Real Will of man coincide!

The operation of nature's harmony is summarized and applied by means of "principles." If facts are sought, research carried on, measurement achieved, "principles" will emerge to guide future action. Frederick W. Taylor and W. F. Willoughby, in their respective fields, express in closely similar language this belief in the emergence of "scientific" principles or laws from a study of the data.[30] Being scientific, resting upon "the facts," these principles are incontrovertible, are as inflexible as the "law of gravity." In scientific management the belief in scientific law finds expression in Taylor's statement, "the development of a science for each element of the work." It is often referred to as the "one best way." In public administration the word "principle" is customarily used.[31] A "principle" is a "one best way" which emerges (we are told) from a scientific study of the facts. Just as there is one best way to shovel coal there is one best way to organize or conduct an administrative activity. Since both "best ways" rest on facts they are, of course, True, and not proper subjects for differences of opinion.

The "One Best Man."—Not only is there a "one best way," there is a "one best man." Different tasks call for different qualities of inheritance and training. The theory of equality is no good; neither is any theory of moral fitness. Rather, for any given task there is, theoretically, one person, or at least a type of person, better suited by measurable qualities than all others. There is a "one man in ten thousand." The chief task of a personnel agency is to find this man and, if his superiority is potential rather than immediate, train him —"the bringing together of the science and the properly selected and trained employee." The case for the influence of scientific management upon public administration at this point is overwhelming. There is no doubt that the transition from the "negative and moral" to the "positive and scientific" attitude in personnel administration was due largely to scientific management.[32]

---

[30] *Cf.* Taylor's *Principles,* and Willoughby's "Science of Public Administration" in *Essays in Political Science,* J. M. Mathews and J. Hart, eds. (Baltimore: 1937), 39–63.

[31] While the notion of "principles" seems to have been developed independently by public administration, it has perhaps been reinforced by scientific management. See, for example, H. P. Kendall, *op. cit.,* and G. D. Babcock, *op. cit.;* M. L. Cooke, *Our Cities Awake* (Garden City: 1918), ch. 4, "The One Best Way."

[32] See Cooke, *Our Cities Awake,* ch. 6; and Mosher, "The Next Step in Civil Service Reform" 10 *Nat. Mun. Rev.* (July, 1921), 386–391.

Perhaps enough has been said to indicate the general similarity between public administration and scientific management. A few more points deserve mention, however. One is the wide acceptance of "efficiency" as both criterion and goal. In each case efficiency has been apotheosized and given a moral content. In each case there has been, especially recently, a broadening of the meaning of the term, as well as suggestions that there are other desirable values of at least equal importance.

Centralization versus Decentralization.—Both disciplines have a decentralizing or "democratic" tendency, and a centralizing and hierarchical, or "autocratic," tendency. Impetus for both of these trends in scientific management clearly derived from Taylor. On the one hand, Taylor regarded himself as "on the management's side"—he was very paternalistic, considered laborers incapable of understanding their own work, wanted a revision of responsibility upward, and insisted on centralized planning and direction. On the other hand, he regarded his system, in which he saw "friendly, intimate co-operation" and the sovereignty of the "facts" or of the "system," as a vast improvement upon "military" organization, in which mere formal authority or brute force rule. "Functionalism" can mean that each person has a range of duties, a sphere of expertise, for which he is uniquely qualified and about which he above all others is entitled to express an opinion or make a decision.

It is in this latter direction that the literature of scientific management has tended to develop. Whereas scientific management found as a datum "centralization" or "military" organization and worked toward decentralization or functionalism, public administration found as a datum far-reaching decentralization and sought centralization, and its corollary, hierarchy. But while there can be no doubt that the two disciplines moved in opposite directions in this regard, scientific management does contain both doctrines, and students of public administration were at liberty to make use of the centralizing aspects—as they did, for example, in condemning boards for administrative purposes.

BIBLIOGRAPHICAL NOTE

On the "second phase of the industrial revolution" in relation to Scientific Management see: Willard E. Atkins, "Frederick Winslow Taylor," in 14 *Encyc. of Soc. Sci.,* 542; Herman Feldman, "Business Administration," in 3 *Encyc. of Soc. Sci.,* 87–90; H. S. Person, "The Origin and Nature of Scientific Management" (ch. 1), and "The New Attitude Toward Management" (ch. 2), in *Scientific Management in American Industry* (New York: 1929), H. S. Person, ed.; and C. B. Thompson,

"The Literature of Scientific Management," in *Scientific Management* (Cambridge: 1914), C. B. Thompson, ed.

In addition to these works I have relied for information about scientific management chiefly upon the following: the *Scientific Management in American Industry* and *Scientific Management* volumes just cited, *passim* (both are collections of essays); Taylor's works, chiefly *Shop Management* (New York: 1911) and *The Principles of Scientific Management* (New York: 1911); *Hearings before a Special Committee of the House of Representatives to Investigate the Taylor and Other Systems of Shop Management* (Wash.: 1912), 3 vols.; The Taylor Society, *Frederick Winslow Taylor: A Memorial Volume* (New York: 1920); First Tuck School Conference, *Addresses and Discussions at the Conference on Scientific Management* (Hanover: 1912); E. E. Hunt, ed., *Scientific Management Since Taylor* (New York: 1924); L. Urwick and E. F. L. Brech, *The Making of Scientific Management: Thirteen Pioneers* (London: 1945); Harrington Emerson, *Efficiency as a Basis for Operation and Wages* (New York: 1909), and *The Twelve Principles of Efficiency* (New York: 1912); H. B. Drury, *Scientific Management: A History and Criticism* (New York: 1915); Yu-Tsuan Ku, An Abstract of a Thesis on *Taylorism: A New Doctrine of the Second Industrial Revolution* (Ithaca: 1931); A. H. Church, *The Science and Practice of Management* (New York: 1914); M. L. Cooke, "The Spirit and Social Significance of Scientific Management," 21 *Jour. Pol. Econ.* (June, 1913), 481–493; F. B. Copley, *Frederick W. Taylor: Father of Scientific Management* (New York: 1923), 2 vols.; Oliver Sheldon, *The Philosophy of Management* (London: 1924); J. D. Mooney, and A. C. Reilley, *Onward Industry!* (New York: 1931); and *The Principles of Organization* (New York: 1939); Luther Gulick and L. Urwick, eds., *Papers on the Science of Administration* (New York: 1937). Various works more strictly under the heading of "business administration," such as Hugo Diemer's *Factory Organization and Administration* (New York: 2nd ed., 1914) have also been useful. The files of the *Bulletin of the Taylor Society, Bulletin of the Taylor Society and of The Society of Industrial Engineers,* and *Advanced Management,* as well as those of the *Bulletin of the International Management Institute* and the first to seventh *International Congress for Scientific Management* are also indispensable in tracing the contours of the movement. Useful bibliographies may be found in Thompson, Person, Feldman, Atkins, and Diemer (363 ff.), and in N. A. Brisco, *Economics of Efficiency* (New York: 1914).

PART II

PROBLEMS OF POLITICAL PHILOSOPHY

Chapter 4

THE GOOD LIFE

The previous chapters considered the rise of public administration and sought to interpret it in terms of its historical setting, leading personalities, and dominant motifs. The object of this and the four following chapters is a more intensive review of that part of the literature of public administration that bears upon five problems in political philosophy: (1) the nature of the Good Life, (2) the criteria of action or the "bases of decision," (3) "Who should rule?", (4) the separation of powers, and (5) centralization versus decentralization.

The Ends of the State

Anyone who writes political philosophy has an idea of the Good Life and at least a faint hope of realizing it—otherwise he would not write political philosophy. When the ends desired seem remote from "reality," subsequent generations call the work a Utopia. In the Utopias the Good Life stands forth most clearly. Here the author, more concerned with ends than means, is at pains to enumerate the values, both spiritual and material, which will be served, and to delineate the right relationship of man to his God, his State, and his fellows.

But the outlines of the Good Life can be discerned in any political philosophy, even in those cases in which the author is "hard-boiled" or "scientific." Machiavelli's ideal is quite clear: a strong nation of healthy, frugal, brave, and aggressive citizens, banded together in a republic if possible, under the rule of a skillful and ruthless prince if necessary. The Marxists, with their sneer at "pie in the sky, bye and bye," themselves promise us pie when—lines of class, race, and nation having been erased and government rendered obsolete—people work for the sheer joy of working, and avidly pursue culture in their off hours. Even those who have advocated the government of society by "science" really mean government by "scientists," *i.e.* men like themselves, who have purposes, such as the eradication of crime or the improvement of the germ-plasm, and think they know how to accomplish these purposes.

65

The Heavenly City of the Twentieth-Century
Public Administrators

Students of public administration have visions of a Good Society, despite their occasional denials and their professional dedication to a scientific inquiry.

Their Good Society is strikingly like a World of Tomorrow futurama or Megapolis' fifty-year plan in scale model. Here at last man has become captain of his destiny and has builded a civilization commensurate with the needs and aspirations of the human frame. It is a civilization primarily industrial and urban—it could hardly be otherwise for "city" and "civilization" are related logically as well as etymologically, and the maintenance of a city nowadays requires industry. It is, of course, a mechanical civilization, for it is the machine that has enabled man to lift himself above his environment and to extend the blessings of civilization to all the members of society for the first time in history. It is quite obviously a "planned" society; such magnificent zoning, for example, would require great imagination in conception and thorough effort and strict obedience in execution. About all we can tell about the form of government must follow from the obvious fact of the planning: it may be "democratic," but the range of government control is unquestionably large and the machinery of administration extensive. It is very probably a "collectivist" society so far as its use of *means* is concerned.

There is probably considerable equality—at least there are no obvious signs of great extremes in wealth, and certainly no evidence of poverty. This fact, together with the fact of planning, indicates that what some people once regarded as their liberties have been curtailed; but that liberty has been given the substantive content—work, food, clothing, shelter, leisure, etc.—that others claimed for it. Speaking in parable, one sees scattered about in the panorama what appear to be churches, but no soaring cathedral dominates the scene; from which we may conclude that, while the claims of the soul are not denied, the emphasis remains mundane.

We may presume that a society which has produced such a civilization has made an ideal of Science. From the clean streets and the general garden-like quality of the city with its spacious parks and fine civic buildings, we may surmise that the citizens are proud of what they have produced, and perhaps bear toward their country and their city some of the warmth of affection borne by Greek writers toward the city-state. But whether this guess is true or not it is beyond doubt that waste, inefficiency, and slovenliness are severely frowned upon by the governing power in this Good Society. The ideal of this Society is evidently one of peace, for none of its energies seem directed toward war.

Do the writings of public administration confirm this as substantially a correct view of the Good Society? Let us "look at the record."

The Mastery of Nature.—There is no doubt that if the Good Life is achieved man will have risen above his environment and made it subservient to his dreams. This applies to his social as well as his non-social environment. The means by which this will be achieved is by an extension of the outlook and the techniques of Science. The "power controlling sciences" will be developed equally with the "power producing sciences." Government and administration, properly conceived and scientifically developed, will make man Master of his Soul; they will realize what political philosophers have only dared dream.[1]

A "Planned" Society.—Planning is the means by which the discipline of Science applied to human affairs will enable man to incarnate his purposes. It is the inevitable link between means and ends. Moreover, it is in itself an inspiring ideal. For once it is realized that there is no natural harmony of nature, no Divine or other purpose hidden beneath the flux and chaos of present planlessness, it becomes immoral to let poverty, ignorance, pestilence, and war continue if they can be obliterated by a plan. Although there is some disagreement as to the nature and desirable limits of planning, students of administration are all "planners." [2]

---

[1] See, for example, A. N. Holcombe, *Government in a Planned Democracy* (New York: 1935), ch. 1. See also M. L. Cooke's *Our Cities Awake* (Garden City, N.Y.: 1918), chs. 3, 9, 10, and 11 for an excellent example of the point of view I have been trying to suggest.

[2] The President's Committee on Administrative Management was stating an article in the credo of all administrative students when it said: "We confidently believe that the universal aspiration for economic security and the increasing enrichment of human lives may be forwarded by substituting the results of careful scientific study for uninformed judgment and political expediency as the basis for the formulation of governmental plans." *Report* (Washington: 1937), 26.

For distinction between different types of planning see: M. E. Dimock, *Modern Politics and Administration* (New York: 1937), 267–268, 374 ff.; Holcombe, *op. cit.,* 140–141; B. L. Gladieux, "Management Planning in the Federal Government," 5 *Adv. Man.* (Apr.–June, 1940), 77–85; on democratic planning, Ordway Tead, *New Adventures in Democracy* (New York: 1939), 105–106; L. D. White, *Introduction to the Study of Public Administration* (New York: 1939), 29–30; on the relationship of organization to purpose in making plans, Max Lerner, "The Burden of Government Business," in *Public Management in the New Democracy* (New York: 1940), F. Morstein Marx, ed., 10; and Lewis Meriam and Lawrence Schmeckebier, *Reorganization of the National Government: What Does It Involve?* (Washington: 1939), 161 ff.

The early reformers were impressed by the magnificence of foreign cities; a new civic consciousness was inspired, a vision of a better life obtained. There was at first a movement to replace the drab and fetid "city hall" by elaborate civic centers, and to extend parks and playgrounds. Gradually the notion crossed the old frontier between public and private, became embodied in such activities as zoning, and has inspired the recent grandiose "city plans."

Scientific management has contributed to thinking on planning, and the depression was the occasion for the extension of planning thought and literature. As early as F. A. Cleveland's address in 1911 at the Dartmouth conference, students began to show an acquaintance with scientific management's thought on planning, and in such publications as *Plan Age* and *Advanced Management* there has recently been overlapping. Planning has followed, in both disciplines, the extension upward and outward of the conception of the range of the discipline. The Depression, of course, so underscored the danger of planlessness that planning became a street-corner fad. There is no doubt that it stimulated administrative students to extend their ideas from the local to the national scale, and from planning for policy-execution to planning for policy-formulation.

Luther Gulick has best expressed the central significance of planning for public administration: a rational apportionment of means to the ends which constitute a full and well-balanced life. Planning, he says, is essential to the Good Life because the Good Life means "nothing too much." "The 'good life' for government as well as for individuals, consists in balance and proportion—'nothing too much' and nothing too little. A city cannot spend all its energies and resources for highways, or for bridges or for schools or for sewers or for police. It must have these things in proportion." [3]

The Extension of the "Public" Interest.—The Good Life will be planned—but to what extent? What do students of administration regard as the proper sphere for government activity? Almost without exception they look favorably upon government, regard it as a desirable instrument for the accomplishment of individual and community purposes, profess indifference or express favor at proposals to extend the range of its operation or control. The only exceptions are those, usually connected with taxpayers' groups, whose primary concern is the reduction of government expense.

[3] "Politics, Administration, and the New Deal," 169 *Annals* (Sept., 1933), 55–66, 57.

The leaders of the early research movement were frank proponents of the extension of government activity. They were interested in reforming government, in fact, to make it a more effective instrument of community cooperation and control. The "new city government," wrote Henry Bruere, must "equip itself for leadership in co-operative effort to promote community welfare." [4] F. A. Cleveland likewise found that "government has a social purpose and . . . *laissez-faire* should no longer dominate our politics." [5]

There is certainly little hint of *laissez-faire* philosophy in the writings of latter-day students. "Our American Government," said the President's Committee in its prolegomena, "rests on the truth that the general interest is superior to and has priority over any special or private interest. . . ." [6]

> Our goal is the constant raising of the level of the happiness and dignity of human life, the steady sharing of the gains of our Nation, whether material or spiritual, among those who make the nation what it is. . . . By democracy we mean getting things done that we, the American people, want done in the general interest.[7]

Good administration, they concluded, will help those who "need the help of government in their struggle for justice, security, steadier employment, better living and working conditions, and a growing share of the gains of civilization." [8]

J. A. Vieg, reflecting on the relationship of "Democracy and Bureaucracy," states his conviction that "today no nation lacking a big bureaucracy and a powerful government has the means of insuring either its liberty or its welfare. This proposition is so plain that it should not need to be labored." [9]

---

[4] *The New City Government* (New York: 1912), 1. Eleven "simple prerogatives of citizenship" are set forth, including "adequate housing at reasonable rents" and "prevention of destitution caused by death, sickness, unemployment or other misfortune." 2.

[5] *Organized Democracy* (New York: 1913), 448.

[6] *Report*, 1.

[7] *Idem.*, L. D. White believes that "in its broader context, the ends of administration are the ultimate ends of the state itself—the maintenance of peace and order, instruction of the young, equalization of opportunity, protection against disease and insecurity, adjustment and compromise of conflicting groups and interests, in short, the achievement of the good life." *Introduction to the Study of Public Administration* (New York: 1939), 7. (By permission of The Macmillan Company, publishers.) These are not self-evident and eternal functions of the State. Most Americans would reject one or more as proper state functions.

[8] *Report*, 45.

[9] 4 *Pub. Adm. Rev.* (Summer, 1944), 247–252, 49. To the same effect V. O. Key: "Unless our civilization collapses completely this is going to continue to be a bureaucratic world." "Politics and Administration," in *The Future of Government in the United States* (Chicago: 1942), L. D. White, ed., 145–163, 146. See also in this volume, J. P. Harris, "The Future of Administrative Management," 164–191, 164–166.

This favorable disposition to government is evident everywhere. Often it takes the form of a refutation of the thesis that money paid in taxes is economic waste.[10] Frequently, approval of the extension of government is indicated by writing of it as a *fait accompli*.[11] Sometimes the writer professes to be "pragmatic" or "factual" about the matter, but indicates his sentiments in the context. And sometimes the writer states openly his faith in the future that may be created by the instrument of government. Thus, J. M. Gaus has written fervently of the part which the administrative process must play in the America of Tomorrow: a "new frontier" created by public administration must replace the vanished West.[12]

Reconciliation of "Government" and "Business"

Perhaps a word should be said on the consistency of this "New Deal" attitude with the general acceptance of "business" by public administration. It is very significant that administrative writers do not generally feel any inconsistency in holding both to the idea of an extended sphere of government influence and operation, and to the ideals of a business civilization. In this, no doubt, they are what the Marxists call "bourgeois"; there is not a hint of doctrinaire socialism in all the literature of public administration.[13] The leaders of the early research movement were business people. Far from thinking in terms of a conflict between government and business, they thought of their work as the extension of business to government.[14] They thought, as most of their successors have thought, that the "tuning up" of governmental machinery and its more vigorous operation will not be inconsistent with the maximum operation

---

[10] For example, Clarence Dykstra, in "In Defense of Government," 189 *Annals* (Jan., 1937), 1–7.

[11] "The conception of government as a policing agency, and concerned with the protection of personal liberty against any and all encroachments, has given way to the conception of government as a housekeeping agency, seeking in an affirmative way to promote the welfare of its citizens." W. E. Mosher, "Public Service as a Career," 169 *Annals* (Sept., 1933), 130–143, 130; *cf.* W. F. Willoughby, in "Introduction" to Gustavus Weber's *Organized Efforts for the Improvement of Administration in the United States* (New York: 1919).

[12] "American Society and Public Administration," in *The Frontiers of Public Administration* (Chicago: 1936), essays by Gaus, L. D. White, and M. E. Dimock, 92–115; see also Dimock's *Modern Politics and Administration*, 383 ff.

[13] American "public administration" has some similarities to British Fabianism, but in doctrinal statement, at least, public administration is cautious and undeveloped in comparison with this middle-class "socialism."

[14] Speaking of commission government in 1912, Henry Bruere—who was more than abreast of the New Deal—said: "It takes away the old fiction that the city's prime business is to serve as the cradle of our liberties, and substitutes the conception of the city as a business enterprise." *Op. cit.*, 92.

of all legitimate business enterprise.[15] After all, it is only a step from this point of view to the opinion that "the purpose of the democratic state . . . necessitates the development of a great administrative machine. Thus, paradoxical as it may seem to the Jeffersonian Democrats, the liberal democratic state must be sustained by a huge bureaucracy." [16] In this post-war period administrative students sought to spearhead the drive for Full Employment Through Private Enterprise—by means of comprehensive governmental action!

The Ultimate Values

The range of planning and of government operation consequently will be extensive in the Good Society—but more important, and logically taking priority, is the question of the values that the planning and control seek to realize.

Individualism.—Certainly the ideal is "individualistic." There is an occasional passage in the literature faintly suggestive of "Oxford" Idealism,[17] but the predominant motif is individualist, utilitarian, instrumentalist. Government is a tool to be used in the services of the individual. It has no *raison d'être* beyond this. Neither state nor nation nor any less inclusive groups have purposes in themselves. They exist only to serve individuals.

Materialism.—The ideal is materialistic. (Perhaps "this-worldly" is more accurate, for the claims of the spirit are encouraged so long as they are confined to what is, if not measurable, at least observable. Thus, slum clearance is both esthetically and morally commendable.) The Good Life is chiefly a matter of the possession or enjoyment of tangible things.[18] It consists, certainly, in the en-

---

[15] Even Herbert Hoover, who found the New Deal a *Challenge to Liberty,* was of the opinion as Secretary of Commerce that "the changed economic situation of the world demands that the functions of the government in aid to commerce and industry be given more concentration and wider scope." "The Problems of the Reorganization of the Federal Government," 9 *Proc. Acad. Pol. Sci.* (1920–1922), 449–452, 450.

[16] E. P. Herring, *Public Administration and the Public Interest* (New York: 1936), 9. See also 398. *Cf.* Dimock, *op. cit.,* 376.

[17] See Cleveland and Buck, *The Budget and Responsible Government* (New York: 1920), ch. 1. This interpretation of the Good Life as "individualist" does not conflict, I think, with the statement that it is also "collectivist." First, the "individualism" of the public administration writers has "equality" as a corollary, as some varieties of individualism do not. Second, public administration's "collectivism" applies only to means, not to ends. The ends to be served are those of the mass of individual persons.

[18] I am not arguing, of course, that students of administration have been a lot of Philistines. Occasionally they have seemed Philistine in attitude, to be sure, but even when they proclaimed that "storm sewers are a joy forever" they hoped that they were laying a foundation for enlightenment and culture.

joyment of a nutritionally adequate diet, a comfortable and healthful dwelling, and plenty of clothing. And it should include a reasonable amount of leisure for movies and picnics, adequate medical attention, and insurance against the hazards of employment and unemployment as well as the uncertainties of old age. It might include playgrounds for the children and an annual vacation with pay. But whatever particular writers consider the minimum amount of goods and services—this is the important point—none of them feel that the chief aim of man is to "magnify the name of God," nor that the proper aim of the State is to become an instrument of the World Spirit. L. D. White, who makes no rash statements, summarized the common faith when he stated that "government and its administrative organs exist to serve and to achieve great human objectives in terms of the health, safety, and convenience of the mass of the population." [19]

Since the Good Life consists to a great degree in the enjoyment of material things, science is emphasized, efficiency and economy demanded, and industrialism highly prized. Science is the key that unlocks nature's doors, the device that lifts man above the vagaries of topography and climate. Waste of nature's treasure and "soldiering" on a job reduce the amount of goods and services available for human consumption and hence are morally reprehensible. Since "civilization" is coterminous with large-scale and widespread enjoyment of goods and services, the question whether industrialization is desirable is tautological.

Peace.—The ideal is one of peace. Even when public administration is stimulated by war or considerations of national safety, the preservation or the restoration of the blessings of peace are the primary concerns. Our feeling of remoteness from danger and our abundant resources have given our writings up to now a flavor distinctly different from those of the Continent, where maintenance of military strength has been a prime desideratum, a means so important it tended to subsume its ends. In this atom-tortured era, the notion that the military life is inherently superior, that peace is ignoble and degrading, would be considered—if taken seriously enough to be considered—stupid, barbaric, and immoral.

Liberty and Equality.—What of the two most common goals of modern democracy: equality and liberty? Students of administration, it is clear, are inclined to a large, if indefinite, degree of

---

[19] *Introduction to Public Administration* (New York: 1939), 209.

equality—at least in the enjoyment of material things. Equality is probably the chief ingredient of their sense of justice. "The gains of civilization," said the President's Committee, "are essentially mass gains. They should be distributed as fairly as possible among those who create them." [20] There is no visible dissent from this dictum.

Writers on public administration have less frequently spoken in terms of liberty, not because they regard it as less important than equality, but because they find the essence of liberty to lie in equality itself. Far from finding liberty and equality incompatible, as do some, they make little distinction in meaning between the two.[21] Liberty for liberty's sake is clearly a meaningless notion; it must be liberty to do and enjoy something. If more people are buying automobiles and taking vacations there is more liberty.

Urbanization.—The Good Life is an urban life. Writers in public administration have rejected the Jeffersonian idea that cities are sores on the body politic and menaces to democracy. They have chosen to reconcile the ideal of democracy not only with the fact but with the ideal of urban life. Urban existence, of course, is closely associated with industrialism, and hence with high production of goods and services. But urban existence is not merely a means which must be endured for the sake of this desired end. City civilization is better and higher; the city is an end in itself. Much of the impetus to public administration came from the municipal reformers, who were genuinely inspired by a City of the Future. So strong is this emotion, at times, that it is not incongruous to compare it to the Greek ideal of the city-state. It is a vision of a community characterized by "love of one's city and willingness to serve," [22] an environment which exercises all of man's essentially human capacities without straining them, a nice adjustment of human talents so that the whole is greater than the sum of the unrelated parts.

---

[20] *Op. cit.*, 25–26.

[21] See, for example, Cleveland and Buck, *op. cit.*, 9–10, where the two terms are defined.

A ringing pronouncement on the value of liberty and its compatibility with administration has been made by C. E. Merriam: "The goal of human aspiration is liberty—self-expression—the unfolding of human personality in constantly richer and more diverse forms. Except as it contributes to this advance toward a higher liberty, all administrative management is as sounding brass and a tinkling cymbal. Our democracy is not menaced by sound administration, but aided by it. On the whole, the strategy of organization, if soundly conceived, will ultimately increase rather than diminish the realm of the personality. The area of personal decisions could and should expand in a new world of far more complex relationship yet with indefinitely broader horizons than those of our ancestors." *On the Agenda of Democracy* (Cambridge, Mass.: 1941), 50–51.

[22] Newton D. Baker, in Introduction to M. L. Cooke's *Our Cities Awake* (Garden City, N. Y.: 1918), x.

Democracy: End or Means?

What form of government will exercise the control and seek to realize the Good Life? Students of administration all profess democracy. Substantively, they regard it as striving toward the ideals which they themselves seek. Procedurally, they have tended to regard it as external or at least incidental to their field of inquiry: administration.

Traditional institutions of democracy in themselves do not guarantee democracy; indeed they may impede it. "It is important to keep prominently before us," prefaced the President's Committee, "the ends of reorganization. . . . There is but one grand purpose, namely, to make democracy work today in our National Government; that is, to make our Government an up-to-date, efficient, and effective instrument for carrying out the will of the Nation. It is for this purpose that Government needs thoroughly modern tools of management." [23] The "will of the nation," it will be recalled, was interpreted as "the steady sharing of the gains of the Nation," "security, steadier employment, better living and working conditions," and so forth. *"Without results we know that democracy means nothing and ceases to be alive in the minds and hearts of men."* [24]

"Democracy will resist Fascism and Communism," J. M. Pfiffner opines, "to the extent that it excels them in maintaining an orderly and just state of human affairs. An adequate material standard of living is an absolute prerequisite to widely disseminated cultural achievements and pleasures. That material standard of living must come through a united national effort applied to research, planning, and rationalized production. . . . The need is for people with faith that democracy can be made to bring happiness and justice for all in this immensely rich America. . . ." [25]

From the standpoint of organization and procedure, the key to the customary view of democracy is found in the politics-administration formula. "The difference between an autocracy and a democracy lies not in its administrative organization, but in the absence or presence of a controlling electorate or representative body outside of the administration with power to determine the will of the mem-

---

[23] *Op. cit.,* 3.
[24] *Ibid.,* 1. Italics mine. *Cf.* F. G. Bates and O. P. Field, *State Government* (New York: 1939), viii.
[25] *Research Methods in Public Administration* (New York: 1940), 24–25. *Cf.* James Hart, "The President and Federal Administration," in *Essays on the Law and Practice of Governmental Administration* (Baltimore: 1935), C. G. Haines and M. Dimock, eds., 47–93.

bership, and to enforce the will on the administration." [26] This quotation summarizes as succinctly as possible the formula which public administration crystallized from Reform and Progressivism, and according to which it sought to reform American governmental institutions. "Democracy," they have believed, under modern conditions could apply only to the deciding phase of the two-fold governmental process. This conclusion flows inexorably from the specialization of function upon which civilization rests, and in any event is forced upon us if we are to "stand up" to autocracy from without. "Autocracy" at work is the unavoidable price for "Democracy" after hours.

This orthodox view has not gone unchallenged. For example, it has been sharply criticized by A. C. Millspaugh who charges administrative students with forgetting political democracy in the search for economic democracy. They have been, he says, "disposed to deal with the relatively narrow questions of administration as if they were separate from the general problem of political democracy. . . . Trapped by superficial analogies and misled by structural appearances, the administrative reorganizers momentarily forgot that democracy is a fundamental issue and a conditioning factor in all aspects of American government." [27] He proposes to discard the "fiction" that democracy has no relevance to administrative organization: "If administration is to reach full stature and functional maturity, it should no longer be viewed as a 'branch' of government but rather as an integral and vital part of the whole interacting democratic system. It should be, not merely subject to or controlled by government, but an active agent in implementing, supporting, and realizing democracy." [28]

There is a measure of justice in this indictment. But it is undoubtedly too severe (and to the extent that "politics-administration" has been recently abandoned and efforts made to make administration "democratic," irrelevant). It is less than fair to say that Woodrow Wilson, Frank Goodnow, and Frederick Cleveland were not genuinely interested in democracy: they were ardently seeking a scheme to save it. And if the President's Committee believes that "without results Democracy means nothing" they are entitled to that interpretation. They may be right.

---

[26] F. A. Cleveland and A. E. Buck, *The Budget and Responsible Government* (New York: 1920), 15. (By permission of the Macmillan Co., publishers.)

[27] "Democracy and Administrative Organization," in *Essays on the Law and Practice of Governmental Administration* (Baltimore: 1935), C. G. Haines and M. E. Dimock, eds., 47–93 (citations by permission of Johns Hopkins Press).

[28] *Ibid.*, 69.

Chapter 5

THE CRITERIA OF ACTION

What have writers on administration held to be "fundamental"? What considerations would they weigh or what techniques for deciding would they use when faced with a demand for decision and action?

Full-blown political philosophies, it is clear, have readily recognizable criteria or procedures for determining "What should be done?" In Platonic philosophy the Idea of the Good, the Form that is greater than the others and indicates their proper proportions, provides the answer. In the view of St. Augustine the Will of God indicates the proper course of action. Locke finds in the pre-political existence and eternal imperative of individual rights a criterion for deciding all questions of the common life. Bentham asserts the notion of "rights" is nonsense, and proposes the Greatest Happiness Principle as a formula for solving all political problems. Hitler finds the purity and continuation of the German blood-stream the desideratum above all others. In a coherent political philosophy the "basis of decision" will be closely articulated on the one hand with the Good Life, and on the other it will indicate "Who should govern?"

The necessity for and the existence of "bases of decision" in public administration can be illustrated briefly. "The chief problem of modern administration is co-ordination," writes a leading student. "There seems to be a tendency for subunits to desire departmental autonomy and self-sufficiency. . . . When this is the case, the less worthy activities, fortunate in possessing aggressive administrative leadership combined with effective citizen pressure, may be developed at the expense of neglecting more desirable ones. Likewise, functions of equal merit might receive unequal consideration." [1] Who decides, and upon what basis, what activities are "less worthy" or "more desirable"? Does the administrative superior decide, as a part of the coordinating process? Do the "people" decide? Does the "will of the people" or the "public interest" decide? And how

---

[1] J. M. Pfiffner, *Municipal Administration* (New York: 1940), 19.

is "effective citizen pressure" distinguished from these? *Whoever* makes the decision, how does he know that the decision he makes is "right"?

The Good Life—and parts thereof, such as equality—"facts" and "science," the "public interest" or "social advantage," "experience," "pragmatism," "principles," and "economy and efficiency" have all been put forth as giving us an answer to, or being techniques for answering, our questions of "What should we do?" Is there a core of consistency among these criteria, despite an obvious antagonism between "pragmatism" and "principles"?

The answer is: Yes. The consistency lies in what they do *not* include. There is no hint of Platonic Realism, nor any variety of Idealism, nor anything as intangible as the "will of the people." The one school of philosophy which is mentioned by name is the "tough-minded" school, Pragmatism.

A Point of View: Utilitarianism, Legal Realism and "Administrationism"

A comparison of public administration with Utilitarianism and with so-called "legal realism" reveals some significant parallels. These three movements are closely similar in temper, in motives, in philosophic presumptions. The chief distinction among them, indeed, seems to lie in the fact that each is concerned primarily with a different "branch" of government. According to the vagaries of time and events, Utilitarians found themselves concerned chiefly with the legislative branch, legal realists with the judicial branch, administrative students with the executive or administrative branch. The nature of the obstacles in the way of realizing the objectives has differed, but the objectives in each case have been substantially the same.

The Utilitarians.—The Utilitarians wanted to do away with "higher law" and other intangible considerations, and to substitute the single test of "utility" as a criterion for public action. Horrified at the habit of mind that accepted cruelties and confusion because they were traditional or sanctioned by a "natural" order, they hoped to revamp the laws and the law-making process, thus to make of Parliament a machine to grind out a New Order, and to create out of the laws a code of pains and pleasures so finely adjusted as to produce almost complete individual well-being and social harmony. "Utility" was conceived to be identical with "the greatest happiness of the greatest number." So far did they go in rejecting the *a priori* and transcendental that they denied any qualitative difference in pleasure—"pleasure being equal, pushpin is as good as poetry."

But as their critics have pointed out, the Utilitarians retained many of the Natural Law assumptions of their predecessors, despite their derision of the philosophical and ethical vaporings of their contemporaries. The rule that, in calculating the sum total of happiness, "each shall count for one and nobody for more than one" was a carry-over of the Natural Law tenet of equal rights. And the Utilitarians accepted, of course, the Natural Order of classical economics. In short, "utility" was not the basic principle its devotees supposed it to be; Utilitarians acted upon fundamental beliefs prior or additional to utility; and even "utility" itself dissolved when J. S. Mill applied to it the mild acid of his criticism.

The Legal Realists.—The American "legal realists" also want to do away with "higher law" and other intangibles that stand in the way of getting things done. They seek to set aside the question "Is it legal?" and to substitute utilitarian, pragmatic, and humanitarian criteria. They deny the *a priori* and the theoretical and put forward the empirical, the instrumentalist, the experimental. Finding an "antiquated" judicial organ interposing itself in the American scheme between the creative legislature (Utilitarians) and the New Order, they sought to educate the members of the judicial organ to their utilitarian function, or failing that to curtail their powers.

The "legal realists" also pose as hardheaded. They have presented their arguments as practical and objective when compared to the "constitutional metaphysics" and "folklore" of their opponents. Their objective is also that of the Utilitarians—the greatest happiness of the greatest number. The phrase is not used, of course; but the meaning is clearly contained in such expressions as "social advance" and "general welfare." As in the case of the Utilitarians also, their basic assumptions accord ill with their objective and "scientific" professions. If there are no "fixed principles of justice," then it is clear that human equality is not such a principle. The legal realists are starry-eyed cynics.

"Administrationism."—Public administration stands in the same relation to the executive branch as Utilitarianism to the legislative and legal realism to the judicial. The aim is the "greatest happiness of the greatest number," presuming practical equality of persons. The same professions of utility, practicality, objectivity, and empiricism are made, the same boast of tough-mindedness. The legislative ways having been cleared of "nonsense on stilts" and the judicial procedure having been freed of "metaphysics," there remains only to use the instrument of administration in an unencumbered, expeditious, practical, and scientific way to insure "pleasure maximized, pain minimized." This is the task of public administration. The point of view is so definite and distinct that it might be tagged as "administrationism."

The Relationship of Public Administration and Legal Realism. —The anti-legal temper of public administration is obvious and its import clear. In fact, one does not need to go far in the literature of public administration to find that if any person is to count for less than one in the New Order it is the lawyer! The lawyer suffers from a meager social outlook, the spirit of the New Management does not abide with him; he represents everything stultifying that Bentham imputed to "Judge & Co." [2]

At a number of points legal realism and public administration are overlapping movements. Frank Goodnow was not only the "Father" of public administration; his *Social Reform and the Constitution* [3] contains much of what was heard, with different "arrangements" and full orchestration, in the days of the Nine Old Men. Felix Frankfurter's *The Public and Its Government* [4] is a contribution to the literature of both fields. John Dickinson's *Administrative Justice and the Supremacy of the Law in the United States* [5] is clearly an important work in either movement. Robert H. Jackson's "The Administrative Process," [6] a defense of administrative tribunals against the courts and "legalism," is another example of the similarity that at times becomes identity. In short, though Legal Realists and students of administration would view Bentham's "felicific calculus" as a too simple formula, they would agree that

---

[2] On anti-legalism see, for example: C. E. Thach, "The Inadequacies of the Rule of Law," in *Essays on the Law and Practice of Governmental Administration* (Baltimore: 1935), C. G. Haines and M. E. Dimock, eds., 269–286; J. M. Pfiffner, *Public Administration* (New York: 1935), 18; L. D. White, *Introduction to Public Administration* (New York: 1926), vii; J. M. Gaus, letter printed in 1 *Pub. Adm. Rev.* (June, 1938—Maxwell School publication), 2.

The anti-legalism of public administration perhaps is brought to its highest pitch in F. F. Blachly and M. E. Oatman's "Sabotage of the Administrative Process," 6 *Pub. Adm. Rev.* (Summer, 1946), 213–227, a diatribe against the Administrative Procedure Act of 1946.

I have objectivity enough to realize that my essay on "Government by Procedure," in *Elements of Public Administration* (New York: 1946), F. Morstein Marx, ed., ch. 17, has an antilegalist bent. In fact during my tour of duty in Washington I often reflected that Bentham let the lawyers off too lightly!

[3] New York: 1911.
[4] New Haven: 1930.
[5] Cambridge: 1927.
[6] 5 *Jour. Soc. Philos.* (Jan., 1940), 143–149. See also Jerome Frank's *If Men Were Angels* (New York: 1942).

the philosopher of Somersetshire had the root of the truth in him: nothing "incompetent, irrelevant, and immaterial" must obstruct the Greatest Happiness Principle.

The Positivism of Public Administration

In a preceding chapter public administration was described as a "positivist" movement. The "Utilitarianism" of public administration, accords with this thesis. Utilitarianism and positivism are quite distinguishable, but they are much similar in spirit: utilitarianism is positivist, positivism is utilitarian. Both are protests against intangible criteria, both propose to substitute measurement for metaphysics. Both claim the sanction of Science—and both seek to "engineer" for Heaven an earthly locus.

The answer of positivism to the problem of the basis of decision is that "science," "facts," "measurement" answer questions of "What to do?" It asserts that what is objective can and should "determine," that the imperative of "the facts" should be substituted for chance and will. This common viewpoint of public administration is well illustrated in the following quotation: "The scientific approach is merely the application of common sense procedure to human problems. It involves securing all obtainable facts, associating or correlating them so as to determine what they mean, and deducing the logical course of procedure therefrom. In other words, solve administrative problems by getting the facts and acting in accordance therewith." [7]

The faith that "answers" result from a scientific observation of "the facts" is illustrated on a different plane by the recorded beliefs of those who favored the establishment of the United States Tariff Commission. The Commission was proposed as an alternative to guess, drift, chance, and the importunities and dishonesties of conflicting interests. The making of rates was to be removed from the realm of "politics" to the realm of "science," to become a matter for "experts." There was a firm faith that there is a relationship of facts in a given tariff situation which, if known, will determine with complete justice the answer to the questions involved. The Tariff Commission has developed as an independent fact-finding body of high repute; but the minor role it has played in rate determination indicates the limitations of "the facts."

Limitations and Objections.—The paradox of the customary positivist position—rigid scientific objectivity on the one hand, hu-

---

[7] J. M. Pfiffner, *op. cit.*, 6.

manitarian zeal on the other—has already been noted. "Science," it should be clear, has no purposes; indeed its lack of concern with values has traditionally been the proud boast of its devotees, sworn to the-truth-no-matter-what-the-consequences. Neither the Greatest Happiness of the Greatest Number, nor any other conception of the Good Life, can find sanction within the four corners of "Science." It is in the name of Self Preservation, or Humanity, not of Science, that frightened scientists seek now to bottle or to harness the atomic genie.

The necessity of rejecting the soothing assumption that questions of "What to do?" are answered by an objective study of the facts has occasionally been recognized. Thus Henry Dennison, writing on "The Need for the Development of Political Science Engineering," said:

> If political science is to furnish the basis for this engineering approach to the problems of government, it must view any community it is studying as a field of forces—psychological, biological, and physical. In view of what it can discover about these forces, it must determine the measures and structures of government which can be expected to use these forces and to relate them so as to bring about development in the direction of the fundamental purpose adopted by and appropriate to a particular social group.[8]

"Purpose," then, from the scientific point of view, is only a datum—not a moral imperative.

> The abstract validity of theories of government or of human rights— whether they may be called moral, legal, or natural—is from a strictly engineering point of view wholly impossible to determine. For the governmental engineer, the only question of fact is what appeal the various theories make in any given social group—what force they exert or may exert, and, hence, what reactions may follow from them or may be expected to result from them.[9]

"From a strictly engineering point of view," it is clear, the Greatest Happiness Principle must be rewritten in the indicative mood, on a parallel with the anthropological observation that Esquimaux are fond of tripe.

The limitations of the "engineering point of view" have recently stirred some uneasiness. One of the most notable evidences is Merle Fainsod's essay, "Some Reflections on the Nature of the

---

[8] 26 *Am. Pol. Sci. Rev.* (April, 1932), 241–255, 246.
[9] *Ibid.*, 251.

Regulatory Process." [10] He there comments upon the limitations of the point of view that reduces the formulation of public policy to conflict between forces—"pressures"—so that it becomes nothing more than "the resultant of a parallelogram of operative forces." [11] He then sets forth the thesis that the regulatory process is most satisfactorily revealed when the analysis proceeds on three interrelated levels: (1) the conditioning factors which make up the institutional context of regulation, (2) the parties in interest who are concerned with the character of regulation, and (3) the actual political instruments which provide the pattern of operative controls. [12]

The analysis which follows is penetrating and subtle, but, except for some phrases in the closing paragraphs suggestive of Idealism ("shared purpose," "crystallization of common purpose"), there is no presentation of a philosophical, ethical, or even technical, basis for policy decisions. In short, the analysis, however keen, does not differ in *kind* from the type of treatment it is proposed as excelling. The fact that regulatory bodies may have more prime force in making policy decisions than some have supposed (which he concludes) is significant from an ethical viewpoint only if their force is different in quality from other forces; otherwise, public policy will still be only "the resultant of a parallelogram of operative forces." [13]

The "Naturalistic Fallacy" of Positivism.—The Idealists' criticism of Utilitarianism and positivism with respect to their "basis of decision" is that they commit the "naturalistic fallacy." This is the fallacy of supposing that any "ought" for human beings can be deduced from any status of affairs in the common-sense, three-dimensional world. The very significance of "ought" lies in the difference it implies from what "is." The most accurate vital statistics about Oshkosh will not determine how many people *ought* to live in Oshkosh; nor can the most accurate statistics on income distribution in Walla Walla determine how income *should* be distributed in Walla

---

[10] In *Public Policy* (Cambridge: 1940), C. J. Friedrich, ed., 297–323. *Cf.* F. Morstein Marx, "The Bureaucratic State," 1 *Rev. of Pol.* (Oct., 1939), 457–472, 457, for a criticism of the "pressure" approach to the study of government.

[11] *Ibid.*, 218.

[12] *Ibid.*, 299.

[13] E. P. Herring's *Public Administration and the Public Interest* (New York: 1936) should perhaps be mentioned at this point. Here, in a number of concrete instances, Herring poses the question: What content has been given to the "public interest" when it has been made the legal criterion for administrative action? His evidence strongly supports the "resultant-of-forces" hypothesis. In practice the "public interest" is given meaning only by the pulling and hauling of private interests—mitigated occasionally by the personal views of the Good Society held by some regulatory commissioners. Admirable as these analyses are, Herring advances us little in the search for a substantive content for the "public interest."

Walla; nor can a four-drawer file of data on a proposed road through Kalamazoo determine *whether* to build the road. If "facts" determine policy why don't the facts of poverty, of disease, of waste, and inefficiency indicate that we ought to have poverty, disease, waste, and inefficiency? Both Utilitarians and positivists, because they commit the "naturalistic fallacy," generally feel no uneasiness at proclaiming "objectivity" while engaged in a humanitarian crusade. Both make the easy assumption that the "facts" about the world are in accordance with (or at least do not deny) their interpretation of and striving toward the Real Will of man.

Pragmatism and Public Administration

Another answer to the question "What basis of decision does public administration accept?" is "pragmatism." There are none among well-known students of administration who have written in a speculative way about pragmatist philosophy; nor by a wide margin is there as much overlapping between public administration and pragmatism as there has been between legal realism and pragmatism.[14] Nevertheless, "pragmatism" is occasionally mentioned in the texts, and the writers often appeal to or indicate that they wish to be judged by pragmatic standards or tests.

A definition of pragmatism would be very difficult and would take us far afield—"pragmatism" as a body of literature cannot be compressed and reconciled in short space. But we are on safe grounds to say that pragmatism is a protest against rationalism, against *a priori* methods of thought, and habits of mind. Its test of truth is usually considered to be chiefly "workability" or "cash value"; an idea is true if it "works," if it has desirable effects when tried. It places emphasis upon experience, and is hence characterized by empiricism. Intelligent use of experience in testing for truth is an experiment; so "experimental" is a term frequently found in pragmatic writings. Since the truth of an idea is determined by (or is) what it does, it is in some sense an instrument. Impatience with the "abstract" or "theoretical," and use of such terms as scientific, experience, empirical, practicability, experiment—these characterize the pragmatic temper.

---

[14] Strangely enough, some of the few defenses in the literature of public administration of the legal and judicial processes are based on essentially "pragmatic" grounds, and bring to mind the writings defending Catholicism, not because of the validity of the tenets of Catholicism, but because Catholicism creates and preserves a desired degree or kind of social order. See, for example, John Dickinson's *Administrative Justice and the Supremacy of the Law in the United States* (Cambridge, Mass.: 1927), 30–31, 357, explaining the "practical advantage" of a system of government based on the theory of the supremacy of the law.

It is obvious, then, that on its negative side pragmatism accords with Utilitarianism and positivism—all are objections to rationalism, *a priorism*, the abstract and theoretical. It also is obvious that on the positive side there are affinities—*i.e.* pragmatism's test of truth is utilitarian ("social pragmatism" is, indeed, a sophisticated rewrite of the Greatest Happiness of the Greatest Number).[15] The present concern is not the abstract truth or falsity of pragmatism, but simply what ideas of a "pragmatic nature" have been enunciated by writers on administration. We may begin, appropriately, with Frank Goodnow.

Axiomatic and permanent principles of law, he wrote in his *Social Reform and the Constitution,* fitted the relatively static eighteenth century with considerable grace, but the dynamic twentieth century not at all. "More and more political and social students are recognizing that a policy of opportunism is the policy most likely to be followed by desirable results and that adherence to general theories which are to be applied at all times and under all conditions is productive of harm rather than good. . . . One may, therefore, without committing himself to all the vagaries of pragmatic philosophy . . . safely say that at the present time most students regard the postulation of fundamental political principles of universal application as the statement of 'mere useless opprobrious theory.' "[16]

Charles A. Beard, another of the Early Giants, discourses in a similar vein. Writing on "The Criteria and Scheme of Municipal Science" he disclaims as a basis of criticism and evaluation "some ideal system evolved by *a priori* reasoning from an abstract concept," but insists rather that his approach is "practical and pragmatic."[17] The sources of his criteria for evaluating a city administration are derived "from a study of administrative law,"[18] experimentation, "actual municipal organizations," and from the "methods employed

---

[15] It is well not to stretch the similarities too far, for it is beyond doubt that the outlines of pragmatist epistemology and metaphysics do not accord with positivist tenents. In particular, pragmatism envisages a rather flexible, indeterminate, and relativist world; positivism regards the things and relations of the world as fixed, determinable, and determining. Since both claim the sanction of "science" it seems probable that one, at least, is swinging on the wrong gate.

[16] New York: 1911, 3–4 (by permission of the Estate of Dr. Frank J. Goodnow).

[17] *The Administration and Government of Tokyo* (New York: 1923), 19.

[18] *Ibid.,* 20. See also the New York Bureau's *The Constitution and Government of the State of New York: An Appraisal* (New York: 1915), 1, on the value of empirical standards as against "theories evolved in the closet of the political philosopher."

by private corporations in organizing and directing their administrative forces."

A. E. Buck, prefacing his *Municipal Finance,* has left us no doubt where he stands. "The approach is from the pragmatic point of view, emphasis being placed on practical and efficient financial administration. The method of treatment is empirical; theory is reduced to a minimum. The criteria used are based on experience and practice." [19] Many others have affirmed their "practical" view. Thus: "Throughout the work there has been a constant effort to make the text practical, rather than theoretical." [20] And: "In evaluation of the work of these . . . departments all criteria have been based on results." [21] One frequently has the impression that a student of administration would like as little to be caught consorting with a Theory as a member of the Anti-Saloon League to be photographed in the back room of the White Rose. [22]

The Literature of Budgeting

Consideration of the literature of budgeting has been reserved until this point because it might be presumed—the essence of budgeting being decisions on public policy—to deal in a highly conscious way with the problem of the proper basis of decision. Instances of serious consideration of this question, however, can be counted on the fingers of one hand.

Paul Studenski, in one of these instances, treats the problem briefly in *Chapters in Public Finance.* He suggests that "social advantage" be used as the criterion of state economic activity. "It is impossible without the concept of social advantage to discuss the public economy and evaluate its activities, since its object should be to secure the maximum well being of society." [23] He admits, however, and discusses, the difficulties of applying such an indefinite

---

[19] New York: 1926, v. *Cf.* M. E. Dimock, *Modern Politics and Administration* (New York: 1937), 338 ff.; M. L. Cooke, *Our Cities Awake* (Garden City: 1918), 266.

[20] F. W. Reeves and J. D. Russell, *College Organization and Administration* (Indianapolis: 1929), 4.

[21] C. E. Ridley, *Measuring Municipal Government* (New York and Syracuse: 1927), 8.

[22] The pragmatic strain in public administration is augmented by the literature of "experimentation." See, for example, W. K. Doyle's *Independent Commissions in the Federal Government* (Chapel Hill: 1939), 92; Felix Frankfurter, *op. cit.,* 49–50; A. N. Holcombe, *Government in a Planned Democracy* (New York: 1935), *passim.*

The pragmatism of public administration is re-enforced by its attitude toward democracy, discussed in the previous chapter: Democracy is instrumental, a tool to achieve the Good Life, and its value lies in how it "works."

[23] New York: n. d., 474.

criterion, finding so many objections that one can only wonder how it can serve at all. In fact, its value could only be procedural, because the discussion leaves no substantive content. Even this dubious comfort vanishes when we learn that those who frame public policy are not "inclined or equipped" to weigh subtle questions of social advantage, that "their decisions are dictated by and large by precedent, pressure from selfish groups, accident, and even their own personal interest." [24]

The problem is canvassed in Mabel Walker's *Municipal Expenditures.* She is frankly skeptical of the value of any theory: "Can the gap ever be bridged between the high sounding theories of the scholar and the rough and ready methods of the public official?" [25]

> The problem of budget distribution is one of mechanics. The final appropriation is the resultant of all the forces in action just as truly as in an analogous case in physics.[26]

She puts aside her doubts, however, and tackles the problem. The marginal utility theory of economics she disposes of summarily —it is a pleasing theory but not a practical guide for budget makers. A "cruder and simpler" method of attack, one "partaking of the pragmatic viewpoint," is to follow the method used in working out "ideal" household budgets that are objective in the sense of being based on averages.

> If the budgets of a sufficiently large number of the most progressive cities could be analyzed and compared, after variations due to peculiar political or geographical exigencies had been eliminated, certain tendencies would be apparent which would point the way for a norm of expenditures consistent with the state of progress at present achieved by society.[27]

Such a procedure cannot be followed unhesitatingly and without qualification, but it is the only thing solid upon which to build.[28]

Wylie Kilpatrick appears to have given the problem the most thorough consideration—consequently summarization may do him less than justice. [29] First, it is necessary to establish five major

---

[24] *Ibid.,* 476.
[25] Baltimore: 1930, 47 (citations by permission of Johns Hopkins Press).
[26] *Idem.*
[27] *Ibid.,* 50. "Progressive city" is not defined.
[28] This procedure would, of course, project present tendencies on a straight line into the future—which few persons would desire, and which we can feel mortally certain will never happen.
[29] "Classification and Measurement of Public Expenditures," 183 *Annals* (Jan., 1936), 19–26, 20.

categories or classifications for measurement, beginning with amounts expended, simply, and ending with a measurement "according to the social values consequent from performing the services." Then the classifications must be brought to bear upon the "four concepts of need, ability, benefit, and character of public administration." [30]

> The initial tool is the classification of expenditure in amounts. . . . Upon this basis may be built the measurement of the quantity of services which accompanies the criteria of need; the measurement of unit costs paralleling the criteria of ability; the measure of social results of services accompanying the concept of benefit; and the measure of the quality of services or administrative efficiency which parallels the criteria of administration.[31]

Kilpatrick's scheme may be useful as a procedure; certainly it highlights some budgetary problems. But on the substantive side he puts a rabbit into the hat at the point of measuring "according to the social values consequent from planning the services" and—leaves it there. What "social values" and how are they measured?

There are perhaps other considerations of the problem of the basis of decision in the literature of budgeting, but if so they are surely few.[32] V. O. Key, Jr., has written on "The Lack of a Budgetary Theory," [33] noting that American budget literature is "singularly arid" on the "basic budgeting problem (on the expenditure side), namely: On what basis shall it be decided to allocate x dollars to activity A instead of activity B?" [34] and reviewing American treatments of the subject. "It is not to be concluded," he reflects in closing, "that by excogitation a set of principles may be formulated on the basis of which the harassed budget official may devise an automatic technique for the allocation of financial resources. Yet the

---

[30] *Ibid.*, 25.

[31] *Ibid.*, 26.

[32] L. D. White states the problem in his *Introduction to Public Administration* (New York: 1939, 215 ff.), but advances only a step in exploring it.

E. A. Fitzpatrick in his *Budget Making in a Democracy* (New York: 1918) has considered the problem, but his contribution in many respects is atypical of American writings on public administration. He accepts the necessity for an ever-increasing amount of public expenditure, and accuses the "executive budget" advocates of narrow-minded parsimony, of treating social problems as though they were fiscal problems merely. He would have expenditure decided by the people's representatives according to the following formula: "Social energy as expressed in public funds must secure in terms of social welfare results greater than the same expenditure privately made." 291—Italicized in original.

[33] 34 *Am. Pol. Sci. Rev.* (Dec., 1940), 1137–1144. See also, J. Wilner Sundelson, "Budgetary Principles," 50 *Pol. Sci. Q.* (June, 1935), 236–263, a brief review of the history of American budget thought, emphasizing the fact that to date Americans have been concerned chiefly with practical and procedural questions. *Cf.* Gerhard Colm, "Theory of Public Expenditure," 183 *Annals* (Jan., 1936), 1–11.

[34] *Ibid.*, 1138.

problem needs study in several directions. Further examination from the viewpoints of economic theory and political philosophy could produce valuable results." [35]

The literature on budgeting apparently shares the same vices (if they are vices) of the "literature of decision" in public administration generally. There is the same "naturalistic fallacy," the presumption that correct answers flow from a procedurally proper juxtaposition of "facts," the same inclination to avoid questions of value by taking refuge in the observation that, after all, the whole matter is one of "pressures." Their defense, if one be needed, is obvious: Idealist and Realists have had nothing to offer but the pleasure of contemplating Eternals and Transcendentals in scholastic quietude; whereas the budgeteers have been waging a crucial campaign against inertia and avarice.

Two patent "bases of decision" in the literature of public administration have not been considered: "principles" of public administration, which are deemed by some to dictate decisions, and "economy and efficiency," professed by many as the bedrock value of the discipline. But these two subjects deserve separate chapters.

Another answer is "functionalism"—the notion that questions are to be decided in terms of the expertise of the field within which they fall, by the master of this expertise, the expert. This matter is considered in the following chapter.

---

[35] *Ibid.*, 1143. Some evidence on both the "Good Life" and the "criteria of action" is to be gained, presumably, from assessing the actions and ideals of those whom administrative students have tended to take as their heroes—Robert Moses, Harold Ickes, Harry Hopkins, W. O. Douglas, Fiorello La Guardia, William Allenson White, Harold D. Smith, etc.

Chapter 6

WHO SHOULD RULE?

Who are competent to govern the Good Society that writers on public administration envisage?

Any political philosophy necessarily must answer the question, "Who should rule?" The rulers of Plato's *Republic* are the Guardians, who rule by virtue of their knowledge of the Good. They are the only ones capable by innate ability and rigorous training to know the Good. At the other extreme are anarchists such as Bakunin and Kropotkin, who find government an evil in itself, and evil because it sustains other evils. Their answer to "Who should rule?" is "nobody." To them, "governing or ruling" and "right or good" are irreconcilable ideas.

The gamut of political theory contains many answers between these extremes. Preparatory to the state of beatific anarchy, Marxists find that the Proletariat is entitled to rule. August Comte proclaimed the Man of Science to be the legitimate ruler. Filmer and Bossuet knew the standard of right and wrong to be Divine Fiat revealed through a divinely designated monarch. Locke found that person (or persons) entitled to rule who knows the extent and respects the imperative of Natural Rights. Burke revealed a country's true and natural rulers to be those who by gentle birth and especially privileged nurture are quick to sense and bold to apply the Divine Purpose, particularly as that Purpose is revealed in the history of His wondrous creation, the Nation. Machiavelli found that person supremely entitled to exercise authority who is most apt at seizing power and aggrandizing the State.

Administrators:
A Democratic Ruling Class

To demonstrate that American students of administration have elaborated theories of "Who should rule?" is an unnecessary labor. The assertion that there is a field of expertise which has, or should have, a place in and claim upon the exercise of modern governmental functions—this is a fundamental postulate of the public administration movement.[1] What is the nature of this claim upon the exercise of political power?

In general the claim is that the conditions of the modern world require a large and skilful body of bureaucrats, administrators, or experts; that the scientific method and the vast changes which it has brought about in the externals of life, the existence of the nation-state (or hope of a world-state) system, and the demand by all classes of society that government be used as an instrument for achieving the Good Life—that these stupendous facts compel us to recognize the necessity for a "governing class." We have become, in the expression of Graham Wallas, biologically parasitic on *Our Social Heritage*. Without a group dedicated to the preservation, exercise, and extension of this social heritage "civilization as we have known it" would be impossible—and civilization as we hope to make it, the vainest of dreams.

"There is no subject more important," Beard proclaims, "—from its minute ramifications of unit costs and accounts to the top structure of the overhead—than this subject of administration. The future of civilized government, and even, I think, of civilization itself, rests upon our ability to develop a science and a philosophy and a practice of administration competent to discharge the public functions of civilized society." [2] Is a Philosopher-King or a Communist or Fascist Party charged with a greater responsibility than preserving civilization?

Rise of the "Administrator"

The notion of professionalism or expertise in government service was at first inclusive, undifferentiated, and uncritical. Until the First Great War, there was as a rule simply a strong feeling that "business methods" ought to be applied to government, that appoint-

---

[1] The objection may perhaps be entered at this point that public administrators do not "rule," but "serve," and hence a discussion of "Who should rule?" is misguided. This objection can easily be met. In the first place, students of administration do not nowadays regard administrators as dumb servants of a legislature, ready to go right or left, stop or start, at its command. In the second place, serving and ruling are not mutually exclusive concepts. Plato's guardians "served"; they were servants of that objective Good upon which their claim to power was based, and they served the whole State by performing a task nobody else could perform. It was a divine right and practically absolute Prussian monarch who stated: "I am the first servant of the State."

[2] "The Role of Administration in Government," in *The Work Unit in Federal Administration* (Chicago: 1937), 1-3, 3 (by permission of Public Administration Service); *Cf.* Max Lerner, "The Burden of Government Business," in *Public Management in the New Democracy* (New York: 1940), F. Morstein Marx, ed., 3-14, 12, reflecting on the idea of a "trained *elite* of administrators and technicians" that will help "rebuild the pattern of our lives," "mould the framework of a culture."

ments to government positions should be by "merit," that we ought to have "experts" in government service. These notions were undefined and overlapping; they were simply the positive side of the reflections that "morality is not enough" and "we can no longer allow the politicians to run things as in the past."

The Businessman as Administrator

There is in the early writings a strong presumption that the businessman is the "expert" who is entitled to rule. The businessman has built this civilization; so he is morally entitled and mentally equipped to run it.[3] Although there was no large-scale desertion of the standard of business until the Depression, there were scattered dissents from the business-man-as-model much earlier. Thus H. G. James, reflecting in 1915 upon the emerging city-managership, asserts: instead of the successful businessman type we must have "a man of liberal training, broad point of view and a comprehensive conception of the real problems of urban life."[4] Nowadays writers speak of "public businessmen," but chiefly to emphasize the difference between the public administrator and the private businessman.[5]

Experts in Government.—Prominent in the early writings is insistence upon the necessity for "experts" in government service. The term was used broadly to connote permanence, training, specialization; to designate the opposite of "spoils" or simple morality, the first of which was wicked, the second irrelevant or inadequate. A. L. Lowell's "Expert Administrators in Popular Government" may be taken as typical of this literature.[6] Lowell's thesis is that we must have experts in government to preserve modern democracy. The specification of "expert" is hardly more definite than "nonlaymen." He specifies, however, trained professional men (physicians, engineers, etc.). There is perhaps in germ the idea of experts in an administrative function, but it hardly reaches beyond the notion of "nonpolitical"; permanence and training-on-the-job are the chief ingredients of expertise in the administrative func-

---

[3] *Cf.* Woodrow Wilson, "The Study of Administration," *2 Pol. Sci. Q.* (June, 1887), 197–222, 209; Moorfield Storey, "The Government of Cities; The Need of a Divorce of Municipal Business from Politics," *Proceedings,* National Civil Service Reform League, 1891, 47–67, 48.
[4] "Some Reflections on the City Manager Plan of Government," *9 Am. Pol. Sci. Rev.* (Aug., 1915), 504–506, 504.
[5] Thus A. N. Holcombe, in *Government in a Planned Democracy* (New York: 1935).
[6] *7 Am. Pol. Sci. Rev.* (Feb. 1913), 45–62.

tion. The year of this essay—1913—is significant. This was the bloom period of the notion that experts are to solve our problems.

The notion that the "expert" is entitled to exercise governmental power is still among us. We have proceeded little, however, in the analysis and rationalization of this claim to power. We are still in the folk-wisdom stage of the pat phrase, "The expert should be on tap, not on top." [7]

The Administrator: Genesis.—In recent years—say since the First Great War—there has emerged from the general notion of permanence, capacity, and expertise in government service a concept of a distinct and definable function of "general administration," not merely a skill in the employment of government, but a skill *in* or *of* government; a function necessary to be performed well, given modern conditions, if government is to realize desirable objectives, and a function requiring great capacity and special training for its most successful performance. It is not stretching a point to say that this function partakes of "governing" and that the persons who perform it constitute something of a "governing class." [8] The writers have been concerned, one way or another, to make this function of administration "democratic" in personnel and procedures. But the "governing class," in the writings, certainly is *not* a mere tool of the legislature, and it *is* a prime force.

The idea of administrators-as-such is closely bound up with the emergence of the notion that "public administration" in itself is a subject-matter field or technique in which one can specialize, a science and art one can learn. W. E. Mosher, for example, was an ardent protagonist of both ideas.

---

[7] I do not mean to deny that this is wisdom. Perhaps it is as much wisdom as we can attain. It stands, nevertheless, in the relationship to an acute and philosophical treatment of the relation of expertise to democracy that the maxim "Honesty is the best policy" stands to the ethical theory of Kant.

There are at least four recognizable usages of the term "expert" in recent writings. Sometimes, and perhaps most precisely, it is used in referring to one who possesses a knowledge and skill which is a part of the body of attitudes and knowledge we call "science"—engineers, meteorologists, bacteriologists, etc. Second, the term may be enlarged to designate one skilful in the exercise of any large and organized body of knowledge. So used, an "expert" is a professional man; and lawyers, accountants, journalists, and teachers join the doctors and chemists as "experts." Third, "expert" may be used to designate one skilled in the special function of administration. Fourth, "expert" may be used, chiefly adjectively, to connote permanence, specialization, and professionalism in government work, regardless of the particular function performed. It seems reasonable to suppose that the problem of the proper role of the "expert" in government is not a simple one, that the answer with respect to one of the above categories need not be valid for the others.

[8] Some of the expressions of opinion quoted below do not refer *solely* to the "administrative class." But I do not think I have done serious violence to the author's meaning in any case.

Certain general principles have been derived as well as a number of standard practices that have met the test of experience. Taken all together such principles and approved practices form the groundwork of a science that in the course of time may take its place alongside such pragmatic sciences as medicine, law, and various branches of engineering. Contrary to prevailing opinion in the past, it is becoming more and more widely recognized that administration is a *ding an sich*.... and that like any other art and science is learnable and teachable.[9]

Administration, in Mr. Mosher's view, is a science and art that combines and uses the results of many specializations. It is, as a matter of fact, the "master trade of all," because it subsumes and synthesizes all others.

It is imperative that we secure the exercise of this "master trade" in our government.

Government is no longer a second- or third-rate industry. . . . Its successful conduct calls for the best brains and leadership available in the country. If we cannot increase the prestige of public employment and give assurance of satisfactory careers in it . . . the permanency of democratic institutions is far from assured.[10]

We *must* be aroused from the notion that government is a side issue in American life. We must launch a campaign with the slogan, "The Best shall serve the State." [11]

The notion that a skilled bureaucracy, particularly a highly competent administrative class, is a necessary "balance wheel" or "cambium layer"—*the* essential organ of a modern democracy—is quite common. One of the better treatments of this viewpoint is by E. P. Herring. The "general will" or "public interest," he finds in his *Public Administration and the Public Interest,*[12] is a fiction. A realistic analysis shows a multitude of special interests competing for favors, creating a welter in which the "public interest" is but the slightest of considerations. The legislative branch, naturally disintegrative or centrifugal because based on representation, is further weakened for the task of securing the "public interest" by our unfortunate political traditions. The administrative agencies in

---

[9] W. E. Mosher, "The Making of a Public Servant," 28 *Nat. Mun. Rev.* (June, 1939), 416–419, 416.

[10] Mosher, "Government Without Patronage," 189 *Annals* (Jan., 1937), 35–41, 41.

[11] "Public Service As a Career," 169 *Annals* (Sept., 1933), 130–143. The more purely "inspirational" or "devotional" pieces are not considered in this essay. The notion that "civilization rests on us" is, of course, a general professional conceit. The burden of upholding civilization rests heavily also upon the shoulders of farmers, plumbers, and teachers.

[12] New York: 1936.

the past have displayed a most lamentable weakness, swaying in the winds of group interest rather than discovering and enforcing the public interest. The President alone has proved strong enough to bring a measure of unity out of conflict. What we need, according to Herring, is a revised and strengthened bureaucracy, headed and reinforced by the President, and having new or revised institutions for representation of interests, planning, and general coordination. Such an arrangement would give stability and purpose, and at the same time realize the democratic goods of freedom, equality, and representation. Indeed, under modern conditions, only by such changes can democracy be preserved. To the legislative body will be reserved the right of deciding upon programs. But the formulation of alternatives and the decisions on implementing broad policies will be a function of the bureaucracy. Only by such a means can the function of the voter be reduced to manageable compass: the expression of yea or nay.[13]

The Administrator: Function and Virtues.—The Chairman of the President's Committee on Administrative Management, Louis Brownlow, has also meditated upon "The New Role of the Public Administrator." The new task of the public administrator "above all else . . . is to concern himself with human relations, with human values, with those deeper economic, social, and spiritual needs of the human beings whose government, in its administrative branch, he represents." [14] He will be more and more regarded not as the agent of a particular government entity, but as a center of social cooperation. He will be less legal and more technical and professional. "He will be more of a success and less of a failure in proportion as he is able to command and utilize broad knowledge, deep understanding, and human sympathy in a synthesis of social wisdom." [15]

Lucius Wilmerding finds that "in classifying civil servants, the primary division is . . . that between those who assist the political officers of the government in the formulation of policy and those who merely carry out orders, accumulate facts, or engage in research. The work of the first group may conveniently be called administrative work. . . ." [16] The qualifications of the administrator give one pause:

---

[13] This line of thought is repeated and extended in his *The Politics of Democracy* (New York: 1940). See 18, 288 ff. See also, A. N. Holcombe, *op. cit.,* 38.

[14] 23 *Nat. Mun. Rev.* (May, 1934), 248–251, 250.

[15] *Ibid.,* 251.

[16] Reprinted by permission from *Government by Merit,* copyrighted 1935 by McGraw-Hill Book Co., Inc.

In the *administrator* such qualities are to be desired as initiative, intelligence, judgment, imagination, open-mindedness, and tact. . . . Although he must be learned in the law, experienced in the political consequences of administrative action, skilled in public finance, and able to understand the purely technical considerations involved in a problem, he is neither a lawyer, a politician, a financier, nor a technician. . . . He . . . is a specialist . . . but . . . not in the limited field of a profession or a science. His specialty is method rather than subject matter. He is a coordinator of knowledge rather than a researcher into the inner recesses of one of his branches.[17]

Here, as ever, L. D. White hews close to the line of the facts, but he finds in the British administrative class many of the characteristics listed in the above catalog of the administrative virtues, and thinks the British example worthy, in outline, to be followed here. Philips Bradley's summary of his (White's) *Government Career Service* is apt: "Briefly put, his thesis is that there is a distinctive administrative function, as yet hardly recognized in this country, but indispensable to the effective organization and conduct of public business. This function, as defined in England, is 'concerned with the formulation of policy, with the coordination and improvement of government machinery, and with the general administration and control of the departments of the public service.' It is independent of, but integrates, the staff and line functions. . . ."[18]

Ordway Tead believes that administration in a modern democracy is a special skill, requiring special training. The administrative techniques of private enterprise will not suffice. "Administration in public service is, under present conditions, distinctive, *sui generis*. . . ."[19] We need an administrative leadership that is vital, intelligent, creative, and democratic. The administrative expert must be able at once to "satisfy the requirements of democratic control and of responsible unified administrative direction." These administrators are not to be "experts in the usual narrow sense in which that word is now employed. They are to be, as the phrase is, 'specialists in generalization,' and in capacities special to democratic leadership."[20]

---

[17] *Ibid.*, 33.

[18] "Administration: The Fourth Power in Modern Government," 27 *Soc. Studies* (May, 1936), 320–327, 327. See also, White's "The Public Service of the Future," in *The Future of Government in the United States* (Chicago: 1942), 192–217, 202–203, in which he envisages the "gradual segregation of an administrative corps" distinct from the "business administration" or "administrative management" group.

[19] "Amateurs Versus Experts in Administration," 189 *Annals* (Jan., 1937), 42–47, 45.

[20] *Ibid.*, 47. *Cf.* P. T. Stafford, "The New Amateur in Public Administration," 29 *Am. Pol. Sci. Rev.* (Apr., 1935), 257–269.

The Commission of Inquiry on Better Government Personnel reported that "there is general agreement on the evidence presented to the Commission that the work of government, performed by appointed personnel, is made up of five clearly distinguishable kinds of service." [21] The first of these is *administrative work, that is, the general management,*" which consists of "organizing, staffing, directing, coordinating, planning, budgeting, and reporting." [22] The others are professional work, clerical work, skilled and trades work, and unskilled work. This program "recognizes the fundamental differences in individuals . . . as analyzed by science and experience." [23]

M. E. Dimock adds the weight of his opinion that "the 'administrator' is no figment of the imagination. He must possess an unusual balance of characteristics and accomplishments which enable him to direct the work of others. He needs physique, nervous energy, special knowledge, imagination, theoretical ability, judgment, perspective, co-ordinating capacity, tact, strength to say 'no,' and ability to inspire others and to create confidence in employees and the public. This enumeration is by no means exclusive." [24]

We may conclude our sampling by a quotation from J. M. Pfiffner : "The development of a class of administrative technicians in America would be beneficial to the survival of democracy and freedom. Democracy will resist Fascism and Communism to the extent that it excels them in maintaining an orderly and just state of human affairs. . . . What is needed is the development of a school of management research technicians who possess the just, wise, and omniscient qualities of Plato's guardians." [25]

The reference to Plato's Guardians is revealing. Laying aside questions of "power" and "authority," it is patent by now that those

---

[21] Reprinted by permission from *Better Government Personnel,* copyrighted 1935 by McGraw-Hill Book Co., Inc., p. 26.

[22] *Loc. cit.*

[23] *Ibid.,* 84. See Herman Finer, "Better Government Personnel," 51 *Pol. Sci. Q.* (Dec., 1936), 569–599, for searching criticism, from the viewpoint of British thought and experience, of some assumptions and conclusions of the Commission of Inquiry on Better Government Personnel.

[24] *Modern Politics and Administration* (New York: 1937), 293. (By permission of the American Book Co.)

[25] *Research Methods in Public Administration* (New York: 1940), 24–25. See also, E. J. Coil, "Planning Staffs in a Democratic Government," 6 *Plan Age* (Feb., 1940), 56–67; and J. M. Gaus and L. O. Wolcott, *Public Administration and the United States Department of Agriculture* (Chicago: 1940), 298–301, on the notion of "specialists in generalization." In the latter occurs the famous quotation from Brooks Adams' *The Theory of Social Revolutions,* that describes the capacity for coordination or generalization as the distinctive administrative quality and as "not only the faculty upon which social stability rests, but . . . possibly, the highest faculty of the human mind."

who are to lead us into Democracy's Promised Land will exercise *functions* as exalted as Plato's Guardians, Machiavelli's Prince, Le Roi Soleil, Comte's Scientists, the Communist Party, or James I.

Recruitment and Training

How will the Administrators be chosen and prepared for the exercise of their responsibilities?

The Administrative Class will be recruited "democratically"—it will not be based on wealth, birth, or social class. It will be an aristocracy of talent. It will resemble—the analogy recurs because it is so apt—Plato's Guardian Class, not Burke's aristocracy of the rich, the well-born, and the able. It will "exemplify the democratic principle of equality of opportunity in accordance with merit."

Recruitment must be on a broad base in order to satisfy democratic principles, and also because "gold," as Plato wrote, is where you find it. But there is another reason for broad recruitment, a reason which E. P. Herring emphasizes: if the bureaucracy is to be the balance wheel of society it should be recruited from all strata of society.[26] A. N. Holcombe finds, to be sure, that there is a concentration of the needed skills in the "middle class," and W. E. Mosher hopes to attract persons from the "abler and more ambitious classes of citizens." But these are not serious limitations upon the above generalizations. Holcombe hopes to make his "middle class" broad enough to include everyone, and Mosher is trying to broaden, not narrow, the basis of recruitment.

The Administrative Class can also be required to have had the benefit of a college education, without doing violence to democratic principles. Thus H. W. Dodds, after a general argument that the establishment of a special administrative class does not nullify democratic ideals, holds that insistence upon higher education is not undemocratic in a land where it is so widespread. Besides, the argument that this requirement is "undemocratic" assumes that the old

---

[26] V. O. Key has expressed very strongly the desirability of broad recruitment of higher civil servants: "We probably do not appreciate our good fortune in not being limited in the recruitment of higher civil servants, as are the armed forces in the selection of their officer personnel, to the uniformly disciplined product of a few educational institutions. (The essentially pernicious nature of the occasional proposal for the establishment of a 'West Point' for the civil service is, by analogy, obvious.) Diversity of social origin is perhaps as significant as diversity of training in determining the character of a civil service. We are not restricted, as some other nations have been, in the recruitment of upper personnel to any particular social class—a purely fortuitous precipitate of events but, nevertheless, one that could well be evocative of self-congratulations." "Politics and Administration," in *The Future Government in the United States* (Chicago: 1942), L. D. White, ed., 145–163, 153 (by permission of the University of Chicago Press).

system was "democratic." It wasn't; it was fortuitous and quite unjust.[27] Pfiffner seconds this view. We need to attract the young intelligent college graduate. After all, college is not a perquisite of the rich in America.[28] Dimock is of the opinion that "whether or not those who reach the top of the administrative career are university trained makes no difference to the public welfare, so long as in the selection and promotion processes the man possessing the necessary co-ordinating qualities is given preference."[29] But "percentages greatly favor," he feels, the university trained man.

Education: Cultural or Professional?—There is rather a sharp difference of opinion among those accepting the need for an Administrative Class as to the type of formal education required. Some wish to see this education primarily "cultural," some—naturally most of the professional students of public administration—wish to see it primarily "professional." Of the first group W. Y. Elliott is an outstanding example. His argument closely resembles those surveyed above until we reach the subject of training. "Our universities," he finds, "do not turn out enough first-rate administrators from their student bodies (the proper recruiting ground of administrators) precisely because we are too much occupied with administration, with the organization of knowledge, and not enough with training students, as well as professors, to think hard, even— I dare say it—to think abstractly. . . . A humanistic culture, intensely philosophical and with a rich historical perspective, is the groundwork of any long-run human development."[30] Felix Frankfurter echoes this sentiment: "Our institutions of higher learning must be training schools for public service, not through utilitarian courses but by the whole sweep of their culture and discipline."[31]

Practically all professional students and teachers of public administration agree upon the desirability of more or less "cultural" education for public administrators. But they assert that administra-

---

[27] Dodds, "Bureaucracy and Representative Government," 189 *Annals* (Jan., 1937), 165–172.
[28] *Public Administration* (New York: 1935), 170–178.
[29] *Op. cit.*, 294.
[30] Reprinted by permission from *The Need for Constitutional Reform* by W. Y. Elliott, copyrighted 1935 by McGraw-Hill Book Co., Inc., 225. There is a present vogue for the "liberal" point of view, a demand for administrators with a "broad point of view," as against "mechanics," "paper pushers." See, for example, R. A. Walker, "Public Administration: The Universities and the Public Service," 39 *Am. Pol. Sci. Rev.* (Oct., 1945), 926–933; V. M. Barnett, "Modern Constitutional Development: A Challenge to Administration," 4 *Pub. Adm. Rev.* (Spring, 1944), 159–164, 163–164; D. M. Levitan, "Political Means and Administrative Means," 3 *Pub. Adm. Rev.* (Autumn, 1943), 353–359, 354.
[31] *The Public and Its Government* (New Haven, 1930), 163–164.

tion is not merely a matter of humane sentiments, broad views, and generalizing faculties, but that it is a thing-in-itself, that it consists of or utilizes knowledge and skills which can be taught and learned by formal instruction. There is some difference of opinion as to what the knowledge and skills are, but the POSDCORB [32] subjects are a substantial core of consistency.[33] A middle view is that "administration" is real, that it can be put on a teach-and-learn basis, but that it cannot, or should not, be separated from a particular subject-matter field. Colleges of education proceed upon this basis, for example, and to judge from their curricula, some schools of public administration do likewise.

The "Compleat Administrator."—We are now in a position to attempt to summarize or categorize the expertise of the Administrator. He must, in the first place, have an unusual natural endowment of physique, stamina, the qualities of personality which enable him to "win friends and influence people," and—particularly—intelligence. He must, in the second place, be educated. We have seen that there are two general views about the nature of this education, but most writers on administration would agree that both "cultural" and "professional" subjects should be included—and that general "social science" subjects should be in the curriculum whether they are considered "cultural" or "professional." [34] Third, he must not only be educated, he must be "educated"; he must "know something," be a "wise" man. A public administrator "should have a knowledge of the place of the public service in its relationship with basic economic and social forces and some realization of the potentialities of government as a means of meeting human needs." [35]

At this point we pass into a region of bald assertion, intangibility, and—faith. Precisely, *in what sense* can one be a "specialist at things in general"? What is one to make of this vague but recurring

----

[32] Planning, Organizing, Staffing, Directing, Coordinating, Reporting, Budgeting.

[33] The most cogent short statement of both sides of the cultural-professional argument that has come to my attention is that of W. E. Mosher and Robert Hutchins, "Shall We Train for Public Administration? 'Impossible,'" 1 *Pub. Adm. Rev.* (Mar., 1938—Maxwell School Publication), 3.

[34] In or out of the literature of public administration, the reasons advanced for training in the social sciences, except where a salable skill is developed, are extremely vague. They can almost be reduced to a feeling that "some good will come of it."

[35] Glen Leet, "The University Graduate in Local Government in the United States," 2 *Local Gov't. Adm.* (Mar., 1936), 85–92, 87. "The concept of the administrator as a clever manipulator is not adequate to the needs of the present and the probable future." G. A. Graham, *Education for Public Administration* (Chicago: 1941), 118.

expression? The reference to Plato, perhaps, is helpful here: what we are dealing with is a theory of a governing class.

The Claim to Power: Shadow or Substance?

Now, the State that Plato sketched is an outstanding example of the application of the idea of "functionalism." A place for everyone, and everyone in his place; each entitled to his place by virtue of being most capable of performing its functions. The principle of functionalism applies to the Guardians as well as the others; they and they alone, by nature and nurture, are fitted to perform the function of ruling. Yet their function is different *in kind* from the others, and it is this difference that titles them to rulership. They and they alone know the Good, and it is the Good, as set forth in Plato's metaphysics and epistemology, that is supposed to answer questions of "What should be done?" If it were not for this competence on the part of the Guardians they would have no authority, not even that limited type of authority that shoemakers and shepherds enjoy, arising from, but confined to, making shoes and tending sheep.

Now, the State which public administration envisages is also functional.[36] There is division of labor and specialization of function on the basis of innate ability—the Commission of Inquiry found a five-fold grouping of human talents based on "science and experience" and conforming "to the natural capacities and characteristics of human beings." As in Plato's State there is a group better fitted by nature and nurture than all others to determine the common destiny. But at this point the similarity ceases. The claim to power of the Guardians is quite clear. That of our Administrative Technicians is anything but clear. We are not informed how their expertise is different *in kind* from that of meteorologists or stenographers. We are not told *why* the will of the Administrative Technician is entitled to prevail in case of conflict. The Administrative Technician, it is asserted, is entitled to prevail because he is a "specialist in generalization," whereas meteorologists and stenographers are not. But "specialist in generalization" is unexplained and unsupported. It is a feat of dialectic levitation.

Major Problems, Minor Answers.—Generally speaking, the literature dealing with the problem "Who should Rule?" is not satisfying; it stimulates rather than nourishes. All of the conflicts and in-

---

[36] This is doubly true of scientific management, which sets its "functional" idea against the military idea of "chain of command."

consistencies in the public administration movement meet at this point; all the unresolved theoretical problems of the movement break the surface of the current. Practically all of these conflicts, inconsistencies, and unresolved problems, it should hurriedly be added, are not peculiar to the literature of public administration but are general problems posed by large-scale, technically advanced, democratic society at the present stage of human knowledge and international relations. The indictment against public administration can be only that, at the theoretical level, it has contributed little to the "solution" or even the systematic statement of these problems.

At root is the fact that democratic ideology and institutions grew up in association with a belief in an underlying harmony, a belief that things need not be "managed" but will run themselves. The democratic philosophy at present is in the travail of being "rethought" to accommodate the concept of management and democratic institutions in the throes of change to accommodate the fact of management. Democratic liberalism has been associated historically with the fact and the ideal of a "plurality of values"—of which ideal, freedom of speech, association, and religion, and "limited government," are the characteristic institutional expressions.

The problems we now face tax not only reason for their solution, they tax the very imagination even to grasp their extent. Is it possible to build a strong bureaucracy unless there is agreement upon the ends to be served (as against agreement to disagree, and plurality of values)? Bureaucracies have never grown up, so far as we are aware, to "mould the framework of our culture" or to "rebuild the pattern of our lives," but for much more immediate and mundane objectives upon which at least the ruling groups were agreed. Science has created a whole new realm of discourse. What is the relationship of the domain of science to administration? to politics? If administrators are to use "science," how far up the governmental pyramid should it extend, what conceptions of "scientific method" are we to accept, and what is the relationship of science to "purpose"?[87] If there is a distinct "administrative" function, what precisely is the nature of its expertise? How should these experts be recruited; how are they to be trained; what, precisely, is the relationship of their curriculum to their functions? Is the expertise of the administrative class merely another example of functionalism, or does it differ *in kind* from the functionalism characteristic

---

[87] I am not overlooking the claim of the pragmatists to have bridged the gap between the realm of science and the realm of value; I would dispute the validity of that claim.

of the civil service as a whole? What is the relationship of the ideal of civil service neutrality to these questions?

These are not irrelevant or captious questions. They are things we are entitled to know about our new Ruling Class. Some facets of these problems have been satisfactorily, even brilliantly, treated. But on the whole the record is unsatisfying. We have had a spate of shallow and spurious answers. And no one has had the temerity in his thinking to attempt to "grasp the scheme of things entire."

The Voice of Dissent

We may conclude by taking note of the most conspicuous dissent from the idea of a "function of administration"—Lewis Meriam's. He is against the idea of a "profession of public service." The "public service" is not one, but many. Each of these services is likely to extend through society generally, not limited to government employment; and in each service subject matter competence is primary.[38] Meriam is skeptical of training for public administration, as such, and he is skeptical of the value of cultural education for administrators. An "administrator" is a certain amount of natural talent, plus certain useful techniques, such as knowledge of statistics, plus training on the job. Emphasis is properly placed upon professionalizing the particular expertise—such as engineering—that the person will use on the job. This conforms to American values and institutional arrangements, educational and governmental.[39]

Against the idea of "specialists in generalization" he sets the notion of solving problems and securing cooperation and synthesis by "staff agencies." These staff agencies are panels of specialists, specialists in a large number of subject-matter fields and specialists in techniques, such as accounting. "It seems to me that our task is not to seek to raise a breed of general administrators or administrators *per se,* but to recapture Frederick Cleveland's idea of the staff agency made up of experts in every necessary field working together to solve the problem of administering this governmental Leviathan. . . ."[40]

There is in this a suggestion of Progressivism's faith in the expert, and a resemblance to scientific management's emphasis upon "functionalism." It is the functionalism of public administration

[38] "Public Service—Occupation or Industry?" 32 *Am. Pol. Sci. Rev.* (Aug., 1938), 718–722.

[39] "The Trend Toward Professionalization," 189 *Annals* (Jan., 1937), 58–64.

[40] *Public Service and Special Training* (Chicago: 1936), 61 (by permission of the University of Chicago Press). See also ch. 13 in *Public Personnel Problems from the Standpoint of the Operating Officer* (Washington: 1938).

unqualified by the assertion that there is a function different from, greater than, and subsuming the others. There is, we can conclude, no reason to believe that a simple administrative machine will solve problems better than one with a *Deus ex machina*.[41]

---

[41] Speaking of his great but little-known brother Mycroft, Sherlock Holmes, with unaccustomed modesty, says (in *The Adventure of the Bruce-Partington Plans*): "Mycroft draws £450 a year, remains a subordinate, has no ambitions of any kind, will receive neither honour nor title, but remains the most indispensable man in the country. . . . The conclusions of every department are passed on to him, and he is the central exchange, the clearing-house, which makes out the balance. All other men are specialists, but his specialism is omniscience. We will suppose that a Minister needs information as to a point which involves the Navy, India, Canada, and the bimetallic question; he could get his separate advices from various departments upon each, but only Mycroft can focus them all, and say off-hand how each factor would affect the other." It is obvious that Mycroft, being omniscient and having a passion for anonymity, would qualify for staff work (assuming he held the proper degree). But his very introversion would disqualify him from becoming an Administrator.

Chapter 7

THE SEPARATION OF POWERS[1]

The problem of separation of powers has been of prominent and continuing interest to administrative writers. In fact, they have given this problem more attention during the past fifty years than have writers on "political theory."

The reasons for this are not far to seek. Separation of powers into three "branches" was an outstanding characteristic of our national, state, and even municipal governments during the nineteenth century. We had, moreover, a strong public consciousness of the separation of powers and an inclination to regard it as a prime virtue of our superior institutions, a "palladium of our liberties."[2] But by the year of Woodrow Wilson's essay, "The Study of Administration," there was already under way a great expansion of governmental activities. This expansion upset old balances, raised questions of the appositeness of the old theory. At the federal level the creation of "independent establishments," beginning in 1883, and at the state and local levels the extreme decentralization of "executive" power, raised a presumption that the "tripartite theory" was being violated, that it should either be reapplied, or else be modified or abandoned. The separation of powers was writ so large in American practice and thought that students of public administration could not have avoided a conscious, serious treatment of the subject. The resulting literature is vast and disparate. There are recognizable motifs, but many variations on the themes, and some widely varying, indeed contrary, opinions. Some of the writing is

---

[1] This chapter treats incidentally the topics of "division of labor" and "specialization and interrelation of functions." These obviously differ from separation of powers; equally obviously relate to it. In an essay of this short scope an attempt to distinguish in each would be over-subtle, repetitious.

[2] It may be appropriate to take notice of two treatments of the subject of separation of powers in works on comparative government: *Cf.* Herman Finer, "The Separation of Powers: False and True," in ch. 2 of *The Theory and Practice of Modern Government*, one vol. ed., revised by W. B. Guthrie (New York: 1934); and C. J. Friedrich, "The Separation of Powers," ch. 11 in *Constitutional Government and Politics* (New York: 1937). These two essays "box the compass" of opinion on the subject of the validity of the tripartite separation, specialization of governmental function, etc.

of a quality with the *Federalist* papers; all of it is interesting, even when, as occasionally it must be, frivolous.

The Current of Reform

Generally speaking, students of administration have been hostile to the tripartite separation of powers. In this they have not been alone; their hostility must be viewed against the background of almost complete lack of sympathy for the principle by American reformism and political science. This lack of sympathy became more widespread decade by decade between the Civil War and the First Great War.[3] It found its justification in the unhealthy condition of our government and politics, it was nourished by admiration for British practice and American business organization; and it found expression typically in proposals to deflate the judiciary, to aggrandize the executive, to distinguish more sharply "decision" and "execution"—reforming each and confining each to its appropriate realm—and to perfect the party as an instrument of popular control.

Gamaliel Bradford and Woodrow Wilson may be taken as illustrative of the general drift of reformist and academic thought. Bradford, in *The Lesson of Popular Government,* found little good to be said for American legislatures; but he found hope for the future in the executive. "No government has ever been permanently able to maintain itself," he wrote ominously, "where a numerous legislature has taken upon itself directly the work of administration." [4]

> At present the question is, by what method can public opinion . . . be most effectively brought to bear upon the powers of government, and we have reached the conclusion that to this end public opinion is to be concentrated on individuals. It is evident that this can only be effectively done in the executive branch.[5]

According to Bradford, not separation of powers, but executive leadership and predominance is the desired objective. Legislative activity should be reduced to control and criticism of the executive.

[3] On this subject and aggrandizement of the executive see C. E. Merriam, *American Political Ideas, 1856–1917* (New York: 1920), 452–453.
[4] New York: 1899, 43–44.
[5] *Ibid.,* 46 (by permission of The Macmillan Co.). "If the executive is to conduct and be responsible for administration, it must of necessity be furnished with such agents as are requisite for that purpose. . . ." 49. References are frequent to the works of James Bryce and Walter Bagehot. Bagehot's forceful essay, *The English Constitution,* seems to have convinced many Americans of the superiorities of cabinet government. Many statements of his could be interpolated into American writings on public administration without in the least disturbing the continuity. See his *Works,* vol. 4 (Hartford: 1889), Forrest Morgan, ed., 59, 64.

Woodrow Wilson made a distinction between politics and administration as fields of inquiry or endeavor in his "The Study of Administration"; [6] and his *Congressional Government* (1885) put the American plan in an unfavorable light in comparison with the British system. His *Constitutional Government in the United States* is an argument for "dynamicism" as against the static, "Newtonian" view of the founders as it is institutionalized in the separation of powers; [7] and in the Presidential office he acted upon a theory of his office antagonistic to the notion of the executive as merely an equal and coordinate branch.

The Classic Works: Goodnow and Willoughby

The appropriate point of departure for consideration of administrative writings is F. J. Goodnow's *Politics and Administration.*[8] This work blocked out the field of administrative study and provided its dialectic defenses. Most subsequent students of administration, even when they have not read it and even when they arrive at quite opposite conclusions with respect to the application of "politics" and "administration," have regarded *Politics and Administration* much as the eighteenth-century literati regarded Newton's *Principia*.

A Simple Theory.—There are, Goodnow argues, "in all governmental systems two primary or ultimate functions of government, viz. the expression of the will of the state and the execution of that will. . . . These functions are, respectivly, Politics and Administration." [9] The distinction between decision and execution was fundamental in the treatment of the separation of powers by Montesquieu

---

[6] 2 *Pol. Sci. Q.* (June, 1887), 197–222, 210 ff.

[7] New York: 1908. See also on reformist and academic hostility to separation of powers: H. J. Ford, *The Rise and Growth of American Politics* (New York: 1898), *passim;* "Politics and Administration," 16 *Annals* (Sept., 1900), 177–188; "Principles of Municipal Organization," 23 *Annals* (March, 1904), 195–222; E. M. Sait, "Participation of the Executive in Legislation," in 5 *Proceed. Acad. Pol. Sci.* (1914–1915), 127–133; L. S. Rowe, "American Political Ideas and Institutions in Their Relation to the Problem of City Government," 1 *Municipal Affairs* (June, 1897), 317–328; E. R. Lewis, *A History of American Political Thought from the Civil War to the World War* (New York: 1937), 471 ff.

[8] New York: 1900. The *Politics and Administration* essay seems to have grown out of a paper read two years previously at the Indianapolis Conference for Good City Government: "The Place of the Council and of the Mayor in the Organization of Municipal Government." Similar ideas were expressed by H. E. Deming in a paper read at the same conference.

[9] *Op. cit.,* 22. However, Goodnow also distinguishes between the "executive" authorities and the "administrative" authorities in a manner similar to that later elaborated by W. F. Willoughby—see below. (Citations by permission of the estate of Dr. Frank J. Goodnow.)

and the Founding Fathers; they simply did not carry their analysis to the desirable and ultimate point of subsuming the "judicial power" under these two primary functions.[10] The distinction between politics and administration is "made necessary by psychological causes."

> Political functions group themselves naturally under two heads, which are equally applicable to the mental operations and the actions of self-conscious personalities. That is, the action of the state as a political entity consists either in operations necessary to the expression of its will, or in operations necessary to the execution of that will.[11]

Complications.—The separation of powers, Goodnow finds, is both a good and a bad thing. More precisely, distinction and division of functions is good, separation of powers is bad. In the first place, the great complexity of political conditions makes it "practically impossible" for the same governmental organ to be entrusted in equal degree with the discharge of both functions. "In every government more or less differentiated organs are established. Each of these organs, while not perhaps confined exclusively to the discharge of one of these functions, is still characterized by the fact that its action consists largely or mainly in the discharge of one or the other. This . . . solution . . . is inevitable both because of psychological necessity and for reasons of economic expediency." [12] We soon learn, however, in considering Montesquieu, that though "the recognition of separate powers or functions of government" is good, "the existence of separate governmental authorities, to each of which one of the powers of government was to be entrusted," is bad, at least if it is followed very far.[13] The unworkability of this "corollary" to the separation of powers, the "separation of authorities," is conclusively proved, Goodnow feels, by American experience. In fact, "no political organization, based on the general theory of a differentiation of governmental functions, has ever been established which assigns the function of expressing the will of the state exclusively to any one of the organs for which it makes provision." [14]

There is always a meeting and mingling of the two functions, and the organs of government to which the discharge of these functions is entrusted "cannot be clearly defined." Moreover:

> It is impossible to assign each of these functions to a separate authority, not merely because the exercise of governmental power cannot

---

[10] The function of the judiciary seems to fall under both decision and execution. On page 12, for example, he holds that courts have both "made the law" and "administered justice." *Cf.* 17.

[11] *Ibid.*, 9.   [12] *Ibid.*, 11.

[13] *Ibid.*, 13.   [14] *Ibid.*, 15.

be clearly apportioned, but also because, as political systems develop, these two primary functions of government tend to be differentiated into minor and secondary functions. The discharge of each of these minor functions is entrusted to somewhat separate and independent governmental organs.[15]

In short, it must be concluded, what seemed at first a clear and simple principle is no longer clear or simple. Some more recent students have taken the name of Goodnow in vain.

The Control of Administration by Politics.—Having discovered the "Primary Functions of the State" to be two, Goodnow proceeds to consider each in more detail. "The function of politics" has to do primarily with the expression of the state will, secondarily with the execution of that will. So far as it has to do with expressing the state will, the ramifications of "politics" are "most extended"; it must deal with such questions as sovereignty and representation. The important point for present purposes is that politics has to do "secondarily" with the execution of state will. This is true because "actual political necessity . . . requires that there shall be harmony between the expression and the execution of the state will."

> Lack of harmony between the law and its execution results in political paralysis. A rule of conduct, *i.e.* an expression of the state will, practically amounts to nothing if it is not executed. . . .

> Now in order that this harmony between the expression and the execution of the state will may be obtained, the independence either of the body which expresses the state will or of the body which executes it must be sacrificed. . . .

> In other words, practical political necessity makes impossible the consideration of the function of politics apart from that of administration. Politics must have a certain control over administration. . . .[16]

The "certain control" may be found either within the governmental system; or if the formal governmental system attempts to enforce a separation of powers, "outside of that system and in the political party," as has happened in the United States. Whether within or without, the existence of this control is necessitated by the fact that "without it orderly and progressive government is impossible."

---

[15] *Ibid.*, 16.
[16] *Ibid.*, 23–24.

It should, therefore, extend so far as is necessary to produce that harmony between the expression and the execution of the state will which has been shown to be so necessary. If, however, it is extended beyond this limit, it at once loses its *raison d'être*. . . .[17]

The problem, then, is to have the "necessary" control of administration by politics, without having too much. This can be accomplished by "recognizing a degree of independence in the administrative as in the judicial authorities," and by "the cultivation of a sound public opinion."

We get further help with the problem of securing the proper control in the chapter on "The Function of Administration." "Administration," we find, is of several kinds, and the proper amount of control varies with the type of administration. Administration may be either of justice or of government. Politics should not intrude in the administration of justice. Administration of government is of several types: purely executive, quasi-judicial, and statistical and semi-scientific. As regards the executive function, there can be no question: it must "of necessity be subordinated to the function of politics." [18]

With respect to the other administrative functions, however, the presumption must be reversed.

> The fact is . . . that there is a large part of administration which is unconnected with politics, which should be relieved very largely, if not altogether, from the control of political bodies. It is unconnected with politics because it embraces fields of semi-scientific, *quasi*-judicial and *quasi*-business or commercial activity—work which has little if any influence on the expression of the true state will.[19]

European countries have recognized this fact and made provision for it: independence of operation and permanence of tenure. The United States must do likewise. And it should extend the same treatment to "that vast class of clerical and ministerial officers who simply carry out orders of superiors in whose hands is the determination of general questions of administrative policy." [20]

There is much else in *Politics and Administration*—but mostly about political parties. Goodnow is seeking administrative responsi-

---

[17] *Ibid.*, 37. Goodnow had previously spoken as though complete control of administration by politics is inevitable, even a separation of powers failing to halt it. *Cf.* 25.
[18] *Ibid.*, 79.
[19] *Ibid.*, 85–86.
[20] *Ibid.*, 88.

bility by perfecting the party as the instrument of popular control. The party is the necessary device both for expressing and executing the state's will; it is an inevitable link in good government (or even in bad government, if it is "popular"). There is much in his treatment of the subject, on the side of analysis, that might have inspired P. H. Odegard and E. A. Helms' *American Politics* or E. P. Herring's *The Politics of Democracy*. But he is an admirer of the British system and hopes, by amending our formal governmental institutions and by reforming our parties, to secure the benefits of that system.[21]

An Appraisal.—Several comments are in order before passing on. The first is that the argument considered as a whole is a somewhat unstable compound. If it is, for example, "impossible to assign each of these functions to a separate authority" because the governmental process is so much of a piece, it is difficult to see why there is a clear case for entrusting quasi-judicial, scientific, and commercial authority to bodies hermetically sealed from "politics." Second, it should be noted that "anti-legalism" is a corollary of a twofold scheme of powers. If there is no third "power," lawyers and judges are puffed up overmuch. Third, it is possible to derive two quite opposite corollaries with respect to political parties from the politics-administration axiom. The first, espoused by Goodnow, is that parties are Good: they concentrate power and enforce responsibility, enable politics to control administration—as should be the case in popular government—and they bind together a system of government constitutionally disjointed. The second is that parties are Bad: they invade the realm of administration proper, the realm which is not supposed to be disturbed by politics; they confuse, impede, and corrupt; the less "politics" and the more "administration," the better.

Finally, it should be observed, Goodnow's approach to his subject is open to several objections in the light of views prevailing today. There is in it some of the nineteenth-century's vogue for an "organic" interpretation of the state. There is in it some of that species of Idealism that conceives the state as an entity with a "will." And the analogy between the individual and the state with respect to "decision" and "execution" is based upon nineteenth-century "faculty" psychology: the "will" is conceived as a distinct and

---

[21] The argument of *Politics and Administration* is recapitulated in ch. 1 of *The Principles of the Administrative Law of the United States* (New York: 1905). See also, "The Limit of Budgetary Control," 7 *Am. Pol. Sci. Rev.* (Feb., 1913, Supp.), 68–77.

homogeneous entity. Any questioning of these assumptions touches the soundness of the analysis at its very base.

Willoughby's Treatment.—The second most influential treatment of separation of powers by an American student of public administration is that of W. F. Willoughby. His *The Government of Modern States,* though formally a text on comparative government, best presents his distinctive viewpoint.

He finds the American threefold division of powers as unsatisfactory as did Goodnow: "examination will show that it cannot stand the test of scientific analysis. . . ." [22]

The threefold scheme is at once too subtle, and lacking in subtlety. It is too subtle because it posits three equal powers when, broadly speaking, government is a process of two parts:

> If the work involved in the administration of any service or enterprise is subject to analysis certain important distinctions appear. The first of these is that between the function of direction, supervision and control, on the one hand, and execution on the other . . . [23]

The Five Powers of Government.—The above quotation comes very close to being the distinction between "politics" and "administration." Yet there are, Willoughby believes, not two, but five "powers" or "functions" of government in a modern democracy: the executive, the legislative, the judicial, the administrative, and the electoral. So the threefold scheme is really a confusing oversimplification. The fivefold scheme of powers—particularly the relationships envisaged among executive, legislative, and administrative—this constitutes his distinctive contribution. These doctrines are the parent stem from which spring many of the arguments on executive-administrative reorganization that have issued from "the ivory tower on Jackson Place."

The "Administrative" Function.—In modern government, Willoughby argues, there is a distinctive function of "administration," often confused with the "executive" function, which must be recog-

---

[22] New York: 1919, 229. The 1919 edition seemed more appropriate for this purpose than the 1936 edition.
[23] *The Government of Modern States* (New York: 1919), 387–388 (by permission of the D. Appleton-Century Co., Inc.). *Cf.* "The Correlation of the Organization of Congress with that of the Executive," 8 *Am. Pol. Sci. Rev.* (Feb., 1914), 155–167, 165. See also his Introduction to G. A. Weber's *Organized Efforts for the Improvement of Methods of Administration in the United States* (New York: 1919); and *Principles of Public Administration* (Wash.: 1927), chs. 1–3, *passim.*

nized and provided for. Pointing out that our government fails to do so, he says:

> In the threefold classification of governmental power no recognition is given to Administration as a separate function or branch of government. Insofar as any account at all is taken of this function in that classification, it is confused with, and treated as a part of, the executive function.[24]

The proper duties of the executive are rather easily defined.[25] It is the administrative function, "the function of actually administering the law" as declared by the legislative and interpreted by the judicial branches, that needs special attention. For it is confused both by the Constitution and in the popular mind, as is clearly indicated in the following passage.

> In framing our Constitution its authors proceeded upon the theory that all of the powers of government were divisible into the three great branches. . . . They failed utterly to recognize or to make any direct provision for the exercise of administrative powers. In consequence of this failure our entire constitutional history has been marked by a struggle between the legislative and the executive branches as to the relative parts that they should play in the exercise of this power.[26]

"The "greatest failure" of the Framers, in fact, was the failure with respect to the exercise of administrative power "definitely to locate authority and responsibility in a single organ." Responsibility

---

[24] *Ibid.*, 231.

[25] "The executive function is the function of representing the government as a whole, and of seeing that all of its laws are complied with by its several parts." *Ibid.*, 232. Speaking of the difference "between the executive and the administrative functions. The former is distinctly political in character. It involves the making of far-reaching decisions in respect to governmental policies. In respect to the actual conduct of governmental affairs it has to do with seeing that policies that are adopted, or lines of action that are decided upon, are properly carried into effect rather than in undertaking the work proper of putting these policies and programs into execution. . . . The latter function, the administrative, on the other hand, strictly speaking, involves the making of no decisions of a political character. Its participation in the making of such decisions is, or should be, merely that of furnishing to the policy-determining organs of government, the legislative and the executive, the facts which should be taken into account by those organs in reaching their decisions. Apart from this, the duties of the administrative branch should consist solely in the execution of orders." *Ibid.*, 385–386.

[26] *Ibid.*, 53. The historicity of Willoughby's argument that the Framers "failed utterly to recognize or to make any direct provision for the exercise of administrative power" seems to me more than a little doubtful. It depends, perhaps, upon how "administrative power" is defined. But certainly some passages in the *Federalist* give support to the contention of others that the intent of the Framers to create a strong executive was subverted by Congressional encroachment. The position of the President's Committee on Administrative Management, for example, seems to be supported by the introduction to Hamilton's "Reeligibility of the President," No. 72 (Ford ed., New York: 1898), 481.

is, in fact, "fairly evenly distributed" between the legislative and the executive branches. Willoughby goes on to say:

> Owing to the fact that the President at the present time in fact exercises large administrative powers and is in appearance the head of the administrative departments the popular opinion prevails that the framers . . . employed the term executive as including what are now known as administrative powers and that it was their intention that the President should be the head of the administration. This is a mistake. There can be no question but that they used the term executive in its technical sense as covering only the political duties of the titular head of the nation.[27]

The President and "Administration."—Nevertheless, in "two important respects" the President was vested with important administrative power by the Framers. He is enjoined to "take care that the laws be faithfully executed," and to nominate, and with the advice and consent of the Senate to appoint, important officers.

The argument becomes very complicated when the position of chief executive is examined. He has, of course, purely executive duties, such as commanding the army and seeing that the laws are "duly enforced"; but he has also been made administrator-in-chief by Congress.

> The chief executive has been given the general status and powers of an administrator-in-chief . . . we have in effect the same person holding two offices. As administrator-in-chief the person holding the office of chief executive plays the dominant role in the work of the administrative branch. In doing so, however, he does not do so in virtue of any inherent powers as chief executive, but merely because the legislative branch, in which final authority in respect to the organization and work of the administrative branch is vested, has, as a matter of policy, made of this officer one to serve in this capacity.[28]

---

[27] *Ibid.,* 252. F. A. Cleveland's reading of the Constitution and of constitutional history is quite different from that of Willoughby. In "The Reorganization of the Federal Government—An Alternative," 9 *Proceed. Acad. Pol. Sci.* (1920–1922), 361–419, Cleveland argues that the intent of the Framers was subverted. They planned, he argues, something much more like cabinet government, an arrangement under which the executive would be vigorous in leadership and possessed of considerable freedom; the legislative and judicial branches being charged with holding the executive responsible, modifying and restraining. Congressional groups, however, arrogated power to themselves, dispersed leadership among committees, and upset this scheme. "Congress reduced the executive to a 'superintendency'; took to itself the function of leadership; and parcelled it out to 'standing committees' . . ." 367. *Cf.* "Need for Readjustment of Relations between the Executive and the Legislative Branches of Government," in *Democracy in Reconstruction* (Boston: 1919), Cleveland and J. Schafer, eds., 443; see also Henry Bruere's *A Plan of Organization for New York City* (1917, pamphlet).
[28] *Ibid.,* 351.

We may close this survey with a statement from an earlier essay in which Willoughby summarized his position. He agrees with other students that the parts of our government are not well articulated, but disagrees as to the remedy. "The attitude of most students is that the only remedy is to abandon this theory and adopt, in whole or in part, that of a union of powers as exemplified in the government of Great Britain. It is with this attitude that the writer wishes to take issue." [29] He favors adjustment within the outlines of the Constitution—*e.g.* a separate organization of Congress for each of its two main functions, (1) law-making proper, and (2) acting as a board of directors.

An Appraisal.—Let us now pause to take stock of the argument. We may first observe that Willoughby's subtleties are largely nugatory; for what is taken from the President with the right hand is returned to him with the left. Second, it seems clear that his argument as a whole would have difficulty in passing the test of consistency. If, for example, the Framers of the Constitution "failed utterly to recognize or to make any direct provision for the exercise of administrative powers," had even "no conception of the function of administration," it is appropriate to ask how Willoughby knows with certainty how they intended administrative authority to be divided, so much to Congress, so much for the President. Third, the details of the argument must not obscure important points of agreement with Goodnow: Willoughby as well as Goodnow is preoccupied with a dichotomy between politics and administration, and Goodnow as well as Willoughby recognizes a function of "administration" apart from and in addition to the "executive" proper.

Recent Interpretations of Politics-Administration

While later treatments of the separation of powers are not confined to a reiteration of the arguments of Goodnow and Willoughby, most of them stem from one or the other, or both, treatments. Almost without exception the writers accept it as plain fact that there are but two parts or functions in the governmental process: decision and execution, politics and administration; that administration is a realm of expertise from which politics can be and should be largely

---

[29] In "The Correlation of the Organization of the Congress with that of the Executive," 8 *Am. Pol. Sci. Rev.* (Febr., 1914—Supp.), 155–167, 160. For a further comparison of the arguments of Goodnow and Willoughby see L. M. Short, *The Development of National Administrative Organization in the United States* (Urbana: 1923), ch. 1. This is also a good brief historical consideration of the theory of separation of powers.

excluded. Here, as he often does, J. M. Pfiffner states most clearly a general sentiment:

> Politics is . . . an inevitable and necessary part of the process of government. It must, however, be controlled and confined to its proper sphere which is the determination, crystallization, and declaration of the will of the community. Administration, on the other hand, is the carrying into effect of this will once it has been made clear by political processes. From these premises, therefore, is derived the keystone of the new public administration—the conclusion that politics should stick to its policy-determining sphere and leave administration to apply its own technical processes free from the blight of political meddling.[30]

Variations on a Theme.—It is important to note, however, that even though two writers may both accept the politics-administration formula as true, they may be completely at variance as to its meaning in practice—as two adherents of dialectic materialism may be completely at odds over the politics of Graustark. Like so many grand and simple truths politics-administration tells us nothing so far as particular actions are concerned. *It tells us nothing at all about the organs to which these functions should be assigned, or the desirable relationships among these organs.*

Statements by Harvey Walker and G. W. Spicer will serve to indicate how the politics-administration notion can be used to support widely divergent points of view.

Walker finds the threefold scheme quite unsatisfactory; and that the dual scheme requires reorganization of state government on the model of the council-manager plan.

> In its most usual form—separation of governmental functions into legislative, executive, and judicial—this doctrine, under modern conditions only introduces unnecessary and undesirable complications into the gov-

---

[30] *Public Administration* (New York: 1935), 9 (The Ronald Press Co.). *Cf.* 12. Pfiffner also makes use of Willoughby's distinction between "executive" and "administrative." 40–41. See also Pfiffner's *Municipal. Administration* (New York: 1940), 10, for a statement on separation of powers. For statements more or less "orthodox" see the following: A. E. Buck, *The Budget in Governments of Today* (New York: 1934), 55; L. D. White, *The City Manager* (Chicago: 1927), 301; J. M. Mathews, *Principles of American State Administration* (New York: 1917), 3, 7; William Anderson, *American City Government* (New York: 1925), 308, 326 n.; C. A. Dykstra, "The Quest for Responsibility," 33 *Am. Pol. Sci. Rev.* (Feb., 1939), 1–25; H. G. James, "The Reorganization of State Government," 9 *Am. Pol. Sci. Rev.* (May, 1915), 294–303; Felix Frankfurter, *The Public and Its Government* (New Haven: 1930), 78: H. G. Hodges, *City Management: Theory and Practice of Municipal Administration* (New York: 1939), 25.
On similar tendencies in scientific management, *cf.* A. H. Church, *The Science and Practice of Management* (New York: 1914), 1; F. W. Taylor, quoted in M. L. Cooke, *Academic and Industrial Efficiency* (Carnegie Foundation Bulletin: 1910), 15.

ernmental system. Most private businesses could not be operated successfully under similar conditions. . . . There are only two phases to
any business, public or private. One is to make the decision as to what
is to be done. That is legislation. The other is to see that the decision
is carried out. That is administration. For the legislative function,
representatives are needed, and the process of election is appropriate.
For the administrative function, experts are needed, and the only method
of securing them which has proved successful is that of appointment
under a merit system.[31]

The distinction between politics and administration is so important as to invalidate the arguments of those reorganizers who would
make the governor the only elected administrative officer, with all
the machinery of administration under his direction.

Such a reorganization violates the principle of separation of politics
from administration, unless it may be assumed that the governor is to
drop his political functions. Since this seems unlikely, those who feel
that the separation of politics from administration is more important to
good government than concentration of administrative responsibility in
the hands of an elected officer prefer to see the state governments organized along lines similar to those of the city-manager plan.[32]

The plan as outlined requires a small, unicameral legislature,
responsible for the selection of a state-manager and a legislative auditor. The state-manager would be a professional administrator, responsible for state administration. The governor would remain as
a political officer, with the duties of sending messages, vetoing acts,
calling special sessions, and acting in a ceremonial capacity. "Under such a plan the chief function of the executive would be that for
which the office was originally designed—to aid the legislature in
formulating public policy. . . . Separation of administration from
policy formation is the *sine qua non* of improved administration in
the state area." [33]

Again it is proper to put the argument to the test of consistency.
If "students recognize that government is essentially a unity," if "all
attempts at classification must be arbitrary and hence unsatisfying," [34]—then why is the case so clear for a twofold separation?

G. W. Spicer, also considering the organization of state govern-

---

[31] *Public Administration in the United States* (New York: 1937), 15–16.
(This and following citations by permission of Rinehart & Co., Inc.)

[32] *Ibid.*, 81. "The case for the dual concept rests upon a pragmatic basis. The
objective of government in a democratic state is to serve the majority of the people
in the way in which they want to be served. In other words, the aim of government is service. . . . Once he [the citizen] has made up his mind and enough others
have made up their minds in the same way the next step is to get his idea embodied
into law. . . . The work which the government does to give effect to a law is
called administration." 4–5. See also 7, 112.

[33] *Ibid.*, 80.   [34] *Ibid.*, 7.

ment and also starting from Goodnow's argument, arrives at quite other conclusions about the position of the governor. Specifically, he takes as his theme Goodnow's statement that "popular government requires that the execution of the state will be subjected to the control of the organ expressing the state will." He makes of this an argument for the union of powers, legislative and administrative, in the person of the governor. After considering the governor in relation to the course of administrative centralization in Virginia he concludes:

> It should be clear that this position of administrative supremacy issued from his position of political supremacy. Without his political power he could not have attained his administrative power, nor effected this vast transformation in the administrative organization. This being so, it follows that administration is continuously subject to political control in this state.[35]

"If the governor is the leader of the legislature and shapes the course of legislative policy, the administration will in the final analysis be subject to his control," [36] and the principle of control of administration by politics will be secured.

Some Important Recent Statements

Three recent treatments of the subject should be noted, both because of their intrinsic interest and their historical importance: those of the President's Committee on Administrative Management, "Brookings," and J. M. Landis.

The President's Committee.—The *Report* of the President's Committee presents what is formally a defense of the traditional threefold separation of powers, practically the only one in the literature of public administration. This formal adherence to the venerable triad, however, must not blind us to what has been occasionally [37] but inadequately recognized: that the members of the Committee

---

[35] "From Political Chief to Administrative Chief," in *Essays on the Law and Practice of Governmental Administration* (Baltimore: 1935), C. G. Haines and M. E. Dimock, eds., 118–119 (by permission of Johns Hopkins Press).

[36] *Ibid.*, 123. *Cf.* J. A. Fairlie, "The Executive in the Model State Constitution," 10 *Nat. Mun. Rev.* (April, 1921), 226–231. The Model State Constitution proposes, roughly speaking, to split the difference between a reorganized state government and the forms of cabinet government: the governor would continue to be popularly elected, but would sit, with his heads of departments, in the legislature, introduce bills, etc.
Fairlie's essay "The Separation of Powers," 21 *Mich. L. Rev.* (Feb., 1923), 393–436, is a scholarly review of separation of powers theories in ancient and recent times.

[37] K. C. Cole, "The 'Merit System' Again," 31 *Am. Pol. Sci. Rev.* (Aug., 1937), 695–698, 696: "Throughout the report, its [the Committee's] members are staunch

had no reverence for the threefold scheme in the George Wickersham-Elihu Root manner, that in its case acceptance of separation of powers was a strategic maneuver. In the interest of building up the Presidency, they sought to make their own the stereotypes and emotions historically used to oppose presidential aggrandizement.

The constitutional principle of the separation of powers, reported the Committee, places "in the President, and in the President alone, the whole executive power of the Government of the United States." [38] However, "the responsibility of the President for 'the executive Power' is impaired through the multiplicity and confusion of agencies which render effective action impossible." [39] Particularly is the principle of separation of powers impaired by the "new and headless 'fourth branch' of the Government." These independent establishments "do violence to the basic theory of the American Constitution that there should be three major branches of the Government and only three." [40]

The independent agencies enjoy power without responsibility, and "leave the President with responsibility without power." Plainly we are required "to make effective management possible by restoring the President to his proper place as Chief Executive. . . ." [41] If this is done the principle of separation of powers will be restored. "The preservation of the principle of the full accountability of the executive to the Congress is an essential part of our republican system." [42] Present confusions impair this principle; the changes suggested will restore it.

"Brookings."—Opposed to President's Committee's position was, of course, the group more or less closely identified with the Brookings Institution. This group took positions with regard to the separation of powers stemming from, or at least similar to, those of the first director of the Institute for Government Research, W. F. Willoughby. The President's Committee finds that the Founders intended the President to be responsible for administration because he is made the chief "executive"; the Brookings group believes that "executive" and "administrative" must be distinguished, and that the Framers gave administrative power chiefly to Congress.

The views of the Brookings group were set forth in the study of administrative reorganization prepared for the Senate Select Com-

---

advocates of presidential power, but they are not above making eloquent appeals to traditional check and balance sentiment in order to get it."

[38] *Report* (Washington: 1937), 29.
[39] *Ibid.*, 30.   [40] *Ibid.*, 36.
[41] *Ibid.*, 31.   [42] *Ibid.*, 43.

mittee to Investigate Executive Agencies of the Government with a View to Co-ordination, the so-called Byrd Committee.[43] In accordance with a general policy of empiricism, fact-mindedness, and practicability—and with a keen ear for its congressional audience —the Brookings group hid its theoretical postulates in a bushel of facts and presented its conclusions in qualified and "objective" statements. The Report does not deign to reply to the argument of the President's Committee that the President should have the direction of the independent agencies by virtue of his "executive" power by arguing that Congress has this power through its control over administration. They simply assume the legitimacy of the Willoughby position,[44] and seek to show that, on practical or pragmatic grounds, the better case is for independence. They seek to establish their case by a full consideration and elaborate balancing of all reasonably weighty arguments pro and con. These arguments need not be repeated here; suffice it that they are, so far as form is concerned, a thorough refutation of the argument of the President's Committee.[45]

Books on the subject of reorganization by members of the Brookings group followed the Byrd Committee's Report. In *Reorganization of the National Government,* Lewis Meriam and L. F. Schmeckebier present three major proposals with respect to executive control "arranged in descending order according to their degree of radicalism from one point of view. . . ."

> 1. To increase materially the actual power of the President without any increase whatever in the congressional control over the President. In fact the increase in power would be achieved under the Constitution by having the Congress delegate some of its powers to the President and by having it forego the exercise of some of the power it now possesses.
>
> . . . .
>
> 2. To increase materially the power of the President but at the same time, possibly through constitutional amendments, to increase the power of the Congress to hold him responsible for the manner in which he uses his increased power.
>
> . . . .
>
> 3. To make no change in the powers of the President as they are set forth in the Constitution, to preserve the division of powers as the

---

[43] *Investigation of Executive Agencies of the Government,* Sen. Report 1275, 75th Congress, 1st. Session.

[44] Their clients, of course, needed no persuading on the point.

[45] It should be added that a proposal for a system of administrative courts is appended to the argument. See 8–9, 787–810.

Constitution provides, but to furnish the President with better mechanisms, particularly through the establishment of adequate staff agencies, to enable him more easily to perform his functions as general manager of the executive branch of the government.[46]

The argument is couched in the same "objective" tone as the Report of the Byrd Committee, but the authors have no trouble concluding that sensible and moderate men will gravitate toward the third of these positions.[47]

J. M. Landis.—Stimulated by the Report of the President's Committee and having some affinities with the Willoughby-Brookings doctrines, is J. M. Landis' *The Administrative Process,* setting forth a distinctive "legal" view. Mr. Landis believes that "administration" is quite real and distinct, a process which should enjoy much independence; but by "administration" or "the administrative process" he means specifically the characteristic activities of the independent regulatory commissions, not the broader aspects of "execution." This administrative function has been developed to fill a vacuum created by the separation of powers.

In terms of political theory, the administrative process springs from the inadequacy of a simple tripartite form of government to deal with modern problems. It represents a striving to adapt governmental technique, that still divides under three rubrics, to modern needs and, at the same time, to preserve those elements of responsibility and those conditions of balance that have distinguished Anglo-American government.[48]

He regards the President's Committee as ridiculously attached to the tripartite scheme—which mere common sense reveals to be unworkable in a strict form. "Administrative" power has evolved to fill a need, and is not simply an extension of executive power.

The administrative differs not only with regard to the scope of its powers; it differs most radically in regard to the responsibility it possesses for their exercise. In the grant to it of that full ambit of authority necessary for it in order to plan, to promote, and to police, it repre-

---

[46] Washington: 1939, 15–17 (by permission of The Brookings Institution).

[47] See their ch. 5, *passim.* "In a government of divided powers, the administrative part of the government is controlled by all three major branches of government—executive, legislative, and judicial." 5. See also: Lewis Meriam, *Personnel Administration in the Federal Government* (Wash.: 1937), 23; F. F. Blachly and M. E. Oatman, *Administrative Legislation and Adjudication* (Wash.; 1934), chs. X–XIII.

[48] New Haven: 1938, 1 (by permission of Yale University Press). See also: "The Administrative Process," *Personnel Jour.* (Oct., 1938), 120–132. *Cf.* Jerome Frank, *If Men Were Angels* (New York: 1942), growing out of the experience of another legalist sitting as a member of the SEC.

sents an assemblage of rights normally exercisable by government as a whole. . . . The creation of that power is, in essence, the response made in the light of a tripartite political theory to the demand that government assume responsibility. . . .[49]

So, according to this view, although originating as a circumvention of the tripartite system, the administrative process ends as its bulwark: it enables us to extend the functions of government without increasing the powers of the executive and thus destroying the balance that is the core of the separation of powers doctrine.

The Rise of Heterodoxy

Recent years have brought a new development in the politics-administration formula, with advocates of the newer theory lining up against the above-quoted authorities in their insistence upon a sharp separation between the two. The disagreement is not generally with politics-administration itself; only with the spirit of rigid separatism. In some measure this is an advance into realism. In some measure it flows from a feeling of strength and security, a feeling that the processes and the study of administration have matured, that they no longer need be isolated from the germs of politics. Administration can even think about invading the field of politics, the field of policy determination.

"Today . . ." declares Leslie Lipson, "the attempt to demarcate clear-cut functions of government is impossible. Government is a continuous process. It is true that the process contains phases. Legislation is one phase, administration another. But these are merged together and at certain points become indistinguishable." [50] Government, conclude H. A. Stone, D. K. Price, and K. H. Stone in a keen discussion of the separation of powers in the city-manager scheme, is essentially a *unity* in operation.[51] They do not question that in some sense government consists of politics and administration; but the notion of the early advocates that there should be a strict separation is held to be unrealistic. The idea that the council alone is concerned with "politics" and the manager alone with "administration" accords neither with actual facts nor the desirable goal.

[49] *Ibid.*, 15–16. *Cf.* C. J. Friedrich's "Responsible Government Service Under the American Constitution," in *Problems of the American Public Service* (New York: 1935), Friedrich, *et al.*, 49.

[50] *The American Governor: From Figurehead to Leader* (Chicago: 1939), 8 (by permission of University of Chicago Press). Lipson disagrees with the "Brookings" view that the principle of separation of powers demands that the executive should not be made strong. What it *does* require is that there should be "reciprocal means of control." 255.

[51] *City Manager Government in the United States* (Chicago: 1940), ch. 12.

C. J. Friedrich, pondering Goodnow's distinction, writes that while it "has a great deal of value as a relative matter of emphasis, it cannot any longer be accepted in this absolute form. Admittedly, this misleading distinction has become a fetish, a stereotype in the minds of theorists and practitioners alike." Politics and administration are not "two mutually exclusive boxes," but "two closely linked aspects of the same process." [52]

K. C. Cole finds that "Ours is a government according to law, which means that the gears of administration must be meshed in some fashion with the gears of constitutional purpose. In short, it is never proper under our system to treat political considerations as if they were extraneous to conclusions about 'good' or 'efficient' administration." [53] J. D. Kingsley considers that "administration is a branch of politics." "We have had, in the field of administration, too much synthetic philosophy disguised as science and not enough examination of the relation of administrative devices and techniques to major political objectives." [54] J. W. Fesler insists, "To isolate administration from policy and government from economics may fatally compromise our capacity for straight thinking." [55] William Anderson states that administrative students "are aware . . . that public administration is closely intertwined with, and dependent upon, the nation's political institution, traditions, and ideals in a general sense. Public administration is not something set apart from, but is an integral part of, the whole system of popular government and democratic ideals." [56] The tone of recent writings strongly suggests that politics-administration, at least in the you-go-your-way-and-I'll-go-mine form, is fast becoming an outworn credo. [57]

---

[52] "Public Policy and the Nature of Administrative Responsibility," in *Public Policy*, I (Cambridge: 1940), Friedrich, ed., 6 (by permission of Harvard University Press). In our quest for responsibility, he believes, we must recognize the inadequacy of "political" responsibility as now existing in parliamentary government. We must recognize, instead, two important facts: that the responsibility of technicians can only be enforced by fellow technicians, that the check must be an "inner check"; and the possibilities that lie in developing, by the proper use of information and citizen participation, a working relationship between administrators and the public which will be reciprocal and emollient.

[53] "Regulation in a Federal System," 3 *Pub. Adm. Rev.* (Autumn, 1943), 375–377, 376.

[54] "Political Ends and Administrative Means: The Administrative Principles of Hamilton and Jefferson," 5 *Pub. Adm. Rev.* (Winter, 1945), 87–89, 89.

[55] "Mobilizing of Industry for the War," 5 *Pub. Adm. Rev.* (Summer, 1945), 257–262, 262.

[56] *Research in Public Administration* (Chicago: 1945), William Anderson and J. M. Gaus, 106 (by permission of Public Administration Service).

[57] See also, E. S. Wengert, "The Study of Public Administration," 36 *Am. Pol. Sci. Rev.* (April, 1942), 313–322, *passim*; D. M. Levitan, "Political Ends and Administrative Means," 3 *Pub. Adm. Rev.* (Autumn, 1943), 353–359; W. B. Munro, *Municipal Administration* (New York: 1934), 5; Felix Frankfurter, "The

Toward a New Theory

Luther Gulick has given us a careful and extended consideration of the politics-administration notion in the light of political theory, the practical operation of administration, and recent governmental trends. His essay, "Politics, Administration, and the New Deal," deserves thorough consideration.

A False Dichotomy.—Discretion, says Gulick, is the essential element in the determination of policy. Anyone who has discretion determines policy, even the most minor employee. "It is impossible to analyze the work of any public employee from the time he steps into his office in the morning until he leaves at night without discovering that his every act is a seamless web of discretion and action." [58] Only in purely mechanical operations is discretion absent. What is one to say, then, about the idea that government consists of two actions, decision and execution; and particularly what can be said for the idea that "politics" can be taken out of administration by devising separate organs for "politics" and "administration"? Some authorities have professed to be able to distinguish between various kinds of discretion, such as "political," "administrative," "technical," "unimportant," etc. "It is, however, not possible to examine the individual acts of individual men in the normal discharge of their governmental work without discovering that there is no such inherent difference in the nature, the purpose, and the character of discretion." The classification of a discretionary act will depend upon its context, upon the "existing institutional set-up" and upon the "prevalent pattern" of values and interests dominant at a given time and place. The generalization that one *can* safely make about discretion is quantitative, that *as a rule* "discretion decreases at each successive administrative or organizational subdivision of work

Task of Administrative Law," *Law and Politics* (New York: 1937), A. MacLeish and E. F. Prichard, eds., 231; J. M. Gaus, "The New Problem of Administration," 8 *Minn. L. Rev.* (Feb., 1924), 217–231, 220; J. M. Gaus and L. O. Wolcott, *Public Administration and the United States Department of Agriculture* (Chicago: 1940), 379; M. E. Dimock, "What Is Public Administration?," 15 *Pub. Man.* (Sept., 1933), 259–262, 262; his *Modern Politics and Administration* (New York: 1937), 19, 30, 132, 140, 168, 232, 234, 237, 241, 326; and his "The Criteria and Objectives of Public Administration," in *The Frontiers of Public Administration* (Chicago: 1936), 116–133, 128, in which he states that we should emphasize that the administrator is "more than a tool, the unquestioning servant of whatever party happens to be in power. Administration plans. Administration is not merely a lifeless form. It is an active, originating, inventing, contriving element in the body politic. Is it not clear, then, that one of the necessary and legitimate objectives of public administration is the consideration of socially desirable ends?" (By permission of University of Chicago Press.)

[58] 169 *Annals* (Sept., 1933), 55–66, 61.

and that this decrease takes place at a faster rate than a simple arithmetical progression." [59]

Seeking a pragmatic and sensible solution, Gulick expresses his belief as follows:

> The reason for separating politics from administration is not that their combination is a violation of a principle of government. The reason for insisting that the elected legislative and executive officials shall not interfere with the details of administration, and that the rank and file of the permanent administrators shall be permanent and skilled and shall not meddle with politics, is that this division of work makes use of specialization and appears to give better results than a system where such a differentiation does not exist. [60]

Different Times, Different Theories.—At any event, Gulick finds the working arrangements of modern government are "not nearly so much the result of theory as of the process of trial and error." Theorizing has always followed the facts and done more or less violence to them because the philosophers and the protagonists of their theories have always had before them a limited set of facts and definite objectives. Thus Locke and Montesquieu conceived civil liberty and freedom from arbitrary power as the highest good, and elaborated a tripartite separation as a means of achieving such an end. Woodrow Wilson and F. J. Goodnow found quite a different set of problems and gave a different answer. To solve the problems arising from a conflict between old democracy and new technology they "divided all government into politics and administration, assigning to certain organs of government the functions of politics, of policy control, and reserving for other organs the expert task of execution of those policies. This theory is equally a product of time and desire." [61] Now, however, we face a new situation and a new necessity. The government is becoming the super-holding company of our economic life. The new task is no less than "devising and imposing a consistent master plan of national life."

> This will require a new division of actual work, and therefore a new theory of the division of powers. While it is perhaps too early to state such a theory, it is clear that it will be concerned not with checks and balances or with the division of policy and administration, but with the division between policy veto on one side and policy planning and execution on the other. [62]

---

[59] *Ibid.*, 61–62.
[60] *Ibid.*, 63.
[61] *Ibid.*, 66.
[62] *Ibid.*

In the New World into which we are entering, Gulick feels, there must be institutional changes in government. The executive will be responsible for the major plan (aided by deliberative and advisory groups) and will have broad powers in its execution: establishing executory agencies, working out interrelations, settling details. The legislature will retain the right of vetoing major decisions and will exercise the functions of audit and investigation. The mass of citizens will control, by party and pressure group, as in the past. "These are the bricks and straws from which the new theory of the division of powers must be constructed." [63]

The final feeling is one of anticlimax, since Gulick does no more than suggest these "bricks and straws." But he has patently given us a penetrating analysis.

"Administrative Politics."—One result of Gulick's essay was the stimulation of another essay on the same subject by G. H. Durham, who took seriously the call for a new theory of the interrelation of powers. The traditional and the Goodnow theories are inadequate, he finds, because they emphasize separation, whereas in fact politics and administration are very intimately related. Since we cannot take administration out of politics, we should devote attention to taking *certain aspects* of politics out of administration. And in doing this we must recognize the increasingly important role of the administrator. "As a guide to a 'new theory of the division of powers' the idea of *administrative politics,* or the interrelations of public administrators in what appear to be increasingly more permanent offices with tenure, forms a more realistic concept." [64]

The party must be adapted to the uses of the new "administrative politics." Since administration cannot be taken out of politics, we should recognize the fact and develop able and responsible political activity by administrators. "Whereas we formerly had administration by campaigning office seekers and their allies, today we have policy-making by administrators and the molding of a new American politics." [65] Government is one, a unity. The party must direct policy, but there must be an integration of administration and party because administrators also form policy. This integration is already taking place in the office of the chief executive, but it must proceed at lower levels also. Parties will "increasingly tend to revolve around associations of administrators. . . ." [66] This development will help

---

[63] *Ibid.*
[64] "Politics and Administration in Intergovernmental Relations," 207 *Annals* (Jan., 1940), 1–6, 6.
[65] *Ibid.*, 2.
[66] *Ibid.*, 6.

unify our parties and our politics, because of the influence of the federal government and the ever-increasing interrelations of administrators at all levels.

Durham is bold. This seems to be a clear recognition that the concept of a corps of New Administrators, experts in things-in-general, does not accord with any rigid division of politics and administration. The functions of the Specialists in Generalization are much too exalted to be confined to mere execution, their virtues much too magnificent to be cabined and confined by ignorant, unscrupulous politicos. They must accept their destiny as a Democratic Ruling Class.[67]

The Executive As Integrator.—Among the more prominent of recent writings on separation of powers—though he does not use the term nor even allude to the judiciary—is an essay by V. O. Key, titled "Politics and Administration."[68] Taking off from an assertion that Goodnow has been misinterpreted and did not argue for a complete separation of politics and administration, Key reviews in a few short pages current governmental tendencies, increased demands upon and problems of administrative agencies, and ways and means by which government may get done what it must do—that is to say, what we give it to do in fact—and still remain democratic and responsible.

Key accepts as established fact large-scale and increasing governmental intervention in economic life, and asserts the necessity of an extensive, highly competent and well-integrated bureaucratic structure to make that intervention successful. He accepts, and argues the desirability of, widespread and growing powers of policy-

---

[67] These two lines of thought are seldom brought into proximity in the writings: (1) conscious consideration of the powers and interrelations of government, and (2) the "function of administration" that is the expertise of the Administrative Class. "Administration" in this sense is something different from the broad meaning given it in Goodnow, the narrower meaning given it by Willoughby, or the quite restricted meaning given it by Landis. "It [administration] is distinguished on the one hand from the making of broad decisions of policy by a legislative body, and on the other hand from the relatively routine tasks of day-to-day execution of established policy, although the line of demarcation cannot be drawn with mathematical precision."—L. D. White, "Administration as a Profession," 189 *Annals* (Jan., 1937), 84–90, 86. This seems clearly to be a power or function of government, this "specialization in generalization." What are its interrelations with the other parts of government? White, in one of the few forthright considerations of this problem concludes that the new administrative corps "will not disturb in the slightest the prevailing distribution of authority to determine and conclude what the state shall do." *Government Career Service* (Chicago: 1935), 23. Perhaps not, in White's scheme of things. But others have not been as restrained in picturing the role of the New Administrator.

[68] In *The Future of Government in the United States* (Chicago: 1942), L. D. White, ed., 145–163.

formulation by the administrative side of the government—though with over-all and ultimate control in the legislature. Probably his main theme is the necessity for integrated policy-formulation, so that we will not divide and waste our forces working at cross-purposes. To achieve this integration we must further strengthen the Presidency and curb centrifugal forces in the administrative hierarchy.[69]

Responsibility—New Means to an Old End?—Among the "bricks and straws" from which a new theory of separation of powers and interrelation of functions should be constructed are undoubtedly some recently expressed ideas about achieving "responsibility" by other means than bridging it directly from administration to the legislature, as the representatives of the people. L. D. White, for example, has described various means by which administrative agencies can sound public opinion directly among their clientele, thus assuring themselves of majority support for their programs.[70] C. M. Wiltse has argued that the close assimilation of ideas and interests between an agency and its clientele that tends to take place over a considerable period of time is not wholly undesirable, as usually thought, but is, in fact, a means by which government is made responsible.[71] And C. J. Friedrich has argued at length for a new conception of an "inner check." Older ideas of external checks, he feels, must give some ground to more realistic ideas of the actual responsibility imposed by professional methods, professional standards, and professional morale and prestige.[72]

Planning—A "Power" of Government?—This discussion of the separation of powers would be incomplete without reference to the subject of planning. Has "administrative planning" or planning-for-

---

[69] "The only point about which the articulation may be organized is the presidency, and the recent evolution of that institution constitutes both a recognition of need and an attempt to meet it." *Ibid.*, 159. "Central direction based on the politically triumphant philosophy of the general welfare establishes a framework of leadership of the efforts of the civil service both in policy initiation and in operation." *Ibid.*, 163.

[70] "The Public Service of the Future," in *The Future of Government in the United States* (Chicago: 1942), White, ed., 192–217, 213.

[71] "The Representative Function of Bureaucracy," 35 *Am. Pol. Sci. Rev.* (June, 1941), 510–515. Wiltse sees administration, or "the bureaucracy," as more or less separate from, more or less connected with, both President and Congress. "The bureaucracy in this sense is the common meeting ground of the President and the Congress, and it is also the ground on which both executive and legislative functions may be brought into direct contact with the public in its organized and institutionalized capacity." *Ibid.*, 511. We have in fact "functional representation" via the bureaucracy.

[72] See the bibliographical note at the end of the following chapter for references to Friedrich's writings and to other writings on "responsibility."

execution been regarded as a separate function or power? Has over-all or "policy" planning been regarded as a separate power or func-tion? To what extent have these two types of planning been dis-tinguished, or confused? Have either or both types been brought into conscious relationship to writings on the separation of powers? In general the answer to this last question is "no." [73] Here is a lacuna in the literature. For it is evident that an administrative organ that plans policy is not consonant with traditional threefold or twofold formulae.

Some Conclusions

A number of observations are relevant at the close of this survey. The first is that, either as a description of the facts or a scheme of reform, any simple division of government into politics-and-admin-istration is inadequate. As a description of fact it is inadequate because the governing process is a "seamless web of discretion and action." As a scheme of reform it is inadequate because it bears the same defect as the tripartite scheme it was designed to replace: it carries with it the idea of division, of dissimilarity, of antag-onism.

Second, Willoughby's treatment of the separation of powers must be credited with being interesting, but rejected on criteria of ac-curacy and usefulness. Our constitutional history has been mis-read, distorted. The subtleties and contradictions involved in taking away the President's "administrative" power with one hand and giv-ing it back with the other only accent the difficulties inherent in our separation of powers system.

Third, we seem to be on the way to a more adequate philosophy of the powers and functions of government, their nature and inter-relation. This new philosophy may not be "true" in any final sense, but it will serve our purposes better than the formulae it replaces. We have been moving in the interpretation of our federal system from "competitive federalism" to "cooperative federalism," and the same tendencies are observable with respect to the separation of powers. There is a close similarity between the rigid politics-ad-ministration viewpoint and that philosophy of federalism that pic-tured state and nation moving "noiselessly and without friction each in its separate sphere." Gulick has probably indicated accurately

---

[73] *Cf.*, however, A. N. Holcombe, *Government in a Planned Democracy* (New York: 1935), 168 ff.; M. E. Dimock, "The Criteria and Objectives of Public Ad-ministration" (cited above), *passim;* W. F. Willoughby, *The Principles of Public Administration* (Washington: 1927), XVIII; J. M. Gaus, "The General Adminis-trative Staff," 3 *Plan Age* (Jan., 1937), 10–14.

many of the "bricks and straws" from which the new theory will be fashioned.

Finally, the new theory must also incorporate or at least take cognizance of the writings on the subjects of planning and a "function of administration" or the need for an Administrative Class. For in the writings these have clearly been elevated to the status of Powers or Functions.

Chapter 8

CENTRALIZATION VERSUS DECENTRALIZATION[1]

"Centralization versus decentralization" is not a classic and recurring problem of political philosophy in the sense that "Who should rule?" has proved to be. Instead, the precedents and analogues are limited to the political writings of modern times, because the problems posed are modern. These problems relate to the nation-state; to large-scale representative government and the ideological force of "democracy"; and to the rise of science and technology, which has transformed the space-time aspects of our life, and has engendered in acute form the problem of "functionalism" or expertise. The literature of federalism versus the unitary state, of local self-government versus centralized administration, of monism versus pluralism in the law, of cultural autonomy versus uniform national culture, of party dictatorship versus corporatism—these are the modern problems in political theory to which the centripetal and centrifugal forces in public administration are analogous, and in relation to which they are seen in their proper perspective.

The treatment that follows is in no sense exhaustive. Broadly construed, "centralizing" and "decentralizing" would characterize so much writing on public administration that a mere listing of titles would fill the space of a chapter. The objective is: (1) to present, in their derivation and present form, the "centralizing" tendencies that have been so commonly accepted as to have been designated "the dogmas of centralization"; (2) to review the most conspicuous dissents from the "orthodox" position; and (3) to summarize the writings that present the case for or suggest a plan of decentralization.

---

[1] By "centralization" and "decentralization" are meant, broadly, all centripetal and centrifugal tendencies. I am not now concerned with the various and more restricted uses that have been made of these terms, nor with distinguishing them from such terms as "integration" and "deconcentration," however useful these distinctions may be for certain purposes. For definitions of these various terms and references on their usage consult: D. B. Truman, *Administrative Decentralization* (Chicago: 1940), 2–3; J. M. Pfiffner, *Public Administration* (New York: 1935), 85; Harvey Walker, *Public Administration in the United States* (New York: 1937), 87–88; G. C. S. Benson, *The New Centralization* (New York: 1941), Introduction and 9.

The "Dogmas of Centralization"

Governmental reformers and writers on administration were confronted with certain conditions. Applying their assumptions to these conditions, they arrived at certain schemes, beliefs, formulae, or principles about the proper nature of governmental institutions.

The conditions that the early reformers found "given" were, on the one hand, appalling mis- and non-governance, and on the other hand, a governmental system based on eighteenth-century documents and conditioned by nineteenth-century frontier democracy. Widespread graft and flagrant corruption, common mediocrity and gross incompetence, debauchery of the electorate and arrogant flaunting of popular will, general public indifference and appalling public ignorance; despoiling of our national heritage by predatory interests aided and abetted by the representatives of the people and the guardians of the law—these were the governmental facts the reformers faced.

These reformers were men of finer sensibilities and—on any reasonable interpretation—deeper patriotism than their fellow Americans. They were not satisfied with the romantic democracy of Fourth-of-July orations, nor with the rationalizations of the "gospel of wealth," nor with their personal opportunities to make the best of a situation offering a rich plunder to the clever. Instead, the practices of realistic democracy offended their nostrils and assailed their consciences. Their hearts were wrung by the squalor, degradation and chaos of the "City Wilderness." They were mindful of Americans of future generations. They were ashamed that the America they loved fell below the monarchies and tyrannies of Europe in common decency, elementary honesty, and simple efficiency. They knew that an *unreformed* America must fail in her Mission of bringing a better way of life to the world.

"Balanced" and "Centrifugal" Government.—The rationale of the eighteenth-century instruments of government was that good government is government limited in its objectives, balanced in its organs, and divided in its powers. These instruments were framed under the dominance of Newtonian conceptions of mechanical balance, in accordance with ancient precepts for preventing tyranny, and in deep-felt fear of government by a majority. But the original institutions, set up and managed by the commercial and plantation minority, had been considerably modified in spirit and in form by the passing of political power into the hands of "the people" and by the ideology of the New Democracy. Governmental forms were adapted to the fact of rude frontier equalitarianism, and the "spirit of the laws" changed even when the forms remained the same. The Founding Fathers wanted government limited, divided, balanced; nineteenth-century democrats wanted it pulverized, dispersed, vulgarized. The former gave us functional separation and territorial division of powers, checks and balances, bicameralism, an independent judiciary, enumerated powers granted, and enumerated and unenumerated rights retained. The latter gave us general manhood suffrage, elected administrators, elected judges, thousands of tiny political units, a theory that in public life one is worth what he can get, and a practice of rotation in office. *Both the "balanced" and the "centrifugal" institutions were warp and weft of the conditions that aroused the indignation of the reformers.*

The outlook with which the reformers confronted the *status quo* has already been indicated—their faith in the imperative of America's Mission; their anguish at the discrepancy between theory and fact, between dream and realization; and their fear even for the continued existence of a republican United States. They believed also in the goodness and rationality of men. That the "real" selves of men desired "good" government they had no doubt. That man is not stained with an indelible stamp of original sin, that he has great potentialities for good, that he is rational and hence educable and perfectible: these tenets they believed implicitly. It was a case of "moral man and immoral society." Man's *institutions* were bad, and they had to be changed to allow his goodness to expand and his rationality to grow.[2] Believing this, they had to reject the then prevailing approach to the problem of better government, that of trying to get "good" or "moral" men to run the government—gangrene cannot be cured by a sprinkling of lavender water.[3]

---

[2] The long intellectual journey of the greatest of the reformers, Lincoln Steffens, ended in a belief that our institutions must be changed root and branch—to nothing less than Communism—if good government is to obtain. Not Adam, not Eve, not the Serpent, but the Apple of privilege, he found at fault. He could not bring himself to doubt the soul of man.

[3] This single quotation is submitted to illustrate—of course it does not prove—the point of view I have been trying to present: "For those whose idea of patriotism is to boast unceasingly that ours are the only human institutions which have attained perfection, that any public expression of doubt or criticism is little less than treason, and that all shortcomings and misdeeds must be charged to the perversity and wickedness, or, at the very least, ignorance and folly, of the people, this book can have no meaning." Gamaliel Bradford, *The Lesson of Popular Government* (New York: 1899), vol. I, vii. (By permission of The Macmillan Co., publishers.)

Centralization: An Inevitable Formula.—Given the evils of bad government existing conjointly with the political institutions of "balance" and "decentralization," and given the purposes and assumptions of the reformers, their conclusions, their prescriptions for good government were inevitable. If government and administration are bad, and man himself is not at fault, it *must* be a case of bad institutions. Since the institutions that exist with and permit the bad are institutions of balance and decentralization, the corrective institutions, by inexorable logic and the patent demonstration of experience, are *centralizing, simplifying,* and *unifying* institutions. The case for centralization seemed so clear, so indubitable, that the measures by which it was prescribed and applied seemed to be "principles," of universal validity, comparable to the Golden Rule, or an axiom from Euclid, or both.[4] And so were born the "canons of integration," the "dogmas of centralization."

This is, of course, an oversimplification of the facts, to indicate the relationship of the political theory of centralization to its historical context. In particular, for the sake of accuracy, it should be recalled that there were important centrifugal tendencies in the body of thought from which the guiding concepts of public administration were crystallized:[5] the initiative, referendum and recall, home rule, etc. We are here concerned, however, not with the nuances, but with the broad outlines of the truth.

What, in general, was the body of faith bequeathed to public administration by reformism and Progressivism? At the heart of the faith was the postulate that "true" democracy and "true" efficiency are not incompatible. When the actual character of each is searched out, and the proper institutions established to express this character, then the resulting government will be both democratic and efficient. True democracy means popular enlightenment and control. What people had been calling democracy was but a travesty on the name. Bossism, corruption, stupidity, waste—*these* could not be the meaning of the American dream. True efficiency, on the other hand, means efficiency over the long pull and in the interests of the most people. The efficiency of autocracy is a hollow mockery: like the showy tree, nothing grows under it. Now, a

---

[4] "Does it concern an independent board or commission?—integrate it. Is it a metropolitan fringe of unincorporated territory?—annex it. Is it a city manager government?—praise it. Is it a small township?—abolish it. Is it a state-local service?—centralize it. Is it proportional representation?—endorse it." J. F. Sly and J. J. Robbins, "Popularizing the Results of Government Research," 2 *Pub. Opin. Q.* (Jan., 1938), 7–23, 11. Thus two writers have condemned the "sweeping cliches" that are substituted for a "realistic," factual approach.

[5] See Chapter 1 for a discussion of these two tendencies.

government that is *really* democratic is also an efficient government: it is sensitive to popular demand, it realizes popular will with intelligence, honesty, economy, and dispatch. Contrariwise, really efficient government is also democratic: it ministers to the real needs of the people it represents. (What these "real needs" may be, we have reviewed in the chapter on The Good Life.)

In general, the articles of faith were plain and unquestioningly accepted. In the first place, the task of the voter had to be reduced to manageable compass, and he had to be prepared better to perform these restricted duties. This meant in practice such improvements as the short ballot and adequate but understandable government reporting. In the second place, there had to be a union of real power with formal responsibility. This would simplify the voter's task, and make effective his demand for efficiency. Third, there had to be a general buildup of executive power, a general strengthening of the executive's power downward and outward, an organization on hierarchical, pyramidal lines. This meant the abolition of boards, the creation of managerial "tools," the formation of larger but more coherent departments. Fourth, there had to be general simplification and rationalization—the abolition of superfluous offices and jurisdictions, reduction of interference by the judiciary. These tenets, of course, are not separable; they are part of a single plan. While there have been some differences of opinion concerning the proper institutionalization of this philosophy, the Man from Mars would not find the differences very significant.

The Rise of Centralization: Reformism.—With logical and historical fitness, survey of the "orthodox" viewpoint begins with Woodrow Wilson's essay, "The Study of Administration." In this precocious paper the outline of the orthodox position is clearly presented:

> Large powers and unhampered discretion seem to me the indispensable conditions of responsibility. Public attention must be easily directed, in each case of good or bad administration, to just the man deserving of praise or blame. *There is no danger in power, if only it be not irresponsible. If it be divided, dealt out in shares to many, it is obscured; if it be obscured, it is made irresponsible.*[6]

The answer to the question What part shall public opinion take in the conduct of administration? is that it shall play the part of "authoritative critic." This means that the present attempt to make

---

[6] *2 Pol. Sci. Q.* (June, 1887), 197–222, 213. Italics mine.

the voter do everything must be abandoned. "Self-government does not consist in having a hand in everything, any more than housekeeping consists necessarily in cooking dinner with one's own hands. The cook must be trusted with a large discretion as to the management of the fires and the ovens." The problem, as Wilson formulated it, "is to make public opinion efficient without suffering it to be meddlesome." [7]

> Directly exercised, in the oversight of the daily details and in the choice of the daily means of government, public criticism is of course a clumsy nuisance. . . . But as superintending the greater forces of formative policy alike in politics and administration, public criticism is altogether safe and beneficent. . . .[8]

On the eve of the First Great War the philosophy of integration had become the working faith of reformism and political science. Herbert Croly is, of course, the one who speaks the authentic tongue of reform in the Progressive era. He reflects, to some extent, the currents of decentralization, at that time flowing strongly; but he represents also, accurately and prophetically, the victory of the centripetal ideas. In his essay, "State Political Reorganization," he urges a strengthened executive and an improved administration as a necessary counterbalance to the initiative, referendum, and recall, which, though desirable, are not in themselves a formula for successful government.

> The progressive democracy is bound to be as much interested in efficient administration as it is in reconstructive legislation. . . . Its future as the expression of a permanent public interest is tied absolutely to an increase of executive authority and responsibility. It cannot get along without an adequate and efficient administrative organization—responsible to the governor, just as the governor is responsible to his constituents.[9]

In *The Promise of American Life,* Croly declares that "civil service reform" alone cannot break the power of the political machine. To achieve this, we must have reform in administrative organization to simplify form and concentrate power. "There can be," he proclaims, "no efficiency without responsibility. There can be

---

[7] *Ibid.* See also: Woodrow Wilson, *Constitutional Government in the United States* (New York: 1908), 197.

[8] *Ibid.,* 215. See Gamaliel Bradford, "The Reform of Our State Governments," 4 *Annals* (May, 1894), 883–902, illustrating a great many of the characteristics of reformism, including the conflation of "democracy" and "efficiency"; and also, of course, his *Lesson,* cited above.

[9] 6 *Am. Pol. Sci. Rev.* (Feb., 1912, Supp.), 122–136, 132.

no responsibility without authority." [10] To "reorganizers" these tenets of political philosophy have seemed so certainly true as to be themselves standards of truth.

The Progressive era was the period in which the doctrines of centralization began to be accepted as axiomatic, the period in which the formulae for reconciling "true democracy" and "true efficiency" became completely crystallized. Generally, the case was accepted as proved in the following years, and the tenets of centralization were used as guiding principles in local, state, and national reorganization schemes. [11] There was practically nothing added to the theoretical argument for centralization until the thirties. In the general quickening of thought stimulated by the Great Depression, the argument for centralization, while it remained fundamentally the same, was somewhat refurbished and supplemented.

An examination of one writer will suffice for the decade following the First Great War. In 1922 J. M. Mathews stated the accepted beliefs clearly and competently. In discussing "State Administrative Organization," he proposes a plan of reorganization designed to make the office of governor the "central pivot point" about which the whole administration revolves. "There is no great danger in conferring on the governor increased power if it is accompanied with commensurate responsibility." [12] There are two problems involved in the general plan: first, the relation of the executive to the legislature, and second, the internal organization of the executive and administrative authorities.

In considering the first of these problems, Mathews recognizes the split between those who wish to abandon the separation of powers entirely by making the governor politically subordinate to the legislature, and those who wish to retain the independent position of

---

[10] New York: 1909, 337. See also, on early centralization currents: L. S. Rowe, "American Political Ideas and Institutions in Their Relation to the Problem of City Government," 1 *Municipal Affairs* (June, 1897), 317–328; National Municipal League, *A Municipal Program* (New York: 1900); C. R. Woodruff, "The Complexity of American Governmental Methods," 15 *Pol. Sci. Q.* (June, 1900), 260–272; H. J. Ford, "The Reorganization of State Government," 3 *Proceed. Acad. Pol. Sci.* (Jan., 1913), 30–36.

[11] At the point that divides the period of creative thinking on the problem of reconciling Old Democracy with the Great Society from the period of more or less unquestioning acceptance of the political philosophy of centralization, stands the New York Bureau of Municipal Research's *The Constitution and Government of the State of New York: An Appraisal* (New York: 1915). This "new *Federalist*" summarizes the thought that preceded it and introduces the dogmas of the next two decades. See especially its statement of "assumptions" on the first page.

[12] 16 *Am. Pol. Sci. Rev.*, 387–398, 397. During this period, state administrative reorganization on principles of centralization was known as "the federal plan"; "This is merely applying to the states the theory of the national government, in which the President is the real head of the administration." *Loc. cit.*

the governor.   Generally speaking, he favors the latter position, because to be successful state reorganization plans "should be in harmony with the general trend of their organic development." [13]   However, although the principle of separation of powers should not be altogether abandoned, governor and legislature can with mutual advantage be brought into much more satisfactory cooperative relationships than now exist.   To this end he proposes such reforms as admitting the governor to legislative proceedings and giving precedence to administration bills.

In answer to the second problem, "internal reorganization, or the readjustment of the relations between the different executive and administrative agencies in the interests of greater unity, responsibility, concentration of authority and efficiency in action," [14] he urges adoption of the short ballot; increase of the governor's appointing power among higher ranks of administrators (including elimination of Senate concurrence and adoption of indefinite terms); the regrouping of administrative agencies on the principle of functional relation into probably not more than a dozen departments; authority to the governor to redistribute functions; and an adequate civil service system on a merit basis.   Finally, as a precautionary measure against any abuse of power, provision should be made, with "reasonable restrictions," for the recall of the governor.

Restatement and Elaboration.—In recent years the argument for centralization has had some very able and very thorough expositions.   For the most part, these accept the early rationale favoring centralization.   But they do not merely repeat the familiar tenets; they present a refutation of the case for decentralization, advance new arguments for centralization, are more subtle in style, and are more philosophical in tone.

---

[13] *Ibid.*, 388.
[14] *Ibid.*, 391.   See also his *Principles of American State Administration* (New York: 1917), ch. 19 (with bibliography); and "The New Role of the Governor," 6 *Am. Pol. Sci. Rev.* (May, 1912), 216–228.   For generally "orthodox" centralization theory see also: A. E. Buck, *The Reorganization of State Governments in the United States* (New York: successive editions of a monograph first appearing as a supplement to the *National Municipal Review* of November, 1919); H. J. Bruere, *A Plan of Organization for New York City* (n.p.: 1917, a pamphlet); J. A. Pfiffner, *Public Administration* (New York: 1935), *passim*, especially ch. 5.   Early writings of F. F. Blachly contrast rather sharply with his later writings on this point.   See: "The Executive Budget in the Light of Oklahoma's Experience," 2 *Southwestern Pol. Sci. Q.* (June, 1921), 21–39: "Who Should Organize State Administration?" 4 *Southwestern Pol. and Soc. Sci. Q.* (Sept., 1923), 95–109.   See also, of course, the *Report* of the President's Committee on Administrative Management (Washington: 1937); and Louis Brownlow's "The Executive Office of the President, A General View," 1 *Pub. Adm. Rev.* (Winter, 1941), 101–105; the chairman of the President's Committee, unrepentant in his belief in the President as the center of force and administrative boss in the federal government.

An outstanding example of these recent writings is Luther Gulick's "Politics, Administration, and the New Deal." He makes a three-point refutation of the decentralization theories. (1) "Isolation" movements are sporadic and unreliable. While improvement may be an immediate result of an isolation movement, this is not due to the isolation, but to the greater energy and attention accompanying the change. Stagnation is likely to be the long-term result of isolation. (2) The "guild" idea, the use of interest and professional groups in administration, is unsound. Guilds are narrow and self-seeking in their outlook. The "public interest" becomes a mere fiction when various interest groups enjoy a substantial measure of autonomy in administration. (3) Independent agencies serving the same area or clientele stimulate jealousies, generate frictions. Independence renders difficult coordination or mollification from without.[15]

His positive argument for centralization contains new points while remodelling the old. (1) Integration has obvious advantages for planning—which most people recognize as a necessary ingredient of the Good Life. A central, neutral authority should determine the proper balance and proportion among special interests and skills; integration makes this possible. And, of course, planning facilitates economy. (2) In the field of management, integration offers advantages unknown to decentralization. It makes possible centralization of general business operations, reduces conflicts and overlapping jurisdictions and services. (3) Integration of authorities and activities in a given area produces the proved benefits of large-scale enterprise—more minute division of labor, more intense specialization of function, greater opportunities for careers, etc. (4) Integration takes advantage of the principle of economy of citizen attention. Democracy in a complicated, modern setting requires that the citizen's task of judging among persons and policies be reduced to manageable dimensions.[16]

Among studies concerning this phase of the national scene, James Hart's "The President and Federal Administration" is typical and outstanding. Hart recognizes the limits of the chief executive's time and energy while yet seeking to make him the fulcrum in both administration and policy determination; he would also provide safeguards against the misuse of concentrated and strengthened administrative powers necessitated by compelling circumstance.[17] Hart

---

[15] 169 *Annals* (Sept., 1933), 55–66, 56–58.
[16] *Ibid.*, 57–59.
[17] In *Essays on the Law and Practice of Governmental Administration* (Baltimore: 1935), C. G. Haines and M. E. Dimock, eds., 47–93. "The proposals of this

premises the need for increasing control of the American economy, and consequently is convinced that an extensive adjustment of powers and functions is desirable. To secure the desired readjustments, constitutional amendments are urged.

He proposes that the President's political power be made commensurate with his legislative responsibility, that the President be strengthened "as the focal point of all policy-determination." To this end, his term should be made to coincide with that of Congress, and he should be given the power of dissolution. Legislation should be in the form of broad outlines, leaving "to the President or his chosen subordinates the invention, selection and experimental adaptation of means to these objectives." [18] While the President will be the center of the administrative structure as well as the focal point of policy determination, the fact must be recognized that limits of time, energy, and area circumscribe his administrative activities.[19] His should be the crucial choices, and he should have a free hand in the selection and control of advisors and all who make minor decisions in his name.

Actual administration should be the duty of a non-partisan and permanent bureaucracy. The "institutional control" of this bureaucracy should be concentrated in the President and exercised by a bureau of general administration attached to his office. To correct injustice and abuse of power, there should be established an administrative court, with judges whose training has not been chiefly com-

---

essay . . . are: to accept bureaucracy as an inevitable concomitant of the twentieth century functions of the federal government; to organize it in accordance with the best-thought-out views on public administration; to provide legal checks upon it through an adequate administrative court; and to retain and strengthen the Presidency as the focal-point of all policy-determination." 59 (by permission of Johns Hopkins Press).

[18] *Ibid.,* 91.

[19] "The picture of the President as on his own initiative exercising a continuous and detailed direction of all phases of administration is . . . a myth." *Ibid.,* 55. On this "myth," see C. S. Hyneman, "Executive-Administrative Power and Democracy," 2 *Pub. Adm. Rev.* (Autumn, 1942), 332–338, 335. "In other words, the world of administration is a *pluralistic* rather than a *monistic* world, and reposes on the loyalty and competence of individual bureaucrats, qualities which thrive best in conditions making for independence of judgment and pride in a job well done. Certainly, to conceive of the President as a potential 'boss of the works' save in situations raising broad issues of policy would be both absurd and calamitous; and for such issues the legislative process is still available, a field in which presidential leadership is today a more vital factor than ever before." E. S. Corwin, *The President: Office and Powers* (New York: 1940), 359 (by permission of New York University Press). Cf. C. E. Merriam, *On the Agenda of Democracy* (Cambridge, Mass.: 1941), replying to Corwin. Having tried to organize the President's job on the theory that it is in all essential aspects except size the same as the job of superintending a factory, the members of the President's Committee on Administrative Management apparently feel defensive. "The proper conception of the executive is precisely what Corwin calls 'absurd and calamitous'—namely, as the director of the works in the area of management." Merriam, *Op. cit.,* 39.

mon law, and having a jurisdiction similar to that of the French Council of State. Existing regulatory boards and commissions should be abolished. Their judicial functions should go to the administrative courts, their policy-determining functions to agents of the President in the appropriate departments; and technical and investigatory functions should be exercised under the control of officers who formulate policies.

We may close this review of the case for centralization by noting an essay by E. P. Herring. He perhaps states most clearly that form of the argument for integration of organization that is based upon the need to achieve integration of purpose—as against integration merely to achieve efficiency, economy, and responsibility. In his "Social Forces and the Reorganization of the Federal Bureaucracy," 1934,[20] Herring already had evidenced the concern for the public interest that was to produce *Public Administration and the Public Interest* in 1936. He views with alarm the selfish aims and disintegrating effects of social and economic interests, and hopes for a "unified conception of state purpose."

"I insist . . . that the dominating purpose of our federal departments should not be to serve a group of citizens however large and influential but rather to carry out a state function." [21] Reorganization is necessary to secure ordinary economy and efficiency, but also, and more importantly, "because of the need of securing a sense of direction and responsible control in the administrative services. We cannot afford a government of scrambled objectives and indefinite leadership. Our administrative organization must be adapted to the public interest and not arranged to suit the contradictory pressures of special interests." [22]

The Case for Decentralization

We turn now to a review of writings on public administration which plead the cause of decentralization, which are "centrifugal" in tendency—first, to the writings that are primarily refutations of the "orthodox" theories.

---

[20] 15 *Southwestern Soc. Sci. Q.*, 185–200.
[21] *Ibid.*, 197.
[22] *Ibid.*, 200.
The *Report* of the President's Committee on Administrative Management (Washington: 1937) is of course a classic statement of centralization doctrine, with its horror of "independence" and its conception of the President as a brooding omnipresence in Federal administration. Federal centralization reaches something of a climax in E. Charles Woods' proposal to reduce the number of Federal departments to perhaps as few as six. See "A Proposed Reorganization of the Executive Branch of the Federal Government," 37 *Am. Pol. Sci. Rev.* (June, 1943), 476–490.

Refutation of Centralization Theory.—While of course there was always objection to centralization philosophy—and a large part of the population is even yet unconcerned or unconvinced—until the early twenties, there was practically no written attempt, academic or professional, to refute this philosophy. There was, that is to say, no attempt to meet it on its own grounds, on the same plane, instead of merely repeating eighteenth- and nineteenth-century language that it had been, in the first place, especially designed to refute. Most prominent among the early questionings of the formulae of reorganization was F. W. Coker's "Dogmas of Administrative Reform," in 1922. The essay is couched in mild terms; Coker agrees with most of the objectives and many of the general methods of the reorganizers. Some of the disagreement is only as to speed or quantity.

The clue to Coker's disagreement lies in the title of his essay: that the general principles adopted for reforming government had hardened into "dogmas," implicitly believed and mechanically applied. He charges the reorganizers, who presume themselves free from pernicious and stultifying "theory," with being not only theoretical, but doctrinaire.

Coker treats first the "principle of economy"—the notion that by eliminating duplication and overlapping, and by integrating related functions, savings can be effected, and suggests that "improvement in our state administration . . . can be achieved better by a piece-meal process—dealing particularly with each case of duplication—than by the more sweeping method of reconstruction followed by the recent reorganization acts." [23]

The principle of concentration of power or authority is challenged, first, on the ground that it is not true "that for all . . . departments unity of power and responsibility is of more importance than continuity of policy and the maintenance of relations of mutual respect and confidence between head and staff." [24] There is no justification in reason or experience for the belief that *all* administrative services are better discharged when carried on by a single head subject to discharge by a chief executive. Moreover, the reorganizers violate their own principle of "economy of citizen attention" by asking the voters to sit in judgment every two years, not only on pressing matters of public policy, but on the conduct of government in the relatively established and expert areas of public health, welfare, and

---

[23] 16 *Am. Pol. Sci. Rev.* (Aug., 1922), 399–411, 408. "Continuous reorganization" is now, of course, a tenet of orthodoxy.
[24] *Ibid.*, 409.

education. The principle of concentration is challenged, second, on the ground that we are "in danger of carrying too far the idea that popular control is advanced chiefly by placing vast powers in one elected officer. . . ." [25] In addition to overlooking all incentives to good service except the acclaim of an informed public opinion, there is a fundamental error in this notion, in the assumption that popular control of executive officers is chiefly through the electoral process: it is "equally exercised" in enacting a law determining a method of administration.

In short, concentration of considerable authority may be appropriate in some cases; but the criteria in any case, and the mode of procedure, must be "pragmatic." [26]

Voice in the Wilderness.—The most thorough and uncompromising of the refutations of centralization philosophy in general, and state reorganization in particular, is that of W. H. Edwards, in a series of essays on "The State Reorganization Movement" appearing in 1927–1928 in the *Dakota Law Review*.[27] Whether the nature of the publishing medium caused these essays to be generally overlooked by administrative students, whether a certain immoderation of language evoked a conspiracy of silence, or for whatever reason, these articles seem not to have been widely known or read. Their obscurity appears not to have been deserved by their merits. The case presented against centralization is essentially a "debater's" case; but as such it is complete.

In the first of these essays, Edwards elaborates the history of the reorganization movement, distinguishing between decentralizing plans (Wisconsin, 1911; New Jersey, 1912) and the "federal" or centralizing scheme, and incisively presents the rationale of each. The second essay, a refutation of the "federal plan," proceeds as

---

[25] *Ibid.*

[26] Coker briefs his case as follows: "Recent systems of reorganization give too little weight to such needs as the following: (1) The need of securing continuity of policy in administrative departments having work of a technical and regulation-establishing character; (2) the need for facilitating the establishment of customs and traditions of non-interference by periodically changing political officers; (3) the need for eliciting the participation of disinterested citizens serving on unpaid boards, exercising powers of investigation, advice and publicity; (4) the need for placing legal authority and responsibility in the particular offices most likely to develop a sense of professional responsibility and pride in connection with the work of such offices; (5) the uselessness of extending the scope of power of any officer beyond the limits of what that officer can actually devote his attention to. Both reason and experience show that, for the administration of many functions, diffusion, rather than concentration, of authority, secures not only more efficient but also more democratic administration." 411.

[27] Vol. I (Jan., 1927), 13–30; vol. I (April, 1927), 15–41; vol. II (Feb., 1928), 17–67; vol. II (May, 1928), 103–139.

follows: (1) The idea that a single man can actually administer anything as vast and complex as a state government is ridiculous.[28] No one man has the capacity or the insight. Limitations of human ability prevent a governor from performing a tithe of the duties he is given on paper in reorganization plans. (2) The reorganizers carry the principle of unity to extremes. Life is complex, and reality is not single and simple. The unity and simplicity insisted upon by the reorganizers, in his view, is a foible of little minds. (3) In practice, increasing the power of the governor results in discontinuity of personnel and policy, the replacement of experts by spoilsmen, the decrease of much needed impartiality in administration of law. (4) The virtues claimed for the "federal plan"—unity, leadership and responsibility—either will not be realized, are undesirable as conceived, or will not in fact result from adoption of the proposed changes; finally, that they exist at all rests upon unsupported assertions.

In the third essay, Edwards considers the objections to centralization raised by research groups and political scientists, and particularly those of such functional interests as education, welfare, and health. He concludes that the objections of these latter groups against placing their services "back in politics"—from which it took a tremendous struggle to obtain a measure of freedom—are overwhelming. The key issue is "the determination of that selective process which will secure the acquisition to office of the most highly qualified technicians available in existing society" and the circumstancing of these technicians so that they will be allowed to exercise their expertise "uncorrupted and unmolested." [29] In this, decentralized administration is superior. Most of the reorganizers, he concludes, are without the courage of their erroneous convictions: each wishes to exempt his special field—finance, personnel, etc.— from the operation of the plan.

In the final essay, a general philosophical, social and economic argument is made for "functionalism," which is the inner logic of modern civilization (references are made to the various pluralist movements then prominent), and which centralization violates. The federal plan means lay dominance and interference with expertise. The State of the Future must recognize the rightful role of expertise

---

[28] Much of the antithesis between centralizers and decentralizers lies in the weasel-word "administer." How much mastery and control, how great a grasp of detail must a man have to "administer" an enterprise? Surely—Edwards could not have been unaware—there have been examples enough of men able to master and direct larger enterprises—economic, military, and governmental—than most state governments.

[29] Third essay, 18.

and give it free play within the field of its competence. Our institutions and traditions, he argues, make the United States peculiarly adapted to the procedure of integrating private expertise and occupational groupings with the formal administrative organization; rather than having a separate parliament of interests and skills, or some such arrangement. Moreover, the necessary integration of expertise and government should take cognizance in its institutional achievement of the principle that "experts perform the highest standard of work when they serve as a 'thought' and not as a 'will' organization. . . ." [30]

The most striking of more recent refutations of centralization philosophy is an essay by C. S. Hyneman, "Administrative Reorganization: An Adventure into Science and Theology." [31]   The title pitches the tone of the argument, which is a root and branch denial of the assumptions and conclusions of the advocates of state reorganization.   He denies that "efficiency" is acceptable as the "first objective of reorganization."   He denies that work of an administrative nature can be divorced from control of policy.   He denies that there is any evidence, compelling to a neutral observer, that single officers are preferable to boards for directing administration (the analogies to business practice being faulty).   He denies that there is any need to accept the whole reorganization program in order to obtain central direction of administration; that there is any objective evidence available on the accomplishments of actual reorganizations—only bald assertion; that the scheme of concentrating power in and attention upon the governor makes him "responsible" for the conduct of administration.

Elected Chief Administrator: Achilles Heel of Centralization. —We may conclude this survey of "non-centralization" writings by noting an essay by Harvey Walker.   Walker is probably outstanding among those who oppose the uniting of an elected chief executive and chief administrator in a single person.   There is no doubt that the anomaly of an elected chief administrator at the heart of the "orthodox" scheme has been a major weakness in the logic of that

---

[30] Fourth essay, 133. See also his "The Public Efficiency Experts," 10 *Southwestern Pol. and Soc. Sci. Q.* (Dec., 1929), 301–312, in which he charges again that the reorganizers have created a position that only a genius could fill but left the position open to dolts and dastards; and his "Has State Reorganization Succeeded?" 11 *State Gov't.* (Oct., 1938), 183–184, claiming that such economies as can be proved in "reorganized" states are due to such reforms as those in fiscal and purchasing procedures, not to increase in one-man control; "A Factual Summary of State Administrative Reorganization," 19 *Southwestern Soc. Sci. Q.* (June, 1938), 53–67, concluding that consolidation has in fact been very limited, that the principle of functional departments has been violated, etc.

[31] 1 *Jour. of Pol.* (Feb., 1939), 62–75.

viewpoint.[32] In "Theory and Practice in State Administrative Organization," 1930,[33] Walker stated the heterodox opinions that he refined and elaborated in his *Public Administration in the United States* (1937), and that were mentioned in the preceding chapter. He begins by questioning the appropriateness of the "federal" and corporate (joint-stock) analogies as used by the centralizers. He proceeds to question the merits of comprehensive as against piecemeal reorganization. He then comes to the heart of his argument: a challenge to the assumption that the governor should head the administration. The governor, he holds, is an executive, political, and ceremonial figure. Administration, for which the governor is probably not trained and for which he has no time, is not his proper function. Moreover, it is not true that popular control results from such concentration of power. There are no safeguards against its abuse except refusal of reelection, impeachment, and in a few cases the recall. As devices to secure good and responsible administration, these are impossibly clumsy. Walker's alternative plan was noted in the preceding chapter and need not be repeated.

The Values of Decentralization.—We turn now to some of the writings that are not cast primarily in the form of a refutation of the case for centralization, but are devoted primarily to pleading the values of decentralization and presenting specific programs for realizing these values. A readily discernible segment of such writings has been produced by those who have found in the practice of industrial corporate interrelations, or in the corporate devices as adapted to government use, a pattern or guide for government action. These writers are likely to accept the desirability of large and increasing government participation in and control of economic life, but still to be apprehensive of the ability of a centralized apparatus to meet the demands of unprecedented governmental size and diversified activity. In the corporation they feel that they have found an organizational form flexible enough to circumvent old rigid and unreal categories of "public" and "private," and to secure the values both of "poised" and "positive" government.

Corporation Theory.—Historically, the most notable among the "corporation" writings is W. F. Willoughby's "The National Government as a Holding Company," which appeared in 1917. The rationale for Willoughby's plan is not presented in the broad social

---

[32] See, however: G. W. Spicer, "From Political Chief to Administrative Chief," in *Essays on the Law and Practice of Governmental Administration*, 94–126.
[33] 19 *Nat. Mun. Rev.* (April, 1930), 249–254.

and economic terms suggested in the preceding paragraph, but rather in terms of "efficiency" and "responsibility." But the plan is both broad and detailed, and has remained the classic exposition of the "holding company" point of view—*i.e.,* the point of view of those "corporation" advocates, primarily antagonistic to concentrating power in the chief executive, who wish to see popular control exercised through the legislature.

To relieve the congestion of business, both in the administrative branch and in Congress, Willoughby proposes "the definite adoption by the government, in making provision for the performance of both its legislative and administrative functions, of the principle, or device, of what is known as the holding and subsidiary corporations form of organization." [34] Such action

> contemplates that Congress shall look upon the general government as but a holding corporation of which it is the board of directors; that, as such, it shall not seek itself directly to manage all the affairs of government, but shall bring into existence distinct subsidiary corporations to direct and administer the affairs of certain of its special services. Essentially this means that each service will be given a legal, administrative and financial autonomy. [35]

The legal relationship will be precisely that of municipal corporations to the states creating them, but administratively the principal will be much more active in supervision and control. It is not proposed to treat *all* government activities in this manner; a core of essential and traditional government functions will remain, as now, under the direct supervision of Congress. But generally, activities of an industrial or revenue-producing character, those administering or exploiting the public domain, and general supply services and manufacturing plants of the government would be so treated.

The advantages of the plan, according to Willoughby, would be of two kinds. First, Congress would not be responsible, primarily and in detail, for administrative operation; consequently it would have more time and attention to devote to the broader aspects of its control function. Second, the plan would improve the administration of individual services by "taking the purely business and technical services of the government outside of the domain of politics." [36] The plan would promote career opportunities and stimulate *esprit de corps* in each service.

---

[34] 32 *Pol. Sci. Q.* 505–521.

[35] *Ibid.,* 507.

[36] *Ibid.,* 513. For a refutation of the "holding company idea" see Luther Gulick's "Notes on the Theory of Organization," in *Papers on the Science of Administration* (New York: 1937), Gulick and L. Urwick, eds., 1–46, 35.

Congress, Willoughby concludes, would in no way abdicate its responsibility. Rather, it should adopt a plan enabling it to exercise its responsibilities effectively.

Marshall Dimock's "Principles Underlying Government-Owned Corporations," [37] may be taken to illustrate the general argument for the government-owned corporation as it has developed in practice in the federal government. Dimock could not be described as an advocate of the government-owned corporation, in view of other of his writings. But this essay, written for the enlightenment of a British public, is a useful compendium of opinion on the subject.

The general advantage of the corporation is independence and elasticity, plus responsibility. "Because of its freedom from governmental intervention in management, the government-owned corporation enjoys the elasticity and autonomy which are required for efficient and progressive administration." [38]

The specific advantages of the corporation in the American institutional context are outlined. "The principal advantages of a government-owned corporation over an ordinary government department are to be found in the ease and independence with which the undertaking's financial affairs and purchasing operations can be conducted." [39] There are legal advantages: the corporation can sue and be sued—the sovereign's immunity in tort is relinquished. There is freedom from the undesirable features of central civil service administration—slowness, inelasticity, unimaginativeness—although, of course, merit principles can be enforced by a competent personnel agency. There is easy adaptability to changing conditions and to the milieu of private enterprise. Enjoying general corporate powers, there is less need for the undertaking ever to seek additional specific powers from the legislature in order to conduct operations successfully.[40] Opposition to government participation in economic life is lessened because of observance of familiar forms, and competition between government-supported and privately supported enterprise is equalized because the corporation, once established, lives off its own income.[41]

---

[37] 13 *Jour. Pub. Adm.* (Jan., 1935), 51–66.

[38] *Ibid.,* 65.

[39] *Ibid.,* 60.

[40] This argument, of course, is hardly designed to convince legislatures of the desirability of the corporate form of administration.

[41] His "Public Corporations and Business Enterprise," 14 *Jour. of P. A.* (Oct., 1936), 417–428, is somewhat more philosophical on the subject of the compromise which the government-owned corporation effects between "public" and "private."

Some students of the government-owned corporation are not convinced of its general superiority. See John McDiarmid, "Government Corporations and Federal Funds," 31 *Am. Pol. Sci. Rev.* (Dec., 1937), 1094–1106. *Cf.* Herbert Emmerich,

Search for Union of Knowledge with Power.—Most notable among the "decentralization" writings that have stressed the part that technical, professional, and "interest" groups can or should play in administration, are those of L. W. Lancaster. The state fabric of the Great Society, Lancaster argues in a series of articles appearing in the thirties, must be loosely knit, in order that knowledge and power shall coincide. Many doctrines of our law and many of the "canons of integration" Lancaster does not regard as simply *wrong:* they are irrelevant to the great problem before us, the problem of synthesizing our political heritage with contemporary scientific and economic facts.

The evolution of modern technology, he argues in "Private Associations and Public Administration," [42] has "short-circuited" the legislature, the institution that democracy evolved to secure the responsibility of its rulers: the qualities that bring political success are not at all those necessary to form a competent opinion on administrative problems. However, "administration" does not face "the people" in the aspect of ruler to ruled, despite the fact that much of our legal language would suggest this. [43] For the same forces that have altered the relationship between the legislature and the people, and between the legislature and administration, have created a new relationship between administration and the people. The fact is, that the knowledge and skills which give administrators their 'claim to power' are not their prerogatives alone, but are diffused throughout society. Indeed, they may exist in greater quantity or higher quality in 'private' persons or groups. A close survey of actual administration reveals that the membrane of the legal concept of "public" is in fact so thin as to permit a very large amount of osmosis.

To the important and compelling facts of expertise and associations of experts, we have made some pragmatic adjustment. "Not only much of our public administration is conditioned by the attitude of so-called private associations but . . . in fact a substantial proportion of it is actually conducted by such organizations." [44] But our political ideology lags far behind.

"Government Corporations and Independent Supervisory Agencies," in *Report* of the President's Committee on Administrative Management (Washington, 1937), 229–303; and C. Herman Pritchett, "The Paradox of the Government Corporation," 1 *Pub. Adm. Rev.* (Summer, 1941), 381–389.

[42] 13 *Soc. For.* (Dec., 1934), 283–291.

[43] His "The Legal Status of 'Private' Organizations Exercising Governmental Powers" is a review of legal doctrines, as the title indicates, but it also develops his characteristic position. 15 *Southwestern Soc. Sci. Q.* (Mar., 1935), 325–336.

[44] "Private Associations and Public Administration," 291. In "State Supervision and Local Administrative Standards," in 1933, Lancaster chides both home

The Search for "Democratic" Administration.—Both the "corporation" advocates and the "professional group" advocates have been incidentally concerned to make administration more "democratic," but there have been a number of persons of widely varying backgrounds and approaches to the subject whose *primary* object has been to bring democracy into the administrative process. These persons have rejected the "orthodox" viewpoint that the meaning of democracy is external to administration; that "administration" in an autocracy and in a democracy are or should be the same, and that the difference between the two types of government lies only in the purposes realized by the respective bureaucracies and the absence or presence of an elected, controlling legislature. These persons, of increasing number during the past decade, have believed that democracy has implications for the administrative process itself. They have rejected the formulae of the centralizers as inadequate to guarantee a democratic way of life. Selecting two illustrative essays simply on the basis of divergence of approach, let us examine the theories of David Lilienthal and Ordway Tead.

Lilienthal's Views.—Lilienthal speaks, with the authority of distinguished public service and the weight of his experience in administering T.V.A., of the urgent need for decentralizing and democratizing administration.[45] He sees the preservation of democracy as the issue at stake. "We must make it work or it will die. To make it work calls for every resource of intelligence, persistence and open-mindedness we can summon." [46] The formulae of centralization do not, he feels, meet these requirements.

"Excessive centralization at the national capital causes interminable delays in arriving at decisions and putting them into effect." [47] This delay is inevitable, despite high quality of the person-

---

rule and administrative centralization advocates for being unreal in their approach, for imagining that anything in the existential world does or could correspond to their concepts. A new approach is urged: recognition of the unity of problems, abandonment of absolute formulae, and stress upon educational, advisory, and cooperative features. 13 *Southwestern Soc. Sci. Q.* (Mar., 1933), 321–332.

Cf. J. D. Barnett, "Representation of Interests in Administration," 12 *Nat. Mun. Rev.* (July, 1923), 347–349; J. P. Chamberlain, "Democratic Control of Administration," 13 *Am. Bar Assoc. Jour.* (April, 1937), 186–188.

[45] "The TVA: An Experiment in the 'Grass Roots' Administration of Federal Functions," address before the Southern Political Science Association, Nov. 10, 1939, Knoxville, Tenn., published in pamphlet form. Lilienthal favors, of course, the autonomy and flexibility that the corporate form of organization has given the T.V.A. But his essay is not primarily on the virtues of the corporate form—the values it has realized are the chief concern. Other forms may realize the same values. "Experimentation is required."

[46] *Ibid.,* 29.

[47] *Ibid.,* 5.

nel at the capital. Moreover, "a central government is bound to suffer from lack of knowledge of local conditions, of parochial customs. In a country as vast as the United States . . . local and regional differences are . . . vital and . . . precious. . . ." [48] Centrally located personnel cannot possibly know these differences and the consequences are of grave import.

There can be no well-founded doubt about the need of the central government to exercise a large and increasing sphere of authority. "Let us concede that if this democracy is to survive and be effective it must entrust the federal government with increasingly larger powers to deal with emerging social and economic problems." [49] The question is: "How can a democracy enjoy the advantages of a strong central government and escape the evils of remote, top-heavy central administration . . .?" [50]

The escape from this dilemma lies in "the *decentralized administration* of federal functions which lend themselves to such technique, and the *coordination in the field of such decentralized activities. . . .*" [51] The essential characteristics of a decentralized administration of federal functions, as determined by the experience of the T.V.A. are three. First, a decentralized administration is one "in which the greatest number of decisions is made in the field." [52] The mere setting up of field officers is not enough. "The field officers must be selected, trained, and supervised with a view to increasing their capacity to decide questions on the ground. They must be able to understand the broad, general policies, and to adapt them to varying local situations." They must not be mere messengers and errand boys.

Second, "a decentralized federal administration must develop as far as possible the active participation of the people themselves." Cooperation, not compliance, is essential. The federal agency "must utilize the services of state and local agencies, supplementing and stimulating, not duplicating, their staff or equipment."

Third, "a decentralized federal administration must coordinate in the field the work of state and local governments, aiming toward common objectives." In centralized administration the coordination is at the top, with resulting delays, jealousies, and jurisdic-

---

[48] *Ibid.*
[49] *Ibid.*, 6.
[50] *Ibid.*, 7–8.
[51] *Ibid.*, 8.
[52] *Ibid.*, 13. All quotations on these three characteristics are from this page. See also, of course, his *TVA—Democracy on the March* (New York: 1944). *Cf.* William Pincus, "Shall We Have More TVA's?" 5 *Pub. Adm. Rev.* (Spring, 1945), 148–152, an incisive inquiry into the implications of Lilienthal's philosophy.

tional disputes. In decentralized administration, the aim is to create a "whole" of purposes, personalities, and instrumentalities which is greater than the mere sum of the various constituent elements.

Tead, Democratic Missionary.—Ordway Tead brings to his 1939 book, *New Adventures in Democracy,* a background of psychological and economic inquiry, association with the scientific management movement, alert participation in industrial and public management. This breadth of experience is reflected in a distinctive series of works, including *Instincts in Industry* (1918), *Creative Management* (1935), and *The Art of Leadership* (1935). He reflects the "democratizing" tendency in scientific management noted above. But he does not merely "reflect"; he is an original, if not a great, thinker.

The subject of Tead's devotion and the object of his endeavors is—democracy. He fervently believes that democracy is a way of life that must permeate the whole of our waking hours. He wishes to extend its spirit and application to the work-a-day world, not to reserve its blessings for "after hours." He urges that thought be given to extending it to public and private administration—"if democracy is to survive and prosper, thousands of American citizens will have to think about these problems. . . ."[53] We must make flesh our word that "self-government and good government are not opposed realities, but when intelligently conceived, are two aspects of the same reality."[54]

Happily, he finds that increasing psychological knowledge, the developments of administrative science, and increasing experience with democratic principles indicate our problem is soluble. In fact, Tead develops two related principles which he advocates as tested formulae for proceeding:

The first is *the principle of the representation of interests,* which says that every group which has a clearly identifiable set of interests is safeguarded in its dealings with other groups only as it has the opportunity for an explicit voicing of its interests in councils where the common problems of the several groups are under consideration. This principle emphasizes in the first instance the rights of the members or constituency.

The second is *the principle of coordination* which says that an organization functions smoothly only as there is definite, informed and advance agreement throughout the groups which compose the organiza-

[53] *New Adventures:* New York, viii. *Cf.* Alfred M. Bingham, *The Techniques of Democracy* (New York: 1942), chs. 5, 6.
[54] *Ibid.,* 4.

tion, both upon its aims and policies and upon the general methods which will give those aims effect; and further, that this advance agreement requires explicit, organized, group or functional representation in deliberations where aims and policies are decided. This principle centers attention on the organization and its smooth working.[55]

These two principles are valid in three different kinds of administrative relationships: "first, vertically in an organization, up and down the line of authority; second, horizontally among a number of operating departments which desire to correlate their activities; and, third, within one department of an organization." [56] They must be applied *to the administrative process itself*. Present types of group organization are not satisfactory. They "are of themselves merely excrescences upon administration and not an *integral* part of it. They do not touch directly upon matters of defining purpose, policy, or method at the point of their *origination* . . . " [57]

Tead suggests applications of his principles in three fields: education, public service, and industry. But these chapters do not, in the nature of the case, lend themselves to summarization. Suffice it to say that they are for the most part far from the beaten trails of administrative thinking; that, while there are recrudescences of employer paternalism, the approach is radically different from the customary—as it would be for anyone who proposes that within administration itself "democracy must be viewed as a positive, fighting philosophy and as a practical program. . . ." [58]

Skepticism and Compromise

Some recent tendencies in writings on centralization and decentralization are discernible. The first is that writers display an increasing disposition to compromise on the subject of centralization versus decentralization. There is less heat in the presentation of the argument and more subtlety in its elaboration. There may even be skepticism about the possibility of finding an argument for cen-

---

[55] Reprinted by permission from *New Adventures in Democracy* by Ordway Tead, copyrighted 1939 by McGraw-Hill Book Co., Inc., 5–6. *Cf.* J. D. Lewis, "Democratic Planning in Agriculture," 35 *Am. Pol. Sci. Rev.* (April and June, 1941), 232–249 and 454–469.

[56] *Ibid.*, 6.

[57] *Ibid.*, 9.

[58] *Ibid.*, 130. For an able presentation of that variety of dissent from orthodoxy characteristic of the Brookings Institution, see A. C. Millspaugh's "Democracy and Administrative Organization," in *Essays in Political Science* (Baltimore: 1937), J. M. Mathews and James Hart, eds., 64–73. This is briefly considered at the end of Chapter 4, above. See also Millspaugh's *Democracy, Efficiency, Stability* (Washington: 1942), especially the closing chapters.

On further approaches to "decentralization" consult the Bibliographical Note at the end of the chapter.

tralization or decentralization which cannot be matched by an equally plausible argument to the contrary.

M. E. Dimock's "Executive Responsibility: The Span of Control in the Federal Government" [59] may be taken as illustrative. Dimock envisages the President as the manager of a great business —the federal government. To fill this position he needs the powers which the "new management" accords the general-manager, such as control of a dynamic personnel agency. Organizational lines should be simplified, lines of authority made hierarchical. On the other hand, decentralization is stressed. All coordinating and deciding should be done as far down the governmental pyramid as possible, administrative regionalism should be explored, and so forth.

Schuyler C. Wallace's *Federal Departmentalization: A Critique of Theories of Organization* [60] may be taken as the prime example of skepticism with respect to the establishment of a convincing case for either a centralizing or a decentralizing scheme. He refuses to accept as "given" the postulates upon which either side has built its case; he judiciously weighs the "factors" inclining both ways in specific organizational problems; finally, he insists that, on the basis of the evidence, the reasonable man must suspend judgment. He is convinced that administrative students (particularly the later ones) have proceeded upon narrow and unexamined postulates; that they are quite in error in presuming that they can divorce themselves from considerations as to the nature of man, from judgments about contemporary social and economic developments, and from decisions about the nature of the Good Life. Administrative study has advanced, but only on "the basis of half-truths and fictions . . ." [61] and a Scot's verdict of "not proved" must be entered for the bulk of what has been presented as scientific truth.

The second observation on tendencies in recent writings is related to Wallace's criticisms. There has grown up the idea that "organization" is *per se* a subject of study, that it can be isolated from other factors for inquiry. The common factors of organizations for various purposes, in various places, and at various times are emphasized; there are presumed to be "constants" that can be isolated and generalized upon. The environment of the organization structure is passed over lightly, while the organization structure itself is intensely regarded. There is talk of a "pure theory of organization." The conclusions of this inquiry are presented not

---

[59] 3 *Soc. Adv. Man. Jour.* (Jan., 1938), 22–28.
[60] New York: 1941.
[61] *Ibid.*, 235. See ch. 8, "Conclusions."

as arguments, but as simple "facts." There is a notion that a "valid" organization conforms to or approaches a norm. Centralization or decentralization is not something, then, to be argued about; a "good" organization will be one which fits the pattern for all proper organization.

Now, it happens that, while the conclusions of organizational "theorists" incline more often than not in the direction of centralization, their significance for this study lies not in what they hold, but in the manner in which they are reached. This matter is investigated in the next chapter.

BIBLIOGRAPHICAL NOTE

As stated at the beginning of this chapter, it is impossible to treat the subject of centralization versus decentralization fully in an essay of this scope. Particularly, in view of its historical importance, it is a matter for regret that all aspects of the philosophy of integration cannot be developed.

On short ballot philosophy see: G. W. Spicer, "Relation of the Short Ballot to Efficient Government and Popular Control," 11 *Southwestern Pol. and Soc. Sci. Q.* (Sept., 1930), 182–192; J. K. Pollock, "Election or Appointment of Public Officials," 181 *Annals* (Sept., 1935), 74–79; H. A. Stone, D. K. Price, and K. H. Stone, *City Manager Government in the United States* (Chicago: 1940), ch. 1— an excellent short history of the movement, with bibliographical suggestions. *Cf.* K. H. Porter, *State Administration* (New York: 1938), 26–27.

On boards and commissions for administrative purposes see: L. A. Blue, "Recent Tendencies in State Administration," 18 *Annals* (Nov., 1901), 434–445; C. E. McCombs, "State Welfare Administration and Consolidated Government," 13 *Nat. Mun. Rev.* (Supplement, 1924), 461–473; W. K. Doyle, *Independent Commissions in the Federal Government* (Chapel Hill: 1939). *Cf.* M. C. Trackett, "The Committee as an Instrument of Coordination in the New Deal," 31 *Am. Pol. Sci. Rev.* (April, 1937), 301–310.

On giving the executive more control over the personnel agency as a "tool" of management see: W. E. Mosher, "Personnel: The Executive's Responsibility," 25 *Nat. Mun. Rev.* (May, 1936), 283–288, and "The Next Step in Civil Service Reform," 10 *Nat. Mun. Rev.* (July, 1921), 386–391; E. D. Graper, "Public Employees and the Merit System," 181 *Annals* (Sept., 1935), 80–89; L. D. White, "Public Personnel Administration," 27 *Nat. Mun. Rev.* (Oct., 1938), 494–498. *Contra:* Lewis Meriam, *Personnel Administration in the Federal Government* (Washington: 1937—pamphlet).

For further approaches to "decentralization" consult: M. L. Cooke, "Notes on Governmental and Industrial Administration in a Democracy," 3 *Soc. Adv. Man. Jour.* (July–Sept., 1938), 139–143 (developing the decentralizing tendencies of the "functionalism" of scientific management—on which general subject see also, of course, the writings of M. P. Follett); J. M. Turner, "Democracy in Administration," 17 *Am. Pol. Sci. Rev.* (May, 1923), 216–230; J. M. Landis, *The Administrative Process* (New Haven: 1938), 24–28; E. D. Fite, *Government by Cooperation* (New York: 1932); D. B. Truman, *Administrative Decentralization: A Study of the Chicago Field Offices of the United States Department of Agriculture* (Chicago: 1940), especially chs. 1 and 10; J. P. Clark, "Joint Activity Between Federal and

State Officials" 51 *Pol. Sci. Q.* (June, 1936), 230–269; W. W. Stockberger, "The Democratic Way of Administration," 2 *Pub. Adm. Rev.* (June, 1939: Syracuse), 3–4; F. Morstein Marx, "Bureaucracy and Consultation," 1 *Rev. of Pol.* (Jan., 1939), 84–100—holding the customary devices of diffusion to be in fact desirable agents of *integration.*

The literature on "responsibility" is not considered in detail in this essay. Consult: F. Morstein Marx, "Administrative Responsibility," in *Public Management in the New Democracy* (New York: 1940), Marx, ed., 218–251; M. E. Dimock, "Forms of Control over Administrative Action," in *Essays on the Law and Practice of Governmental Administration,* 287–321; C. J. Friedrich and Taylor Cole, *Responsible Bureaucracy* (Cambridge: 1932); Friedrich, "Responsible Government Service under the American Constitution," in Friedrich *et al., Problems of the American Public Service* (New York: 1935), 3–72; and Friedrich's essay in *Public Policy, I* (Cambridge, Mass.: 1940), 3–24; Herman Finer, "Better Government Personnel," 51 *Pol. Sci. Q.* (Dec., 1936), 569–599, and "Administrative Responsibility in Democratic Government," 1 *Pub. Adm. Rev.* (Summer, 1941), 335–350.

PART III

SOME FUNDAMENTAL CONCEPTS: A CRITIQUE

Chapter 9

PRINCIPLES, THEORY OF ORGANIZATION AND SCIENTIFIC METHOD

The concept of "principles" has been prominent in American public administration. Many "principles" have been asserted, defended, elaborated. Much writing has assumed that principles exist, are cognizable, and valid.

Where did this concept arise and what has it meant to administrative writers? In what sense can principles of administration be said to "exist," be "true" or "valid"?

"Cosmic Constitutionalism": Conflation of Moral and Physical Necessity

The idea of principles of administration arose from and is colored by the idea of a "cosmic constitutionalism" that has been a prominent aspect of American thought. This idea of a "cosmic constitutionalism" is characterized by a conflation, a fusion and confusion, of the ideas of moral and physical necessity. How this conflation came about is an oft-told tale.

Two Ideas of Law.—A heritage from the medieval world to the modern was a very strong belief in and respect for "law." The world, in the medieval scheme of things, was conceived as organized and moved in accordance with various types of laws, all nicely adjusted each to the other, and extending from the mind of God to the minutest concerns of His creatures. Through the churches, by means of such political philosophers as Hooker and such jurists as Suarez and Coke—by many means, this notion of a world run by law was adapted for and transmitted to the modern world.

Meanwhile, on the ruins of ancient thought, the structure of modern science was being erected. This science, in its most characteristic and spectacular aspects, also spoke the language of "laws" or "principles." In Western culture, generally, there occurred an overlapping and fusing of these two notions of "law" or "principle."

In some respects this fusing was quite natural. The notion that God—or the Author of Nature—runs the world by laws did not seem inconsistent with the discovery of the laws of thermodynamics: the latter simply are God's laws discovered by man.[1]

There is, however, an area of disagreement between these two notions of law, and the frequent failure to discern it has been a source of much confusion. In essence the notion of moral necessity or "higher law" is this: that right and justice are objective; that there is something "out there," independent of man—God, Platonic Forms, the World Spirit, the Laws of the Universe, etc.—that sets a pattern of behavior obligatory upon good men. The meaning of "law" for science is bound up with profound disputes over such matters as the existence and nature of causality. But it can be stated with assurance that such laws are *not* in essence normative laws—*i.e.* laws that purport to tell man what he *should* do. The distinction between the two types of law is clear. Moral laws purport to tell us *what ought to be true,* and their "meaning" lies in the fact of discrepancy between what ought to be true and what is actually (generally or universally) the case. Physical laws purport to tell us what is *actually the case,* and they are "laws" only if they describe or coincide with "reality."

"Higher Law" and the American Faith.—Faith in law of all kinds, and particularly belief in "higher law," was an outstanding characteristic of American communal psychology in the nineteenth century—and continues strong, though diminished. There are, so the belief holds, laws or principles according to which any good and permanent society must be built. These laws are cognizable by man, and it is obligatory upon him to discover and obey them. Man is disclosing more clearly these fundamental principles and following them more diligently; hence he is progressing—however slowly, he is on the road to perfection. Usually, although not necessarily, this belief has had a theological coloring. "The basic postulate of the democratic faith," writes Ralph Gabriel, "affirmed that God, the Creator of man, has also created a moral law for his government and has endowed him with a conscience with which to apprehend it. Underneath and supporting human society, as the basic rock supports the hills, is a moral order which is the abiding place of

---

[1] Students of social phenomena were "taken in" by and contributed to the fusion of the two notions of law. The "laws" of classical economics are the prime example. These laws, in the view of the Great Names, are at once (1) statements about what is inevitably true of economic life, and (2) statements of what *ought* to be true about economic life.

the eternal principles of truth and righteousness. The reiteration of this doctrine of the moral order runs through mid-nineteenth-century social and political thought like the rhythm of the drums through the forest scene of O'Neill's *Emperor Jones.*" [2] There are principles governing man's society just as there are principles inexorably determining the paths of the sun and the moon. *Man violates these principles at his own peril.*

Our thesis has been stated: that the notion of "principles" was derived from, or colored by, this notion of "cosmic constitutionalism"; that the traditional principles of public administration are really closely akin to the "principles" of the *philosophes,* of St. Thomas, of Cicero and of Plato. The imperative of higher law is always conceived as derived from what is most valid, most powerful, most highly honored. Historically, this has most frequently been God. But in late nineteenth- and early twentieth-century America it has often been SCIENCE.

Reformism and "Principles."—The mingling of the normative and the scientific conceptions of law in Reformism is so evident as to be indisputable. Consider, for example, a discourse upon civil service reform by George L. Prentiss: "We may boast never so loudly of our democratic freedom; there is one and only one way of preserving it unimpaired—namely, by conforming in all things to the divine laws of social order and well-being. These laws are as immutable as that of gravitation; there is with them no respect of persons or of forms of government, and if violated, they are, to say the least of it, quite as sure to avenge themselves upon republican transgressors as upon those of any other name." [3]

The moral imperative of the "merit principle" in administration was made quite clear also by Charles J. Bonaparte: "All men who have sufficiently reflected and are sufficiently informed to entertain an intelligent opinion must and do think alike on the subject; . . . no one who has any claim at all to public attention really doubts that the principle of civil service reform is just and benevolent; if he says that he doubts this 'principle' in official conduct, he does so, just as he may commit theft or adultery, knowing that he does wrong." [4] We can "make no bargain with iniquity."

[2] *The Course of American Democratic Thought* (New York: 1940), 14.

[3] *Our National Bane* (New York: 1877, pamphlet), 2. "*Wherever a wrong principle is admitted and acted upon, there an abuse will, in due time, make its appearance.*" 3. Italics in original.

[4] "Civil Service Reform as a Moral Issue," in 1889 *Proceedings,* National Civil Service Reform League, 43–48, 43–44.

Principles vs. Empiricism.—Among the early writers the method of "principles" was distinguished from "mere empiricism." The language in which they express the superiority of "principles" over "empiricism" is that of other "higher law" adherents. There is the same discernment of a structure of permanence and significance beneath the flux and ephemerae of immediately apprehended phenomena. There is the same assertion that the "principles" of this "real world" should guide man's activities.

Organizations such as the National Municipal League, wrote Dorman B. Eaton in 1899, "have done much to make it plain that no superficial or merely empirical dealing with municipal affairs will give us tolerable city government; they have made it clear that great questions of principle are involved. . . ." [5] The object of administrative study, declared Woodrow Wilson, "is to rescue executive methods from the confusion and costliness of empirical experiment and set them upon foundations laid deep in stable principle." [6] Small wonder that G. A. Graham observed recently that "the orthodoxy of today is perhaps more heavily loaded with nineteenth-century connotations than we like to think." [7]

How the "canons of integration" became the "stable principles" of public administration was seen in the preceding chapter. Here, we need only point out that the dictates of Right Reason have seemed quite different to others in other times; faced with other problems, they discerned other dictates of the "real world."

Principles of Public Administration

It would be impossible to prove, beyond question, that "principles" in public administration in more recent times have been higher-law concepts; the case can only rest upon the similarity of the language. But it would be more difficult to prove to a disinterested spectator that they actually have the sanction that is claimed for them—that of science. Before inquiring what "science" is, however, it will be instructive to note the traditional treatment of

---

[5] *Government of Municipalities* (New York), 5.

[6] "The Study of Administration," 2 *Pol. Sci. Q.* (June, 1887), 197–222, 210. "The empirical influences which now pervade the sphere of government will also decline, and the management of public affairs will take on a more scientific character." H. J. Ford, *The Rise and Growth of American Politics* (New York: 1898), 371.

[7] *Education for Public Administration* (Chicago: 1941), 57. The similar treatment of "principles" by public administration and scientific management, as well as borrowings from scientific management at this point, was discussed in Chapter 2. See N. A. Brisco's, *Economics of Efficiency* (New York: 1914), 93 and 102. *Cf.* H. J. Bruere, *The New City Government* (New York: 1912), 368; and M. L. Cooke, *Our Cities Awake* (Garden City: 1918), 97.

"principles" by administrative writers; and the extent and nature of revolt against principles among administrative writers.

Principles in Theory.—Best known of the writers giving prominence to the notion of principles is W. F. Willoughby. Any student of the subject would be blind to overlook Willoughby's real contributions to administrative study. But he would be mistaken if he thought Willoughby's statements on methodology a contribution, or that Willoughby's real contribution has any but a purely formal connection with the methodology he professes.

Administration, wrote Willoughby in 1919 when the discipline was struggling for existence and needed every scrap of prestige, is "if not a science, a subject to the study of which the scientific method should be rigidly applied."

> Though the problems of administration are of great complexity and vary with the conditions under which each operation of government is carried on, there are certain fundamental principles and practices which must obtain in all governmental undertakings, if efficiency and economy in operation are to be secured.[8]

For the solution of the problems of public administration it must be recognized that two things are necessary:

> First, a greater fund of exact information than has heretofore been available; second, the formulation and adoption of scientifically determined principles of administrative organization and procedure.[9]

In 1937 Willoughby made a formal statement of his views about science and the discovery of principles. "There are," he wrote, "fundamental principles of general application, analogous to those characterizing any science, which must be observed if the end of administration, efficiency in operation, is to be secured; and . . . these principles are to be determined, and their significance made known, only by the rigid application of scientific methods."[10] If true principles can be established and "brought home to those responsible for determining governmental conditions, a great improvement in the manner in which public affairs are conducted will result."[11] In short

---

[8] Introduction to G. A. Weber's *Organized Efforts for the Improvement of Methods of Administration in the United States* (New York: 1919), 30 (citations by permission of The Brookings Institution).

[9] *Ibid.*, 8.

[10] "The Science of Public Administration," in *Essays in Political Science* (Baltimore: 1937), J. M. Mathews and J. Hart, eds., 39–73, 39 (by permission of Johns Hopkins Press).

[11] *Ibid.*, 42–43. This is reminiscent of Calvin Coolidge's classic dictum, "The business of the legislature is to discover economic laws, and to enact them."

"administration constitutes a science in the sense that it is a subject that needs to be inquired into in a scientific spirit, and that it comprehends fundamental principles that can only be established when studied in this scientific manner." [12]

Principles in Practice.—The manner in which "principles" has characteristically been applied to the subject matter of administration can be illustrated by excerpts from the writings of Harvey Walker. Walker's treatment is selected because it is typical of statements by other writers who have used the term without definition or explanation. "The principles of public administration," he writes in 1933, explaining American conceptions to British students, "are derived from the most successful technique used in governments or in private business. For convenience they are classified under the following heads: (1) organization, (2) budget, (3) accounting and auditing, (4) purchasing, (5) personnel, and (6) miscellaneous services. . . ." [13] In his *Public Administration in the United States* he undertakes to state the principles of organization. "The first . . . is that administrative work may be most efficiently organized by function." (This seems to assert something "scientifically" true of any organization.) "A second principle which must be followed in setting up and operating an administrative mechanism in a democracy is that every officer should be responsive to public control." (Since it rests upon a philosophy of government, this is obviously normative.) "A final principle is that staff and line activities should be separated and the staff functions placed under the immediate control of the chief administrative officer of the government." [14] (Is the sanction moral or physical?) A little later he notes that "the organization of the British city violates most of the principles of public administration accepted in the United States" [15]—yet, he says, it works admirably!

The Pragmatic Revolt.—In recent years there have been some attempts to deal more consciously, carefully, and critically with the notion of principles. To these we will turn in just a moment. First, however, it should be noted that a considerable number of administrative students have simply abandoned the "principles" approach to administration in favor of a more "pragmatic" attitude.

---

[12] *Ibid.*, 57.

[13] "An American Conception of Public Administration," 11 *Jour. of Pub. Adm.* (Jan.), 15–19, 15.

[14] New York: 1927, 61–62. (By permission of Rinehart & Co., Inc.)

[15] *Ibid.*, 86. Another writer states that "practical situations" may present problems "the only solution for which may be the violation of organization principles."

The widespread abandonment of "principles" may be put down generally to the increasing maturation and sophistication of public administration. But several sources of the "pragmatic" or "sophisticated" approach are discernible. In the first place, there is the fact that the "principles" asserted have generally been the "canons of integration." Hence it has been natural for dissenters to deny the general concept as well as specific principles—thus the group associated with the Brookings Institution.[16] Second, factual studies of broad conception and thorough execution induced in some persons the conviction that asserted "principles" were but hasty, unproved generalizations; and a strong feeling that administrative reality is much more subtle than it had been supposed, and intimately and inextricably bound up with "what is administered." Third, the elaboration and popularization of pragmatic philosophy induced a temper of mind more hospitable to a world of "loose ends," relativity, and experimentation; and opposed to belief in "principles."

A passage from A. B. Hall may be taken as a typical illustration of the attitude of those who have thus abandoned the "principles" approach. He does not find a critique of the concept necessary—he merely "sloughs it off" in favor of newer and more vital considerations. Students of politics, he finds,

> are becoming increasingly aware that problems of public administration can be adequately understood only in the light of the policies to be administered. Administration cannot be studied in a vacuum. The nature and scope of administrative techniques are conditioned largely by the content of the policies involved. The theory that all the different and diverse functions of government could be fitted into a uniform, symmetrical administrative set-up has become obsolete. A more pragmatic, experimental point of view now prevails. There may be certain fundamental principles of human behavior universally applicable to the problems of administration, but they are so few in number that they afford but little aid to the political engineer who must take a new policy and translate it into an effective system of administration.[17]

A. C. Millspaugh has many times expressed similar views on the contingent and valuational nature of administrative organization

---

[16] The fact that the Brookings Institution is a center of the "pragmatic" school is circumstantial proof of my assertion above that Willoughby's talk of "science" and "principles" had no necessary connection with his real methods of administrative study, nor with his intimate beliefs about "good administration." The Institution has generally followed its first director's methods and accepted his characteristic beliefs—while ignoring the authority he claimed for them.

[17] In preface to A. C. Millspaugh's *Public Welfare Organization* (Washington: 1935), vii (by permission of The Brookings Institution).

and procedure. Thus:

> What the organization should be depends on a variety of considera-
> tions. Among the important factors . . . are the functions to be per-
> formed, the relationships of one function to another, the technical or
> non-technical nature of activities and operations, the effectiveness or
> ineffectiveness of present agencies, and the availability of funds, which
> in turn depends upon the amount and distribution of taxable resources.
> . . . In other words, administrative organization is experimental and
> evolutionary. . . .[18]

The "pragmatic" approach reaches a logical climax in Schuyler
Wallace's *Federal Departmentalization: A Critique of Theories of
Organization,* in which even the pragmatic Brookings "revisionists"
are charged with having "inarticulate major premises" which determine their answers to administrative problems. Wallace conducts
a meticulous survey of the pro's and con's of centralizing and decentralizing arguments—and draws no conclusion except that "it
should be apparent that any intelligent decision as to the type of administrative organization best suited to the needs of the country
depends not upon some simple formula but upon the studied consideration of a multitude of factors. Some of these are seemingly
only remotely connected, if at all, with the process of administration;
they are, nevertheless, of transcendent importance." [19]

Does this bring us full cycle and leave us again "weltering in
empiricism?"

---

[18] In *Report on a Survey of Organization and Administration of Oklahoma,* by
the Institute for Government Research (Oklahoma City: 1935), 4. *Cf. Public Welfare Organization,* 73; *Crime Control by the National Government* (Washington:
1937), 26 ff.; "Democracy and Administrative Organization," in *Essays in Political
Science* (Baltimore: 1937), 64–73, *passim;* Lewis Meriam and L. F. Schmeckebier,
Reorganization of the National Government: What Does It Involve? (Washington:
1939), 49 ff., especially 83 ff.; and Meriam, *Public Service and Special Training*
(Chicago: 1936), 21–22. See also on the Brookings group their report for the
Byrd Committee: *Investigation of Executive Agencies of the Government,* Senate
Report 1275, 75th Congress, 1st Session (1937), 12 ff., especially 24–25.

[19] New York: 1941, 227 (by permission of Columbia University Press). *Cf.*
J. M. Gaus, "A Quarter Century of Public Administration," 5 *Adv. Man.* (Oct.–
Dec., 1940), 177–179, 179. Much of the literature of decentralization discussed in
the preceding chapter is explicitly or by general tenor "anti-principles." Literature,
ignoring or repudiating the politics-administration formula, is also anti-principles in
tendency.

Commenting recently upon the "relative youth and inarticulateness of public
administration as an organized field of human knowledge" F. Morstein Marx says,
"As yet its basic data have been neither fully brought together nor grouped analyti-
cally in such a way that practical men in need of principles may assume with confidence to operate on verified hypotheses. Half-truth still stalks unchecked through
the beginning science of public management. Premature generalization still parades
in the guise of axiom." *"The Lawyer's Role in Public Administration,"* 55 *Yale Law
Jour.* (April, 1946), 498–526, 525. For notes on present tendencies—"general
tendencies that have made public administration more relation-conscious and less
authority-minded"—see Part II of this essay.

Critical Treatments of "Principles"

We come now to a consideration of three attempts to deal carefully and critically with the concept of principles. They are by L. D. White, Herman Finer, and E. O. Stene.[20]

L. D. White: Critical Common Sense.—White, in an essay entitled "The Meaning of Principles in Public Administration," applies his extraordinary gift of common sense to the problem and gives us a common-sense answer. Consulting the dictionaries he discovers, among other meanings, "a standard accepted as a guide to action."[21] He observes that American students have been *par excellence* men of action; he then questions what meaning can be and should be given to principles as guides to action.

"Would it not be desirable," he asks, "to restrict the use of the term to mean a hypothesis or proposition, so adequately tested by observation and/or experiment that it may intelligently be put forward as a guide to action or as a means of understanding? Without expecting experimental or laboratory verification as a *sine qua non,* would it not be desirable to understand that a principle implies (1) an original hypothesis, (2) adequate verification, and (3) in consequence the statement of a proposition possessing the quality of generality and conforming to truth at least in the pragmatic sense? In such a sense a principle would be a safe guide for responsible students and leaders of public administration to suggest as a rule of action."[22]

An objection is noted, and commented upon. The objection and the comment are crucial:

> Here the objection may be raised that it is impossible to state what degree of verification by observation suffices to warrant calling a proposition a principle. There may be no ascertained mathematical degree of verification which separates principle from non-principle. All we desire to insist upon here is that too many hopes, assertions, and opinions have been called principles, and that too few hypotheses have been subject to conscious verification in their making.[23]

---

[20] Other essays might be added. See, for example, M. E. Dimock's "What Is Public Administration?" 15 *Pub. Man.* (Sept., 1933), 259–262, in which he rails against "sweeping generalizations," "dogmatic certainty," and the "hard and fast principles" characterized as "scientific" by their proponents. *Cf.,* however, his "The Study of Administration," 31 *Am. Pol. Sci. Rev.* (Feb., 1937), 28–40, in which he states that "there are universal rules to be uncovered" and that "principles of administration are applicable to all fields of human activity." There is no explanation given for this apparent *volte face.*

[21] In *The Frontiers of Public Administration* (Chicago: 1936), 13–25, 17. Citations by permission of The University of Chicago Press.

[22] *Ibid.,* 18–19. [23] *Ibid.,* 20.

White leaves all the important questions unanswered, all the logical distinctions blurred. The meaning of "truth," the meaning of "verification," the relationship of "experiment" and "observation" to verification, the crucial difference between principle and non-principle—these are at the heart of the problem. What his treatment amounts to is a warning that we must be sharp about using our wits and careful about using our tongues. With this we can all concur. But it does not compel us to conclude, as he does in his final paragraph, that "a principle, considered as tested hypothesis and applied in the light of its appropriate frame of reference, is as useful a guide to action in the public administration of Russia as of Great Britain, of Irak as of the United States." [24] Or at least it can be insisted that the qualifying phrase "applied in the light of its appropriate frame of reference" contains enough force to vitiate the assertion.

Herman Finer: Logical Distinction.—One of the more acute treatments of "principles" is that of Herman Finer—an Englishman—in his essay "Principles as a Guide to Management." There are, he states, two kinds of principles. There is the principle which is an "objective scientific statement of cause and effect." [25] There is also the principle that is a norm, a moral precept—"a statement of values and final design." The two types are related, for the first type "is partly based upon the second type . . . because in our everyday lives we are not merely guided by what is desirable, but are compelled by what is possible. And we plane down our desires and values by what is possible." [26] The causative principle need not be as definite as a law of physics. It is a guide to action, an indication of cause and effect from the "accumulated teachings of actual experience." Knowledge accumulates with experience; and it is a simple and non-controvertible fact that there is a fund of knowledge with respect to cause and effect in the field of management that will aid a manager in achieving moral principles for which he may be striving. In some cases, it is possible to generalize with almost mathematical certainty, if x, then y. But even where no such definiteness exists, study and thought reveal probabilities, probabilities that can be utilized in public administration.

---

[24] *Ibid.,* 27.

[25] 17 *Pub. Man.* (Oct., 1935), 287–289, 287. See also a report of a round table discussion of "Principles of Public Administration," 1933 *City Manager Yearbook,* 265–288, in which Finer sets forth his views. Apparently speaking extemporaneously and subjected to "heckling," Finer turns as a weathercock in the winds of opinion. But he gives a fine statement of several viewpoints!

[26] *Ibid.*

Several observations are appropriate. First, Finer's analysis of *types* of principles is not complete enough to account for all possibilities. There are patently two types of "principles" that fit the formulae, if *a,* then *b.* One type, the causative, Finer has identified. It is enough to note here that it is by no means a simple matter. "Causation" is a matter of mystery and dispute among philosophers and scientists; certainly since the critical philosophy of Hume, the common-sense notion of causation has been (in the words of Bertrand Russell) "little better than a superstition." Some branches of scientific thought have indeed found it possible to get along without the common-sense concept; their (dynamic) "laws" are merely statements of the relationship of two states of a given system at different *times,* whatever be the final answers to the metaphysical problems. Mathematical formulae of probability occupy a position in physical science that should be pondered by "social science" students intent upon copying science.[27]

There is another type of "principle," however, that fits the pattern, if *a,* then *b.* It is the principle of "formal implication." This principle exists in the realm of formal logic and its special branch, mathematics; it *prescribes* a relationship between formal concepts. This principle may also *describe* "causation"—*i.e.* it may be used to "follow" causation, to "predict" the future. But it is not dependent upon causation, either for its existence or its validity. It moves from basic concepts (axioms, hypothesis, etc.) to conclusion; it does not inquire into the "truth" or "validity" of the basic concepts except incidentally and circumstantially; it does not produce in the conclusion more than is given in the premises—which is its great merit. Euclidian geometry is illustrative. As a system of formal implications, it is valid irrespective of whether the geometry of the world is Euclidian or non-Euclidian.[28]

---

[27] Whether this "probability" concept is in conflict with the "laws of conservation" adduced below, the reader must decide. F. S. C. Northrop, whose analyses are relied upon extensively, finds no irresolvable conflict between the idea of a "relation of necessary connection" between the states of a system at different times, and the concept of probability in quantum mechanics and field physics. *Cf.* "The Philosophical Significance of the Concept of Probability in Quantum Mechanics," 3 *Philos. of Science* (April, 1936), 215–232 and "Causality in Field Physics in Its Bearing upon Biological Causation," 5 *Philos. of Science* (April, 1938), 166–180.

[28] These three types of "principle"—the normative, the causal, the formal—may not exhaust all the possibilities. Certainly, there are other "legitimate" uses of the term. It is, for example, properly used (according to the dictionaries) to designate the "elements" or "rudiments" of a thing. Thus one could speak of the "principles of public administration" just as one would speak of the "elements of chemistry." He would not mean in the first place the "laws" or "formulae" of public administration, nor in the second place the 90-odd constituent "elements" of the world. In ordinary discourse "principle" is, in fact, used quite loosely in this and other senses—as no doubt it is occasionally in this study.

The second matter is Finer's statement that the two types of principle are closely related, that the normative type is partly dependent upon the causal "because in our every-day lives we are not merely guided by what is desirable, but are compelled by what is possible." There is comment above (in Chapter 5) upon the "naturalistic fallacy": the fallacy of believing that an "ought" for human beings can be derived simply from the "facts" of the existential world. In truth, the fact that "in our every-day lives we are not merely guided by what is desirable, but are compelled by what is possible" (which no sensible person would deny) does not prove that moral principles are "partly based" upon physical principles. On the contrary, it would seem to prove that moral principles are rather "partly impeded" by what is possible. Certainly, various types of philosophers would dispute Finer at this point. Those who believe in a realm of autonomous values, for example, would deny, root and branch, any necessary dependence of the spiritual upon the physical. Any evidence that it does so, in fact, is always countered by the postulate that it *ought* not!

The opposite approach to the problem should also be noted. Those among the "real" scientists who have had a keen perception of what they are about certainly have rejected any organic connection of their realm to that of "values" or "norms." Scientific morality has consisted in hewing to the line of "what?" and "how?" and letting the chips of "why?" and "for what purpose?" fall as they may. Only pseudo-scientists have attempted to derive moral principles from the findings of science—imperatives about the mission of a race, for example, from the data of anthropology.

E. O. Stene: Precise Statement.—The third of the recent careful and critical essays on principles is Edwin O. Stene's "An Approach to a Science of Administration." [29] Stene's essay is a culmination and close joining of two related tendencies: (1) the effort, extending now over half a century, to state scientific principles of public administration, and (2) the attempt to delineate a "pure theory of organization." As to the first, Stene's analysis may be no more incisive than that of others, but his statements are perhaps more carefully guarded, his formulations certainly are more precise. As to "theory of organization," Stene builds upon the most notable works in this field,[30] attempting to generalize upon them and to formulate their data as irreducible causal relations. The proposi-

---

[29] 34 *Am. Pol. Sci. Rev.* (Dec., 1940), 1124–1137.
[30] Those in *Papers on the Science of Administration* (New York: 1937), Luther Gulick and L. Urwick, eds.; works by C. I. Barnard, James Mooney, and others.

tions he sets forth make no distinction between public and private organization.

Stene begins by observing that, though writers on public administration place much emphasis upon the possibilities and importance of scientific principles in their field, few have sought to state their basic premises. When they announce a principle it is by name only, not "in terms of precise causal relations which can be verified or which can serve adequately as bases for further reasoning." [31] Stene digs for bedrock. He seeks to lay bare some fundamental postulates that will serve both to interpret the mountains of empirical administrative data and as the basis for further theoretical statement.

Since Stene's treatment is itself a summary, an attempt to formulate fundamental concepts of the greatest possible generality in the fewest possible words, it is hardly possible to "summarize" his remarks. An indication of their nature must suffice.

Stene proceeds by means of "definitions," "axioms," and "propositions." The fundamental concept, the first definition, is that of *organization*. "Organization" is a genus of which *administration* is a species. He concludes that the "primary elements of every social organization" are (1) persons, (2) combined efforts, and (3) a common purpose, or a common task to be performed. The following definition is set forth:

> *Definition:* A formal organization is a number of persons who systematically and consciously combine their individual efforts for the accomplishment of a common task.[32]

He then reasons as follows. The "effectiveness of an organization" is measured by the extent to which it carries out its purpose, and

> The degree to which an organization accomplishes its task depends upon three primary factors; namely, (1) the accomplishments of individual members, (2) the number of members, and (3) the coordination of individual efforts. . . . The third, with which this article is particularly concerned, is the factor which determines the efficiency of the organization.[33]

---

[31] *Ibid.,* 1124–1125.

[32] *Ibid.,* 1127.

[33] *Ibid.,* 1128. "Coordination involves several essentials, among which are (1) the attachment of individual accomplishments to the common task, (2) the avoidance of individual activities which interfere with or nullify one another, (3) the performance of all activities necessary to make any given individual accomplishment contribute to the common purpose, and (4) the timing and placement of individual activities in such relationship to each other that the common purpose will be accomplished." 1128.

Now, since all things that aid in attainment of organizational objectives operate through coordination, therefore

> the principle of coordination, which I state here in terms of causal relationship, may be classed as the first axiom in a relational theory of administration:

> *Axiom I:* The degree to which any given organization approaches the full realization of its objectives tends to vary directly with the co-ordination of individual efforts within that organization.[34]

Having stated this "basic axiom," Stene proceeds to examine the things that tend to facilitate or impede coordination. He rejects the "principle of leadership and command" as next in importance to that of coordination. This "leadership" point of view ignores the fact that routine coordination proceeds in any established organization without need of leadership, that "the organization has acquired a *habit* of coordination." Stene then makes a definition of "organization routine," [35] and uses it as the basis for his first "proposition."

> *Proposition I:* Coordination of activities within an organization tends to vary directly with the degree to which essential and recurring functions have become part of the organization routine.[36]

At this point, having illustrated the usage of "axiom" and "proposition," the survey must be broken off. Suffice it that the analysis extends to three axioms and five propositions.

Stene's essay, it was stated, represents the furthest extension of two tendencies: the "principles" tradition in public administration, and the quest for a "theory of organization." Standing in this position, it probably displays more virtues and fewer vices than do most other works in either category. There are certainly fewer sins of commission than in most writings on "principles"; and in clarity and definiteness of statement it excels. In comparison with other "theory of organization" writings it displays similar virtues. It is thus because it brings to a focus many important questions and has important generic qualities that the criticism below is made to turn upon it.

---

[34] *Ibid.*
[35] *"Definition:* Organization routine is that part of any organization's activities which has become habitual because of repetition and which is followed regularly without specific directions or detailed supervision by any member of the organization." 1129.
[36] *Ibid.*

Theory of Organization

First, however, our use of the term "theory of organization" warrants further explanation. There has grown up the idea that "organization" *per se* is a field of inquiry, a subject of study. In this, the common aspects of all organization are stressed, particularities of actual organizations lightly regarded. The distinction between public and private administration is minimized or declared nonexistent. There are deemed to be "constants" in organization that can be isolated and made the subject of "scientific" propositions.

The sources of the "pure theory of organization" notion are several. It is, of course, an aspect of the general drift to "positivism," "objectivity," and "science" that was discussed in the introductory chapters. It doubtless has drawn support from the divorce of "administration" from "politics," from the presumption, expressed as early as Wilson, that for democracy "the question of efficiency is the same . . . as for any other kind of polity. . . ." [37] It seems also to be related to the idea of "the one best way" of scientific management, and to the notion, prominent in the scientific management movement, that "the facts" relevant to a particular problem are ascertainable by scientific inquiry and, having been discovered, determine proper conduct. The "facts" are presumed to be constants and to be measurable, just as are the factors involved in steel-cutting. The formulae for efficient steel-cutting are the same in the Urals as in the Appalachians. Organization can be studied in the same way, and with much the same results. The issue of this inquiry is a theory of organization universally valid or right; any organization is valid—or, for that matter, is an organization—only to the extent that it conforms to the norm, or at least utilizes the "principles" of organization. [38]

Perhaps the most striking aspect of "theory of organization" is its rationalism. In the pages of Fayol and Urwick one recaptures some of the spirit of Condorcet and Bentham. People are conceived as fundamentally rational, society as fundamentally a rational construction. People are fundamentally the same; one studies society scientifically by looking for "lowest common denominators." People and organization parts are regarded more or less as though

---

[37] "Democracy and Efficiency," 87 *Atlantic Monthly* (March, 1901), 289–299, 296.

[38] See J. D. Mooney, "The Principles of Organization," in *Papers on the Science of Administration* (New York: 1937), L. Gulick and L. Urwick, eds., 91–98, 91–92.

they were the interchangeable parts of modern machinery. There are "principles" to which they must conform.[39]

This idea is sometimes set forth in radical and dogmatic terms. Thus Urwick, in his "Organization as a Technical Problem," [40] confesses that "personal factors intrude" and that they "cannot be ignored." Yet he insists that "individuals are the raw material of organization." "The idea that organization should be built up around and adjusted to individual idiosyncrasies, rather than that individuals should be adapted to the requirements of sound principles of organization, is as foolish as attempting to design an engine to accord with the whimsies of one's maiden aunt rather than with the laws of mechanical science." This is a truly remarkable statement. Do the "laws of mechanical science" have an existence apart from the "idiosyncrasies" of the metals, fuels, and lubricants that constitute an engine?

Others, though insisting that there are principles of organization which should be followed, are more tolerant of the circumstances of time, place and person. Thus J. M. Pfiffner believes that "there are certain broad principles of administrative organization which have been proved sound"; but still "practical situations may present perplexing dilemmas the only solution for which may be the violation of organization principles." [41]

Similarly, the President's Committee on Administrative Management stated its belief that there are "canons of efficiency" that have "emerged universally wherever men have worked together for some common purpose, whether through the state, the church, the private association, or the commercial enterprise." [42] But still the Committee found occasion to observe that:

> Government is a human institution. . . . It is human throughout; it rests not only on formal arrangement, skill and numbers, but even more on attitudes, enthusiasms, and loyalty. It is certainly not a machine, which can be taken apart, redesigned, and put together again on the

---

[39] A limerick by one of my friends in Washington expresses the idea well:
An eager analyst named Belter,
Said: "Away with this helter-skelter.
To me the Art
Of organizational chart
Transcends that of Bruegel the Elder."

[40] Citations from *Papers on the Science of Administration* by permission of the Institute of Public Administration 49–88, 85. I have, perhaps, in seeking to characterize the general movement, given the impression that the "organization theorists" are a readily recognizable group with substantially identical opinions. This is not the case. "Theory of organization" is simply a broad tendency in both public administration and scientific management.

[41] *Municipal Administration* (New York: 1940), 19.

[42] *Report* (Washington: 1937), 2.

basis of mechanical laws. It is more akin to a living organism. The reorganization of government is not a mechanical task. It is a human task and must be approached as a problem of morale and personnel fully as much as a task of logic and management.[43]

Opposition to the "pure theory" point of view is usually in the nature of, or identical with, the "pragmatic" opposition to principles, noted above. The attack is from two sides. Organization theorists are held to be too narrow in that they seek to consider organizations apart from the purposes which motivate and justify them—or else they treat "purpose" as something to be measured and manipulated. On the other hand, organization theorists are held guilty of unjustifiable generality, of ignoring the specificity which is the very "stuff" of actual administration. Short quotations from G. A. Graham will illustrate both of these criticisms. ' (1) "We often forget that all organization is for a purpose. The forms and devices of organization are means to an end. They cannot be appraised apart from their use and purpose. The academic dispute over principles of organization frequently reflects an unidentified disagreement over objectives." (2) "We are also prone to forget that organization is necessarily related to a specific situation. That is, it is an organization *of* something as well as *for* a purpose . . . in public affairs, an organization is not concerned with its members alone; it is an organization of forces in the entire governmental system, perhaps in the entire society." [44]

The "Brookings group" has expressed the most vigorous objection to considering organization *per se* a field of inquiry. "Questions of sound organization," write Lewis Meriam and L. F. Schmeckebier, "cannot be successfully divorced from questions pertaining to the fundamental policy of the government. The establishment of fundamental policy, moreover, frequently involves an arbitration or reconciliation of the interests or points of view of conflicting elements in the body politic. Since organization is undertaken to give effect to policy, questions of policy must be considered together with questions of organization." [45]

---

[43] *Op. cit.*, 34. See also J. M. Gaus' "A Theory of Organization in Public Administration," for a combination of "organization theory" with an insistence upon the importance of human purpose and individual uniqueness, in *The Frontiers of Public Administration* (Chicago: 1936).

[44] "Reorganization—A Question of Executive Institutions," 32 *Am. Pol. Sci. Rev.* (Aug., 1938), 708–718, 708.

[45] *Reorganization of the National Government: What Does It Involve?* (Washington: 1939), 161 (by permission of The Brookings Institution). Criticism of organization theory parallels and overlaps that of principles. Consult the items cited above in that connection.

A. C. Millspaugh similarly finds that:

An administrative organization established without reference to the form and philosophy of the government in which it operates would be shortsighted and unrealistic. Administrative organization should bear its fair share of the burdens of democratic government. . . . Administration alone is inadequate as a social force; it attains its maximum power only when it lends its strength to the larger structure of government.[46]

Recent writings evincing a deep respect for the irrational aspects of human organization attack the "pure theory" school from still another direction. A number of such items display a wholly new interest in the massive emotional substructure of organizations and in the structure of "informal organization" which always supplements and sometimes supplants the formal organization. Discussing the consequences of "bureau shuffling" reorganization, Dimock writes: "I do wish that we administrative people could acquire a deeper appreciation of how serious a matter it is to dig up a flourishing tree and transplant it into someone else's back yard. It takes time to re-establish the root structure and during that time the tree withers." [47]

In a lively and refreshing essay, H. C. Mansfield and F. Morstein Marx have recently discussed aspects of "informal organization" that are not unknown to discerning filing clerks but have all but escaped the attention of students intent upon reducing life to the simplicity of an organization chart.[48] Noting that study of informal organization is "still in its infancy" they give the spotlight for the first time to such phenomena as "men behind the throne," "clubs and clusters," "the old school tie," and even the influence of the boss's personal secretary.

---

[46] *Public Welfare Organization,* 73 (by permission of The Brookings Institution). In a recent essay Gaus argues that "the study of public administration must include its ecology." *Reflections on Public Administration* (University, Alabama: 1947), 6. See also, E. S. Wengert, "The Study of Public Administration," 36 *Am. Pol. Sci. Rev.* (April, 1942), 313–322. The "pure theory" school appears to be on the verge of a general retreat.

[47] *New Horizons in Public Administration* (University, Alabama: 1947), 35— a symposium by Dimock and others. See also ch. 3, an essay by Donald C. Stone on the role and methods of the governmental executive. Stone discusses intelligently (but with an air of surprise) the implications of the discovery that the executive cannot rely upon formal authority and the power of command alone in achieving organizational objectives.

[48] Ch. 13 in *Elements of Public Administration* (New York: 1946), F. Morstein Marx, ed. "It can hardly escape the sharp-eyed observer that administrative bodies —and indeed all organizations, whether legislatures, political parties, labor unions, business enterprises, universities, churches, armies, or professional associations— respond in fact to a variety of informal patterns of influence among their membership." 294 (by permission of Prentice-Hall, Inc.).

Scientific Method and Public Administration

Judgment upon "pure theory of organization" must await consideration of a matter that is fundamental both to it and to the search for principles of public administration: "scientific method."

It must be reported that, with few exceptions, the notions of science and scientific method held by the writers are unable to withstand critical examination. It appears that, unless we except the few trained in some branch of engineering technology, there are among the writers no persons trained in the methodology of an established science.[49] Moreover, so far as the evidence of bibliography indicates, few writers on administration are acquainted with the literature of scientific method: historical, expository, critical, comparative, etc. In short, while students of administration have often invoked the name of science, mere declaration that this or that is scientific does not in fact make it so.[50]

Science and Common Sense.—"Scientific method" is not, as often thought, identical with or an extension of "common sense."[51] Despite the fact that so eminent a person as Thomas Huxley characterized science as common sense, this view must be rejected, both *prima facie* and upon any thorough summary of the evidence. The material "gifts" of science all do violence to common sense; the radio, the aeroplane, the photo-electric eye, etc. And the picture of the world presented by theoretical science—sub-microscopic, microscopic, telescopic, etc.—not only violates common sense, it strains the educated imagination.

Science and Empiricism.—It is necessary to deny also that empiricism is the essence of science. Empiricism and experimentalism, both have a prominent place in the methods of physical science. But

---

[49] Of course the writer is not a "scientist" either!

[50] If "science" be defined—as some writers on administration have defined it, when pressed—simply as "a body of organized knowledge" or even as "knowledge," then of course public administration is a "science." This definition has sound etymological foundations. But most people mean by the term something more, or different from, "a body of organized knowledge"; and most writers on public administration have meant to assert more than that. They have meant a certain *type* or *quality* of knowledge and procedure. Certainly there is little advantage in being "scientific," if the criteria for that status admit also cookery and sword-swallowing.

[51] For my comments upon "scientific method" in this chapter, I am primarily indebted to discussions with F. S. C. Northrop. I have also made use of his *Science and First Principles* (New York: 1931); "The Method and Theories of Physical Science in Their Bearing upon Biological Organization," *Growth* (Supplement, 1940), 127–154; and "The Impossibility of a Theoretical Science of Economic Dynamics," 56 *Quart. Jour. Econ.* (Nov., 1941), 1–17. Northrop is not, of course, responsible for my views, which on some matters differ in important respects from his.

there is much in scientific method which is nonempirical and non-experimental. This close identification, in America, of science with empiricism seems to be the work of persons who espouse pragmatic philosophy, and have sought to give pragmatism the prestige of the "philosophy of science." [52] The popularity of pragmatism seems to have given empiricism and experimentalism a vogue among writers on administration. It has been noted how writers first attacked, but now embrace, empiricism—all in the cause of Science.

Science and "Facts": The Role of Theory in Fact-Finding.— A still more fundamental objection to expressed notions of scientific method must be filed with respect to the "accumulation theory." By "accumulation theory" is meant the notion that if enough facts are accumulated, enough data filed, more and increasingly fine measurements made, sufficient experience studied and experiments recorded, then a science of administration will somehow "emerge," a science with answers to problems of "What is the case?" and—more wonderful—answers to "What should we do?" [53] In the scientific management movement, this notion was put forward in the formula, "in the past the man has been first, in the future the system must be first"; the "system" emerges from, *is immanent in,* the "facts" of existence and emerges from them when they are recorded and manipulated; what is "out there" is obligatory upon man in the same manner as it is in Natural Law. The same motif occurs again and again in the literature of public administration: The scientific approach "involves securing all obtainable facts, associating or correlating them so as to determine what they mean, and deducing the logical course of procedure therefrom. In other words, solve administrative problems by getting the facts and acting in accordance therewith." [54] Even those who recognize the rational and deductive aspects of scientific method place them in subordination to "accumulation." [55]

---

[52] *Cf.* Charles W. Morris, *Pragmatism and the Crisis of Democracy* (Chicago: 1934), and *Logical Positivism, Pragmatism and Scientific Empiricism* (Paris: 1937).

[53] We may, as the following statement suggests, be entering a new era. But its understatement indicates the strength of the faith in facts. "There are many questions which cannot be answered by research. . . . We cannot, in a word, escape the responsibility of using our own judgment in many cases." G. C. S. Benson, *The New Centralization* (New York: 1941), 166–167.

[54] J. M. Pfiffner, *op. cit.,* 63.

[55] Thus Luther Gulick in his "Science, Values and Public Administration," in the *Papers,* 191–195, 194. See also his *The Scientific Approach to the Problems of Society and Government,* 15 *Univ. of Buffalo Studies* (March, 1938), 27–34.

This generalization may not be true of Stene, whose conception of the methods of the physical sciences seems to me substantially correct.

The objections to the "accumulation" theory as a means of adducing rules of conduct have been considered above (see the discussion of the "naturalistic fallacy," in Chapter 5). It must be pointed out, however, that there is much reason to believe that it is quite as inadequate as an explanation of the methods of treating physical science data. Its inadequacy lies in the fact that not enough importance has been assigned to the role of "mind" in the development of science.[56]

Administrative students can be charged with a failure to discern the place that ideas play in *creating* and *defining* "facts." They have presumed that "facts" exist apart from fact-finding people, that they are autonomous, cognizable, and more or less free and equal "somethings." It is this failure to inquire into the concept of "facts," the acceptance merely of man-in-the-street notions on the subject, that is responsible for the passion to apply a measuring stick to everything within the purview of the Administrative State. Scientists do not, someone has observed, rush about in a state of great nervous excitement, counting all the leaves on all the trees.

The truth is, there is no such thing as "pure fact" divorced from all concepts and theory. The reasons for this have been clearly expressed by F. S. C. Northrop:

> The popular fallacy that science is concerned only with facts and has nothing to do with concepts and theory rests upon the failure to draw a distinction between what may be termed observed fact and described fact. "Observed fact" may be defined as that which is immediately apprehended apart from all concepts and theory; "described" fact is observed fact brought under concepts and hence under theory. To have purely observed fact apart from all concepts a scientist could merely stare at his data and never report his observations. . . .[57]

The Role of Theory in Science.—Not only is there no such thing as communicable "fact" apart from idea or purpose, but modern science in its advanced aspects is independent of observed fact in a very important way. Apparently, the "real" or "natural" sciences have a primary and a secondary stage of development. In the primary stage, the procedure is chiefly descriptive and inductive

---

[56] We will not argue the case of some Idealists that this world of "physical" reality is a reflection or aspect of a mind or minds. It is worth noting, however, that most people who, since the time of Bishop Berkeley, have considered the matter seriously, have concluded that the common-sense world of public objects is not immediately apprehended. (This is not true of Kantians; but Kant's epistemology is far removed from common-sense notions.) What *are* immediately apprehended are primitive sense-data that, it can be *experimentally* proved, vary from person to person for the same "objects."

[57] "The Method and Theories of Physical Science," 129–130.

(though by no means free from theory, as we have indicated). In this stage the science moves in the realm of "concepts by inspection," *i.e.* concepts which acquire meaning through reference to directly apprehensible data. Eventually, it is found impossible to comprehend the empirical data, to "make sense of it," without recourse to a fundamentally different procedure. This procedure is the introduction of "concepts by postulation." The meaning of a concept by postulation is not given by the deliverances of sense-awareness. Instead, its meaning is "proposed" or "imagined"; and it is defined "syntactically" by its relationship to other concepts by postulation.[58] Thus, the fundamental concepts of the physical sciences refer to such things as electrons and electro-magnetic propagations, which (at first and directly, at least) are unobservable. These "concepts by postulation" can be verified empirically only by verification of the theorems deduced from them; and this procedure (as Northrop has shown in his discussions of "epistemic correlations") is highly complicated and not in accordance with generally received ideas upon the subject. Even so, since the logical formula by which verification takes place contains a fallacy (that of "affirming the consequent"), it is impossible to prove logically or experimentally that *only* the specified concepts by postulation explain the empirical data. For this reason, scientists attempt to propose every *conceivable* theoretical possibility, to demonstrate that not only is a given theoretical system confirmed by natural or experimental phenomena, but that it is the only theoretical system so confirmed. In doing this, previous error is frequently discovered, and the result is that the conceptual basis of science is constantly shifting. To perform the two functions of "proposal" and "verification," a division of labor has developed, so that in such a science as physics there are both "theoretical" and "experimental" physicists. Stene notes this distinction in his essay, and seeks to perform the theoretical function for administrative study.

The scientific inadequacy of the factual approach in public administration is now patent. It is no defense of present procedures

---

[58] "*A concept by postulation is one the meaning of which is proposed for it by the postulates of the deductive theory in which it occurs.* The crucial factor to note in this definition is that one does not determine the meaning of a concept by postulation by inspecting something which is directly observable; instead, one must examine the postulates of the deductive theory in which the concept occurs. Apart from these postulates, such a concept is a meaningless mark. For example . . . the word 'electron' is a fundamentally different concept and refers to a radically different entity in quantum mechanics from what it did in the electro-magnetic theory of Lorentz. This happens because it is a concept by postulation rather than a concept by inspection, and the postulates of quantum mechanics are different from those of Lorentz' theory." *Ibid.*, 131–132.

in the study of public administration merely to point out that, even according to the analysis here presented, the "natural history" stage of a science comes first and that few students would claim that it has passed beyond that stage in this field. There is not adequate appreciation of the role that theory must play even in the *primary* stage of a science. Scientific theories do not necessarily emerge from, or rely upon, a large accumulation of data or repetition of instances.[59] To use the apocryphal example of Newton and the apple, it was not because Newton saw many apples—or anything else—fall, that he was able to formulate in his mechanics the laws of gravitation. As Newton himself stated, the basic concepts of his system, such as mass and momentum, are not common-sense notions at all, but theoretical concepts. The heaping up of facts with a blind faith that a science must eventually emerge if the pile becomes large enough can only be characterized as naive.

Scientific Method and "Values."—So far it has been assumed, as students of administration have frequently assumed, that the subject matter of administrative study lends itself to "scientific" treatment in the same manner as do tantalum atoms, spiral nebulae, and frog embryos. An attempt has been made to show what, on that assumption, would be a "scientific" relationship between administrative students and their subject matter. But it may not be true—is not true—that the subject matter of administrative study is characteristically or chiefly of the same nature as that of the "real sciences."

A physical science problem is a problem of "What is the case?" An administrative problem is characteristically a problem of "What should be done?" Administrative study, as any "social science," is concerned primarily with *human beings,* a type of being characterized by *thinking* and *valuing..* Thinking implies creativeness, free will.[60] Valuing implies morality, conceptions of right and wrong. *It is submitted that the established techniques of science are inapplicable to thinking and valuing human beings.*

---

[59] See the first and final chapters of *Science and First Principles, passim.*

[60] This is admittedly a cavalier treatment of the fundamental question of free will versus determinism. But a few considerations may be brought forward: (1) It is because the material of science is not "free" but "determined" that scientific predictions achieve their accuracy. (I am disregarding recent "probability" theory.) (2) There is an inverse correlation between what is *apparently* an area of free will in human concerns and the predictability of these concerns. (3) As Morris Cohen has observed, even if human affairs obey causality rules, it may be true that because of the infinite complexity of human affairs, these affairs would not demonstrate any "laws" at all to a finite being in finite time.

It is not denied, of course, that human beings exist in a "natural" order, that in some sense they are a part of it, obey its laws, are compelled by it. It is not denied that some administrative matters are susceptible to treatment in the mode of natural science. Many of them are thus amenable, and should be so approached. But it is asserted—as administrative students have been increasingly admitting or asserting—that administration is generally suffused with questions of value. We submit that these questions of value are not amenable to scientific treatment. We hold it to be a fundamental error that "if a science of cause and effect could be worked out, it would be possible to tell what government should do and when the response should be made." If mechanical cause and effect obtained in the realm of human affairs no one would *need* to tell the government what to do; what it does would be predetermined, fixed, and invariable. It is only because free will exists in the realm of human affairs that it is necessary or possible "to tell what government should do and when the response should be made."

The essentially normative nature of administrative problems becomes evident when one examines some of the "principles" proposed with respect to them. Consider the following: "The fundamental principles of efficient administration—namely, expert administrators and concentration and centralization of administrative powers—have been consistently honored in their breach in American municipal government." [61] The real nature of such statements is made evident when paraphrased as a scientific discussion: "The fundamental principles of thermodynamics—namely, that energy is neither created nor destroyed by any transformation of it from one form to another; but that the amount of energy unavailable for work tends toward a maximum—have been consistently honored in their breach in American engineering." Or consider the following: "The checks and balances system makes it necessary and inevitable to violate public administration's central principles." [62] Compare: "The sympathetic nervous system makes it necessary and inevitable to violate biology's central principles."

Possibility of a Theory of Administrative Dynamics.—Not all "principles," however, are discussed in such patently normative terms. Stene's "axioms" and "propositions," notably, use only the indicative mode. They seem also "true" or self-evident in a sense in which such a proposition as "there should always be an appointed

---

[61] H. G. James, *Applied City Government* (New York: 1914), 54.
[62] M. E. Dimock, "The Study of Administration," 31 *Am. Pol. Sci. Rev.* (Feb., 1937), 28–40, 34.

chief-executive" is not true or self-evident. The question arises, therefore, in what the difference consists; and whether Stene's principles are of the nature of the formulae of science. Northrop's essay on "The Impossibility of a Theoretical Science of Economic Dynamics" is germane. For there is a similarity between Stene's formulation and the theoretical formulation of modern economics.

Northrop's thesis is that the nature of the subject matter of economics makes impossible a science of economic dynamics. The nature of a scientific theory of dynamics is that it is "an empirically verified deductive system, providing primitive concepts and postulates defining the present state" of the system "in such a way that, once its quantitative values were determined empirically, the theory, through its postulates and theorems, would enable one to deduce a future state of the system without any further appeal to empirical factors." [63] The data of such a science are from and about the objective or existential world; it is presumed that the world of which we have knowledge from sense data is a "public world," *i.e.*, it exists independently of the perceiving subject and the "truth" about it is in some sense the same for all people. In addition, a science with a theoretical dynamics is one for which the "principle of mechanical causation" is presumed to hold. "This presupposes that all future effects are the result of causes or properties of the elementary subject matter which are present now. This is to affirm that this subject obeys conservation laws." [64] Thus, in Newtonian mechanics, the laws of conservation of momentum guarantee this for momentum; and the acceptance for space of Euclidian metrical properties constant through time guarantees it for position.

Economics does not meet these specifications. In the first place, the subject matter of economic theory is not objective or existential. The subject matter is "economic goods," and the fundamental concept is "value" or "valuation." An "economic good" is not an objective, physical object or activity, but it is, instead, "a relation between such an object or activity and an individual person—a relation, moreover, which exhibits itself introspectively in the person's interest in and desire for that object." [65] The subject matter to which economic theory refers is "not objective in the sense either of the immediately inspected sense-data or the verified naturalistic factors. As Professor Robbins has put it, 'There is no quality in

---

[63] *Op cit.*, 1. "In short, a theory of dynamics exists for a given science when its concepts are sufficient to designate the specific state of a system at a given time and its postulates permit the deduction of a specific state for any future time." 1–2.

[64] *Ibid.*, 9.

[65] *Ibid.*, 4.

things taken out of their relation to men which can make them economic goods. There is no quality in services taken out of relation to the end served which makes them economic. Whether a particular thing or a particular service is an economic good depends entirely on its relation to valuations.' " [66]

In the second place, the procedure of economics in attaining a "publicly valid" theory has been quite different from that of a natural science. Natural science attains publicly valid theory by virtue of its reliance upon objective phenomena; it is able to make statements about the *specific* qualities of phenomena that can be empirically verified; [67] in a deductively formulated science, the specific qualities of a system at one time can be exactly formulated or correlated with the specific qualities of that system at another time. On the other hand, economics has as its subject matter "valuations," given introspectively for single individuals. Since individuals differ, a different "science of economics" might result for each person. To meet this difficulty, to make economics "publicly valid," economists proceeded "by ignoring the specificity of the private valuations which vary from person to person" and by basing their discipline "upon the generic property of the concrete immediately inspected wants apart from their content and concrete specific character." [68]   In short, they postulated

> merely that any individual inspects wants of some kind and that these wants take on an order because of the individual's preferences. Although the particular valuations are relative, varying from person to person, and thus do not have public validity, the fact that any individual does make valuations of some kind, which in every instance do order themselves, is not a private, relativistic fact but a fact which is true for everybody. In this manner a science which found its subject matter to be constituted of private, introspected, relativistic, personal valuations nevertheless attained a theory which is publicly valid.[69]

The reasons why economics cannot achieve a theoretical dynamics now are apparent. Its basic concepts, seemingly made imperative by the nature of the subject matter, refer only to the *generic* properties of a system; whereas the basic requirement of a theoretical dynamics is concepts defining the state of a system at a given time with respect

[66] *Ibid.*, 5–6. In the nineteenth century bustles were economic goods; in the twentieth century they are a source of low humor. Before the armistice the products of the production lines are economic goods; one minute after they are economic waste.

[67] The postulates cannot be empirically verified, as we noted above; the theorems derived from them can be.

[68] *Ibid.*, 6–7.

[69] *Ibid.*, 7.

to its specific as well as its generic properties. Moreover, even were this not the case, a dynamic theory would be impossible because of the requirement with respect to conservation laws in the system. There is no "relation of necessary connection" joining the specific state of a system at a given time to a specific state at any other time. Instead, future supply and demand are uncertain; in some measure they are subject to free will instead of determinism.

All of this does not prove that economic theory is worthless— as some have held—but merely that it is not scientific theory in the sense of natural science. Its uses are in fact considerable.

In the first place, says Northrop, it does provide a theory of economic statistics (albeit, not completely satisfactory); that is, given certain characteristics of the state of a system at a given time, we can deduce other characteristics of that system at that same time. In the second place, it *gives aid* with respect to dynamical problems. One who is acquainted with the generic qualities of an economic system and also has knowledge of its contingent, specific and empirical characteristics can, by means of speculative extrapolation of present tendencies, frequently determine the general outline of future economic phenomena. Certainly he is better situated than the mere empiricist.

A Theory of Administrative Statics.—It seems clear that "theory of organization" in general, and Stene's formulation in particular, have characteristics in common with modern economic theory; and that in a general way the potentialities and limitations of economic theory apply to the study of organization.

Stene, it will be recalled, began by defining a formal organization as "a number of persons who systematically and consciously combine their individual efforts for the accomplishment of a common task." His basic axiom he states as: "The degree to which any given organization approaches the full realization of its objectives tends to vary directly with the coordination of individual efforts within that organization." Attention is directed to the phrases "accomplishment of a common task" and "realization of its objectives." *These are normative conceptions.* What is the significance of their existence at the very foundation of theory of organization?

The significance of "purpose" or "task" or "aim" in theory of organization is the same as "value" or "valuations" in economic theory. The data of administrative study are not organizations as such, any more than the data of economics are objective, physical objects. *The data of administrative study are organizations in rela-*

tion to purposes. "Purpose" is not a constant that can be assumed or an irrelevancy that can be put aside. Instead, it is fundamental to the concept of organization. Organization *qua* organization, is a meaningless notion. Paraphrasing Robbins' statement about economic goods, *"There is no quality in organization and procedures taken out of their relation to man's purposes which can make them administrative goods."*

Further analysis substantiates this viewpoint. The word "coordination" occurs in eight of Stene's definitions, axioms, and propositions, and in the remainder it is clearly implicit. The "first axiom in a rational theory of administration," he tells us, is the "principle of coordination." "Coordination," then, is a fundamental concept.[70] But coordination for coordination's sake is meaningless. "Coordination" must be explained in terms of purpose—as Stene does explain it ("organizational objectives").

Or let us turn to another analysis of organization, that of Luther Gulick. Gulick takes as his point of departure "division of work." "Theory of organization . . . has to do with the structure of coordination imposed upon the work division units of an enterprise. . . . Work division is the foundation of organization; indeed, the reason for organization."[71] This clearly is putting the cart before the horse. The division of labor (or labor itself) does not exist for its own sake. It exists, as Plato observed at the dawn of political theory, to promote man's purposes. Gulick does get around at a later point to considering the role of "ideas" in coordination. He then observes that "the power of an idea to serve as the foundation of coordination is so great that one may observe many examples of coordination even in the absence of any single leader or of any framework of authority."[72] If this is true it seems a strange perverseness to begin a discussion of organization by saying that work division is "the reason" for organization.[73]

But to return to Stene and the similarity between his formulations and those of economic theory. The closeness of this similarity of

---

[70] Northrop states that there must be "relations" as well as "elements" among fundamental concepts. Thus "preference" is the relation among wants or valuations. In terms of this analysis, coordination is presumably a "relational" concept.

[71] "Notes on the Theory of Organization," in the *Papers,* 3–45, 3.

[72] *Ibid.,* 38. J. M. Gaus' essay, "A Theory of Organization in Public Administration," in the *Frontiers,* shows considerable appreciation of the role of purpose.

[73] If the fundamental nature of the concept of purpose is recognized, we may be spared such reports as those of the elaborate experiments at the Hawthorne plant of the Western Electric Company. These experiments are held to prove that an individual's attitude toward himself, his associates, his employment, his place in society and his future—in short, his integration of personality about purpose—affects the amount and quality of his work. Has any reasonable person ever doubted this?

the two is accentuated by the similarity of language and by an analysis of the nature of Stene's allegations. Axiom: "In any particular type of organized activity, coordination tends to vary inversely with the number of persons directly participating." [74] Compare: "The quantity of a commodity which buyers will purchase tends to vary inversely with the price." [75] In their essential nature, Stene's propositions are like those of economics; that is, they define the generic, not the specific, qualities of the system to which they refer. While there is no reason to believe that Stene has made a final statement of administrative theory (which, after all, is much younger than economic theory), he has achieved a theory that seems "publicly valid." By use of the qualifying phrase "tends to vary," by ignoring the specificity of any administrative situation, and by speaking in completely general terms he has achieved statements that seem "true." [76]

It would seem that Stene has most closely approached a statement of "administrative statics," similar to theoretical economic statics. On the analogy of economic statics, an administrative statics would enable one to deduce from given characteristics of an administrative system at a given time other characteristics of the system at the same time; it would enable one, by supplementing theoretical formulae with empirical, contingent data, to predict the future of that administrative system more accurately than if he possessed only the empirical data. At the same time, the impossibility of there being "laws" or "principles," in the sense of the physical sciences, must be recalled. Administrative study, no less than economic study, is at its heart normative. Determinism does not apply to free will; "conservation laws" do not apply to purposive human beings. This is the overwhelming significance of the phrase "tends to vary" in the axioms.

The Problem of Natural vs. Cultural Factors.—There is another problem implicit in this discussion, but not yet clearly stated. It is the problem, inherent in any social study, of distinguishing between "natural" and "cultural" factors, of deciding the proper or the

---

[74] *Op. cit.,* 1131.

[75] C. L. James, *An Outline of the Principles of Economics* (New York: 1934), 76.

[76] It may be that though "true" Stene's statements are useless. Certainly a frustrated "And so what?" is the first reaction to his "axioms" and "propositions." One might, to suggest a possible analogy, build up a system of propositions about books, beginning with definitions and proceeding to axioms such as: "The proportion between red books and blue books tends to vary inversely with the burning of red books and the printing of blue books."

necessary relationship between the two. (The discipline of anthropology, which by its nature finds the problem posed in an acute form, is deeply fissured by the controversies engendered.) Students of administration have not yet considered this problem in a serious way.

The nature of the problem can be demonstrated in economics. The generic qualities of valuation and preference apply to any economic system whatsoever.   This is true because all human beings make valuations and order them by the relation of preference.   It does not follow, however, that the deductions of modern economic theory from these postulates are necessarily true.   (The "deductions" may be faulty logically, they may be conclusions from empirical data not universally valid, they may flow from introspection valid only for the particular writer.)   In fact, many students of economics are ardent in a contrary opinion.   Socialists, for example, think it is both mistaken and immoral to presume that human beings must always act according to the "ideal" laws of a system of private enterprise.   They believe it is possible to educate people to quite different modes of economic behavior.   "Anthropological" economists go the socialists one better.   They regard the economic theory of a given society, ours included, as a species of folklore, and hence "true" only in the sense in which, say, the religion of the Bantus is true.[77]

These considerations are relevant to "principles" and "theory of organization."   It is probably the case that statements can be made about cooperative efforts that apply to *any* cooperative effort by *any* group of humans—if the statement is in broad enough terms.   The

------

[77] This may be a good point to consider Luther Gulick's statement ("Science, Values and Public Administration," in *Papers on the Science of Administration* (New York: 1937), Gulick and L. Urwick, eds., 192) that "in many of the subsidiary but fundamental fields of social knowledge it is possible to put values and ends to one side, or to assume them as constants, just as is done in the pure sciences." The instances he cites hardly prove his point. For example: "Gresham's law with regard to dear currency and cheap currency has validity entirely outside of any notion of what is 'good' or 'bad.' " This "law" is related to values in a more fundamental way than in "the social appraisal and application of the principles deduced," although that itself is fundamental. "Dear currency" and "cheap currency" are not categories of nature, but categories of human value. Apart from the question of complete empirical truth of the proposition in our era, which is very doubtful, there is no reason to believe that the phenomena involved are not related to the peculiar values of a modern, pecuniary society.

(We may note that even with respect to the natural sciences, while it is generally agreed that the truths of science are true irrespective of the nature of the perceiving subject, some persons, even neo-Kantians among the scientists, dispute this. But even granting this, both scientists and philosophers emphasize that the truths of science about the world are answers to questions which it has occurred to *human beings* to ask, and that there is hence no *a priori* reason why they are the only truths or the final truths about existence.)

problem from this angle is finding a use for propositions so broad. On the other hand, when statements with qualities of specificity are made, the problem immediately arises whether the statements are true (if they are true) for *any* organization *qua* organization or whether they are true only because the people concerned are of a given culture pattern and in a certain space-time context.[78] It may be the case that people with different culture patterns vary significantly with respect to cooperative endeavor. In fact, Salvador de Madariaga argues this very plausibly in his *Englishmen, Frenchmen, Spaniards.*[79]

Reflections on Science and Common Sense

This discussion may be concluded with some reflections upon common sense, experience, and science. It has not been our purpose to disparage study of administration; but rather to aid, if possible, in placing it on firmer foundations. To this end, its present foundations have been subjected to severe tests. The possibility must now be admitted that these tests are too severe or are not germane. On this presumption, what should be said?

To begin with, it is no part of our object to discredit "common sense," or a "scientific approach" to the study of administration. Common sense is a rare quality, a precious virtue. And administration is in great need of a scientific approach.

For the purposes of the above analysis a sharp distinction was made between common sense and scientific method, and "scientific" was further narrowed in meaning to refer only to certain assumptions and procedures of such advanced disciplines as chemistry and physics. These distinctions in meaning rested upon real distinctions

---

[78] I am omitting consideration of the problem of individual or racial variations with respect to qualities of organization or cooperation—a tremendous additional complication. This is done to simplify the problem under consideration, not because of a light estimate of the importance of individual and racial variation.

Another point omitted from consideration is that of the "uniqueness" of an administrative situation. Is it or is it not significant that there is no exact repetition in human affairs, that the exact configuration of the data in a given administrative problem has never occurred before and will never occur again?

[79] London: 1928. The analyses of the "organization theorists" proceed in almost complete disregard of other types of analyses of the phenomena of human cooperation—for example, those of social psychology. A cross-fertilization might produce an analysis more pungent, more profound. For other types of approaches see: R. M. MacIver, *Society* (New York: 1931); E. J. Urwick, *A Philosophy of Social Progress* (London: 1920, revised edition); L. T. Hobhouse, *Social Development* (New York: 1924); A. N. Whitehead, *Adventures of Ideas* (New York: 1933). See also works by Morris Ginsberg, Graham Wallas, Leonard Woolf, Ernest Barker, and Gerald Heard. (A philosophical touch will be found in *Public Administration and the United States Department of Agriculture* (Chicago: 1940), by J. M. Gaus and L. O. Wolcott, 289–290.)

of fact, and demonstrated glib assumption and faulty analysis. But perhaps these distinctions did not reveal the whole truth; perhaps they ignored in each case a legitimate residuary meaning.

Common Sense as Wisdom.—Rightly conceived, common sense is indeed a desirable quality in administration and in administrative study. Conceived as general facility of mind, as balance of emotions and "reasonableness" of judgment, as adherence to and progress toward the Golden Mean or Wisdom, we shall never have enough of common sense in human affairs. It is possible that much of administrative study is, and must be, directed toward achieving "common sense" in cooperative endeavor.

The nature of much of the literature suggests that the problems considered and the answers given are essentially "common sense" problems and answers. For example, what to do about Miss Jones, secretary, of long service and otherwise satisfactory, who takes her "sick leave" a day at a time for vacation purposes?[80] From this point of view, administrative common sense is a sort of extension of the social experience or "folk wisdom" of the community. Certainly, much of the literature of centralization and decentralization, respectively, is summarized in the maxims "too many cooks spoil the broth" and "don't put all your eggs in one basket."[81]

Can Common Sense be Communicated?—Granting the desirability of common sense, the question nevertheless remains: to what extent can common sense be "accumulated," "sharpened," made "more sensible"; and in what sense can it be "taught"? (There is little doubt that in some sense we learn, socially as well as individually, from "experience." It is worth noting, however, that the historians, whose profession it is to study human experience, engage in profound and acrimonious argument about what it is we can learn from the past—and some of them deny we can learn anything of value in deciding present or future conduct.)

To take an example, to what extent is it possible to "sharpen" common sense with respect to the "span of control"? There is certainly an advantage in bringing the idea to the attention of anyone managing organized effort; perhaps he or those he controls are not

---

[80] "Why, it's just what they teach in the damned teachers' colleges. 'If the room is too warm, turn down the heat and open a window. If the room is too dark, turn on the lights or raise the shades.'"

[81] On this point see Herbert A. Simon's interesting essay, "The Proverbs of Administration," 6 *Pub. Adm. Rev.* (Winter, 1946), 53–67, 53. On the analytical side Simon's essay is corroborative of many of the points made in this discussion.

making the best disposition of time and energy; this idea may be the clue to greater success. `Still, he might achieve the same general idea by thought and experience—if he is blessed with "common sense"! Certainly people found the general idea valid and acted upon it long before it was "discovered." So far as we are aware, nobody has ever proposed, even in fantasy, that a general give orders directly to all his privates. And on the other hand, the early declarations that there is a certain number of persons that is the *correct* number to control have given way recently to "relativistic" treatments, sensibly concluding that the number to be controlled depends upon the purposes to be realized, the individual capacities concerned, the nature of the work.

Perhaps the proper termination of this discussion is a broader definition of the meaning of "science." There is undoubtedly a temper of mind characterized by general awareness, preciseness, and a disposition to inquire into things. It is called the "scientific outlook," and is opposed in its tenor to acceptance of custom, rule-of-thumb procedures, and "fuzzy" thinking generally. This temper of mind is by no means identical with "common sense," but neither are the two antithetical; in fact there tends to be a measure of overlapping. Perhaps it is the case that common sense in cooperative endeavor *can* be "sharpened," made more "sensible" or effective by the application of this general outlook. We believe it *is* the case.

A final warning. This does not mean that administration can become a "science." The above conclusions on this point are still valid. The "scientific outlook" indeed would lead one to conclude that it is not "scientific" to try to force upon a subject matter a method not suitable to it; that instead *the nature of the subject matter must define the method.* Many administrative matters simply are not, by their nature, amenable to the methods of physical science.[82]

[82] In a discussion that parallels the essential arguments of this chapter Robert A. Dahl reaches similar conclusions: "No science of public administration is possible unless: (1) the place of normative values is made clear; (2) the nature of man in the area of public administration is better understood and his conduct is more predictable; and (3) there is a body of comparative studies from which it may be possible to discover principles and generalities that transcend national boundaries and peculiar historical experiences." "The Science of Public Administration: Three Problems," 7 *Pub. Adm. Rev.* (Winter, 1947), 1–11, 11. His analysis of the "ecology" of the British civil service gives particular weight to the third of these conclusions.

Chapter 10

ECONOMY AND EFFICIENCY

" 'Efficiency with economy,' " remarks an English writer on administration, "is too hackneyed a phrase to have much meaning nowadays; it suffers from being a combination of two of the most abstract words in our language."

This indictment is a serious one. For "economy and efficiency" have inspired reformer and researcher, teacher and student. They have often been held to be the ultimate administrative values, serving to unify and direct all inquiry.

The Rise of Economy and Efficiency

"Economy and efficiency" are related historically to, and were engendered by, the transition in American life from nineteenth-century to twentieth-century conditions.[1] They have been used as weapons of attack and defense in a political struggle. They have, indeed, been "key concepts" in a political philosophy; that is, concepts difficult to define precisely because they are themselves regarded as ultimates, in terms of which other concepts are defined. He whose purpose is historical understanding must approach them with imagination and sympathy as he would *imperium* and *sacerdotium* or "the laws of Nature and Nature's God."

"Economy and efficiency," together with other concepts, such as "scientific," replaced a "moralistic" approach to governmental improvement. Dorman B. Eaton's *Civil Service Reform in Great Britain* (1879) may be taken to illustrate the moralistic approach. In this classic work "efficiency" is seldom, if ever, mentioned; and "economy" occurs infrequently. Instead, such words as "fidelity" and "honesty" sprinkle its pages. Appeal is made to national pride; emphasis is placed upon "the disgrace to republican institutions."

By the turn of the century, however, it was generally agreed that morality, while perhaps desirable, is not enough. Democracy

---

[1] *Cf.*, however, W. H. Edwards, "The State Reorganization Movement," 1 *Dak. L. R.* (April, 1927), 15–41, 18 *n*, pointing out that "efficiency and economy" was used by Thomas Benton in praise of Andrew Jackson—uttered in the same breath with "rotation in office."

must be *able*. Its citizens must be alert and active. The machinery of government must not waste time, money, and energy.[2] The prodigal utilization of our resources must be remedied. If our good purposes fail because of inefficiency—as it appears they may— then *inefficiency is the cardinal sin*.

The Baptism of Efficiency.—In short, a term generally regarded as descriptive, "mechanical," became in fact invested with moral significance. To a considerable extent the exaltation of efficiency must be regarded as the secularization, materialization, of the Protestant conscience. The tenet of efficiency is an article in the faith of "muscular Christianity."

A century's-end essay by C. R. Woodruff evidences the rising force of "efficiency." "The Complexity of American Government Methods" is, as the title suggests, a diatribe against the divisions and dispersions of the American system of government. According to Woodruff, this loosely knit system, established to prevent tyranny in a simple agricultural society, encourages boss-rule and fosters inefficiency and corruption. He urges that we equip ourselves with responsible and efficient governments, adapted to meet our new problems. "Efficiency is of the first consideration in business affairs; it must be first in political affairs." [3]

W. H. Allen's *Efficient Democracy* demonstrates the "moralization" of efficiency. "To be efficient," proclaimed the Director of the New York Bureau of Municipal Research, "is more difficult than to be good. . . . *The goodness that has lasting value to one's fellow-man will be greatly increased and more widely distributed if efficiency tests are applied to all persons and all agencies that are trying to make tomorrow better than today.*" [4] "Goodness" is a "false criterion," for there is no agreement on its meaning and content. Viewed realistically, "good service" means "efficient service."

The high point in the popularity of "efficiency" came in the years immediately preceding the First Great War. It was a rallying cry of Progressivism. Indeed, it was recognized as a "movement" within the larger movement, and became in certain circles a veritable fetish. While it is not literally true, as W. E. Mosher remarks, that the phrase "economy and efficiency" was "first coined by the

---

[2] The prominence of mechanical metaphor in this literature has already been noted. See, for example, W. E. Weyl, *The New Democracy* (New York: 1912), 315.

[3] 15 *Pol. Sci. Q.* (June, 1900), 260–272, 272.

[4] New York: 1907, vii (by permission of Dodd, Mead & Co.). Italics mine.

bureau movement," [5] students and reformers of many kinds became quickly and thoroughly enthusiastic about this new approach during the Progressive years. Woodruff felt moved to remark in 1913 that "efficiency is a word which has been introduced into our municipal vocabulary within a very few years." [6] The bureau movement was certainly instrumental in its popularization.

It is instructive to review the treatment of efficiency by an interpreter of the Progressive era. Seeking to distill the essence of "the efficiency movement" B. P. DeWitt wrote:

> The movement is incapable of any concise definition, and in fact of any definition at all, because it is itself a protest against generalizations and definitions, standing for the specific study and solution of particular problems. The fundamental ideas underlying the efficiency movement are that there is no panacea for municipal ill; that municipal home rule, commission government, and city managers are merely means to an end; that municipal problems depend for their solution upon the same scientific study and analysis that banking and railroad problems require; that any attempt to remove inefficiency and waste must be continuous and not intermittent; that honesty and good intentions cannot take the place of intelligence and ability; and finally that city business is like any other business and needs precisely the same kind of organization, management, and control.[7]

To this liturgical passage he added the following characterization: "The efficiency movement repairs and adapts the machinery of government which the home rule movement frees, the commission movement simplifies, and the social movement uses in the interest of the people." [8] "There are everywhere," wrote another prophet of the era, "signs of an increasing recognition by our more democratic governments that to fulfill their functions they must be efficient." [9]

---

[5] "Reflections on Governmental Research," 28 *Nat. Mun. Rev.* (Oct., 1939), 725–727, 727.
[6] "Simplicity, Publicity and Efficiency in Municipal Affairs," 2 *Nat. Mun. Rev.* (Jan., 1913), 1–10, 7.
[7] *The Progressive Movement* (New York: 1915), 320 (by permission of the author).
[8] *Ibid.*, 339.
[9] W. E. Weyl, *op. cit.*, 313. See also on the efficiency movement: Henry Bruere, "Efficiency in City Government," 41 *Annals* (May, 1912), 3–22; J. L. Barnard, "Training in the Schools for Civic Efficiency," 67 *Annals* (Sept., 1916), 26–33; F. A. Cleveland, *Chapters on Municipal Administration and Accounting* (New York: 1909), 359; Woodrow Wilson, "Democracy and Efficiency," 87 *Atlantic Monthly* (March, 1901), 289–299. With relation to scientific management see: Harrington Emerson, *Efficiency as a Basis for Operation and Wages* (New York: 1909), and *The Twelve Principles of Efficiency* (New York: 1912), *passim;* N. A. Brisco, *Economics of Efficiency* (New York: 1914), *passim.*

Exegesis and Apostasy

"Economy and efficiency," as we believe and argue below, are intimately bound up with "values" or "valuations." For this reason there can be great differences in the meaning ascribed to them. Thus, because they have the appearance of being "impartial" or "scientific" terms, they have occasionally served the ends of those whose purposes might be regarded as more or less reprehensible if stated in another idiom. There have always been reformers and students, chiefly associated with some bureaus of municipal research and taxpayers organizations, whose *primary* purpose is the lowering of taxes, no matter what the cost in human values. "Efficiency" means for them, economy, and "economy" means less money spent by government, more retained by taxpayers—simply that.

Efficiency versus Economy

On the other hand, many writers soon felt obliged to indicate that they meant by "economy and efficiency" something other and greater than penny-pinching. In the down-to-earth language of Walter Weyl in 1912, "it is important that efficiency be not identified with lessened governmental expenditures, with a cheeseparing and a special care for the preservation of governmental lead pencils and the soap and towels in the public offices. In these days of rapidly expanding governmental functions the bark of the 'watchdog of the treasury' is not the epitome of political wisdom." [10]

This attempt to make clear that by "economy and efficiency" is not meant, or should not be meant, anything narrow, niggardly, or mechanical has continued down to the present day. Thus L. D. White speaks out on the subject of "the administrative gods, effi-

---

[10] *The New Democracy* (New York), 313 n. (By permission of The Macmillan Co., publishers.) *Cf.* the statement by the New York Bureau of Municipal Research, *Citizen Agencies for Research in Government* (New York: 1916), viii. The ethical meaning of economy and efficiency for the bureau movement is indicated also by Henry Bruere in *The New City Government* (New York: 1912), 5, 103: "It is the gap . . . between needs and services which affords the opportunity for introducing efficiency methods into city government." Others found it necessary to protest at an early date against a too narrow interpretation of economy and efficiency. Thus L. D. Upson: "A most common test of the character of government is economy, although that is no fairer criterion of worth than it is with shoes, furniture, or tobacco. Cheap government is not necessarily good government." "City Manager Plan in Ohio," 9 *Am. Pol. Sci. Rev.* (Aug., 1915), 496–503, 496. *Cf.* W. H. Taft, *Message of the President of the United States on Efficiency and Economy in the Government Service* (Washington: 1912, 62nd Congress, 2nd Session, House Doc. 458), vol. I, 3; W. B. Munro, *Principles and Methods of Municipal Administration* (New York: 1916), ch. 1; E. A. Fitzpatrick, *Budget Making in a Democracy* (New York: 1918), 291–292; M. L. Cooke, *Academic and Industrial Efficiency* (Carnegie Foundation Bulletin, 1910), 70.

ciency and economy," in his dialogue with T. V. Smith on the state of the civic arts: "Don't misunderstand what we administrators mean when we use the shorthand of efficiency and economy. . . . When we say efficiency we think of homes saved from disease, of boys and girls in school prepared for life, of ships and mines protected against disaster. . . . We do not think in terms of gadgets and paper clips alone. And when we talk of economy, we fight waste of all human resources, still much too scanty to meet human needs." [11]

Similarly, J. M. Pfiffner, noting the fact that the research movement in local government has been based generally upon the assumption that the spending of less money by local government is in itself a desirable end, remarks:

> the inherent desirability of lower governmental expenditures is by no means a scientific conclusion, and it may not even be amenable to scientific proof. There are many other value criteria affecting expenditure. There are those who could present rather convincing data in favor of much greater expenditure than has ever been undertaken in public health, education, and recreation.[12]

"Social Efficiency."—In recent years there has been a tendency to speak of "social economy" and "social efficiency," and to contrast these expressions with earlier and narrower usages of economy and efficiency. "Social economy" and "social efficiency" are, indeed, used as instruments for attacking "economy and efficiency." "Present indications are," writes A. C. Millspaugh, "that the 'efficiency and economy' movement has already slipped from primary to secondary significance; not unlike other political remedies which in their day have been confidently prescribed and enthusiastically swallowed." [13] The prevailing movement toward simplification, symmetry, and internal consistency, he believes, "stresses purely administrative, rather than governmental or social, efficiency. It tends to

---

[11] L. D. White and T. V. Smith, *Politics and Public Service* (New York: 1939), 7–8 (by permission of Harper & Bros.). *Cf.* White, *Trends in Public Administration* (New York: 1933), 11.

[12] *Research Methods in Public Administration* (New York: 1940), 19. (The Ronald Press Co.). See also: J. K. Coleman, *State Administration in South Carolina* (New York: 1935), 15; C. A. Dykstra, "Public Administration and Private Business," 14 *Pub. Man.* (April, 1932), 117–119, 118.

[13] "Democracy and Administrative Organization," in *Essays in Political Science* (Baltimore: 1937), J. M. Mathews and J. Hart, eds., 64–73, 65 (citations by permission of Johns Hopkins Press).

The term "social efficiency" appears as early as the Progressive era. *Cf.* L. D. Brandeis, "The Road to Social Efficiency," in *Business—A Profession* (Boston: 1914), 51–64; C. E. Reitzel, "Industrial Output and Social Efficiency," 59 *Annals* (May, 1915), 125–132.

produce immediate and superficial results, instead of, and perhaps at the expense of, ultimate and fundamental values." [14]

In his essay on "The Criteria and Objectives of Public Administration," Marshall Dimock also seeks to leave behind the "mechanical" meaning of efficiency. Any rigid or mechanical interpretation of the term, he believes, is inappropriate because good administration is not coolly mechanical: it is intensely human, warm and vibrant. More than that, "there is no true efficiency which is not also social efficiency." [15]

Efficiency, it is true, is a major objective of public administration, but it must be "socially and humanly interpreted." Efficiency is a matter of quality, and hence "quantitative and mechanical methods of measurements must perforce be far from complete." [16] With his proclamation that "efficiency, like happiness, is subtle," efficiency becomes completely divested of the firm denotative quality once presumed to be its virtue.

The significance of "social efficiency" is clear: it is a convenient symbol for the concept of the Good Life entertained by these administrative writers. This Good Life, we observed in an earlier chapter, is essentially Utilitarian, for its social philosophy can be summarized in the phrase, "the greatest happiness of the greatest number." Far from being a "scientific" term of precise denotation "efficiency," or "social efficiency," is highly charged with emotion, jam-packed with social philosophy. [17]

In addition to those who have used "social efficiency" and "social economy" to attack narrow interpretations of efficiency and economy, there are those who have rejected these concepts outright, at least as primary considerations. Thus C. S. Hyneman finds that the "efficiency and economy" of the reorganizers is addressed primarily to large taxpayers. "There are," he believes, "many grounds for dis-

---

[14] *Ibid.*, 70. See also his *Local Democracy and Crime Control* (Washington: 1936), 244–245.

[15] In *The Frontiers of Public Administration*, (Chicago: 1936), essays by J. M. Gaus, L. D. White, and M. E. Dimock, 116–133, 123. Dimock also has recently spoken out against those who believe that "efficiency and democracy are mutually exclusive. If we keep our perspectives intact, I think we shall see that each strengthens the other and that, separated, they both grow weak." *New Horizons in Public Administration* (University, Alabama: 1945), a symposium, 22.

[16] *Ibid.*, 122. *Cf.* Dimock, "The Study of Administration," 31 *Am. Pol. Sci. Rev.* (Feb., 1937), 28–40, 39.

[17] The "utilitarian" nature of the philosophy is evident in the context. For example, such passages as: "Efficiency is personnel satisfactions. First of all, the employees of the enterprise must be happy in their work. This is an end in itself. After all, society is simply the totality of all the bodies of persons who do the work of the world. Therefore . . . to be efficient you must produce satisfaction. . . ." Dimock, *The Frontiers of Public Administration*, 125 (by permission of University of Chicago Press).

content with American state government besides its inefficiency and wastefulness. What does the administrative reorganization program, designed to achieve efficiency and economy, offer to the man whose chief concern is for certain other qualities in his government—whose chief concern is that vision and courage predominate in the execution, adaptation, or modification of policy?" [18] An organization adapted to *doing* may be quite inadequate in other important respects.

Efficiency as a Concept of Administrative Hygiene.—A quite distinctive treatment of efficiency is that by A. C. Millspaugh in *Crime Control by the National Government*. The science of administration, he says, "is about where medicine would be without pathology."

> Physical diseases were recognized and treated in the morning twilight of recorded history, when nothing to speak of was known about anatomy, physiology, and hygiene. The concept of positive health is a development of our own day; and the rules of hygienic living appear to have evolved largely from the accumulated knowledge of the nature and causes of disease. [19]

In political science, however, "anatomy and physiology, the principles of hygiene, and the concept of positive health were early developments." [20] Plato sketched a Utopia, and we have had many others. Similarly in the study of administration we have been "able to learn without much difficulty the essentials of structure, functions, and operations. We early envisaged an ideal of administrative well-being; and this ideal we have been calling Efficiency." [21]

The student of administration proceeds as a hygienist rather than a pathologist:

> The student of administration feels fairly confident that he has found a number of conditions and factors that are favorable to administrative well-being. So he says to his patient: "I don't know exactly what ails you, if anything does; and I have no sure means of finding out. But, in any case, I can tell you how an administrative organization in your position, in your surroundings, and with your responsibilities ought to be constituted." [22]

---

[18] "Administrative Organization: An Adventure Into Science and Theology," 1 *Jour. of Pol.* (Feb., 1939), 62–75, 66.
[19] Washington: 1937, 235 (citations by permission of The Brookings Institution).
[20] *Idem.*
[21] *Ibid.*, 236.
[22] *Idem.*

This mode of procedure is not wholly ridiculous, but what we urgently need is a study of administrative pathology. We must stop assuming that there is but one uniform type of inefficiency—there are as many kinds as there are varieties of disease.

"Efforts to measure efficiency," continues Millspaugh, "have three ends in view. The first is to determine whether, at any given time, an agency, or a subdivision or employee of it, is doing a satisfactory quantity or quality of work." This pursuit inevitably leads one to the problem of a standard of measurement. "Accordingly, the second purpose of efficiency measurement is to make possible impartial statistical comparisons of separate agencies." Finally, "the third purpose of measurement conceives efficiency in social terms and looks to the ultimate effects of administrative activity." [23]

The Measurement of Efficiency.—In recent years there have been a number of attempts to treat the concepts of economy and efficiency carefully and critically, to sharpen them into working tools. Certainly the most elaborate and perhaps the most incisive analysis of the notion of economy and efficiency occurs in C. E. Ridley's and H. A. Simon's *Measuring Municipal Activities*. Here the authors, attempting to establish measuring techniques upon a firm basis, were inevitably led to inquire with great care into the meanings and interrelations of economy and efficiency.

These writers make a basic distinction between the "adequacy" of a service and the "efficiency" of a service. Adequacy is the "absolute measurement of accomplishment," whereas efficiency is "the accomplishment relative to available resources." It is not the function of an administrator, since human efforts are finite, to establish a Utopia. It is his function to "maximize the attainment of the governmental objectives (assuming that they have been agreed upon), by the efficient employment of the limited resources that are available to him." [24]

Now, "the efficiency of administration is measured by the ratio of the effects actually obtained with the available resources to the maximum effects possible with the available resources." The terms "effect" and "resource" need definition in turn: "The term *effect* as used here includes any effort, performance, or result. The term *resource* as here used comprehends money expenditure, effort, or performance considered as productive of effect." [25] Efficiency, it is

---

[23] *Ibid.,* 237–239.

[24] This and following citations from *Measuring Municipal Activities* (Chicago, 1938) by permission of the International City Managers Association. 3.

[25] *Ibid.* Italicized in original.

concluded, "can therefore be measured at a number of different levels. There is an efficiency of accomplishment of results (1) relative to money expenditure, (2) relative to effort, and (3) relative to performance. There is efficiency of performance (4) relative to expenditure, and (5) relative to effort. Finally, there is efficiency of effort (6) relative to expenditure." [26]

One criticism of this scheme is anticipated: "In defining efficiency the phrase 'maximum effects possible' was employed. In practical situations, it is seldom possible to determine this 'maximum.' But, though it be impossible to measure absolute efficiency, relative efficiencies can be computed, and that is all that is required in practical problems." [27] Relative efficiencies are adequate for the purposes of management.

Efficiency: The "Good" of Public Administration.—One of the most careful treatments of "efficiency" is by Luther Gulick in his essay on "Science, Values and Public Administration."

"In the science of administration," he announces, "whether public or private, the basic 'good' is efficiency. The fundamental objective of the science of administration is the accomplishment of the work in hand with the least expenditure of man-power and materials. Efficiency is thus axiom number one in the value scale of administration." [28] However:

> This brings administration into apparent conflict with certain elements of the value scale of politics, whether we use that term in its scientific or in its popular sense. But both public administration and politics are branches of political science, so that we are in the end compelled to mitigate the pure concept of efficiency in the light of the value scale of politics and the social order. There are, for example, highly inefficient arrangements like citizen boards and small local governments which may be necessary in a democracy as educational devices. . . . It does not seem to the writer, however, that these interferences with efficiency in any way eliminate efficiency as the fundamental value upon which the science of administration may be erected. They serve to condition and to complicate, but not to change the single ultimate test of value in administration.[29]

"If it be true," asks Gulick, "that continual intrusion of varying scales of value has served to hinder the development of all the social

---

[26] *Ibid.*
[27] *Ibid.*
[28] In *Papers on the Science of Administration* (New York: 1937), Gulick and L. Urwick, eds., 191–195, 192 (citations by permission of Institute of Public Administration).
[29] *Ibid.*, 192–193.

sciences, may it not be well to minimize this difficulty. . . ? This, it seems to the writer, is already possible in the study of public administration by regarding all value scales as environmental with the exception of one—efficiency. In this way it may be possible to approximate more nearly the impersonal valueless world in which exact science has advanced with such success." [30]

Efficiency: End or Means?

Having examined these treatments of economy and efficiency, let us ask again the original question: Is it "too hackneyed a phrase to have much meaning nowadays"?

The inquiry can be simplified by eliminating "economy" from detailed consideration. Some who speak of economy mean simply the spending of less money on the objects of administration or on the process of administration. Those who are more "sophisticated" about economy explain that there are different types or degrees of economy, and that "true" economy may mean spending more rather than less money. If they attempt to explain "true" economy they do it *in terms of efficiency*. Efficiency is therefore the fundamental concept.

What is the meaning of efficiency? While dictionaries list seven or eight "meanings" for "efficient" or "efficiency," there are but two fundamental meanings. One of these meanings might be called the philosophical. It is the notion of energy, force, or cause. In giving this meaning such phrases are used as "operating agent or force" and "impelling or efficient cause." [31] The other meaning might be called the mechanical or scientific. Its essence is the idea of proportion or ratio: actual results in comparison to energy expended or to possible results.[32] Clearly "efficient" is used in the literature of public administration in both these senses. Generally they are not distinguished: efficient becomes a synonym for "competent," "productive," "capable." When an attempt is made to use

---

[30] *Ibid.*, 193. *Cf.* W. F. Willoughby, *Principles of Public Administration* (Baltimore: 1927), IX; President's Committee on Administrative Management, *Report* (Washington: 1937), 2; Lewis Meriam and L. F. Schmeckebier, *Reorganization of the National Government: What Does It Involve?* (Washington: 1939), 11; Leslie Lipson, *The American Governor: From Figurehead to Leader* (Chicago: 1939), 245–246.

[31] From *Webster's New International*. The frequent definition of efficient by use of the word "efficient" suggests that it has given the lexicographers some difficulty.

[32] "Effective operation as measured by a comparison of actual and possible results; effectiveness as compared with capacity to perform or with cost in energy, time, money, etc." "The ratio of the energy or work that is obtained from a machine . . . etc., to the energy put in." From the *New International*.

"efficient" with preciseness (*e.g.* Ridley and Simon), the notion of ratio is emphasized.

Efficiency: "Value" by Courtesy.—From the point of view of the thesis that administration is largely or essentially normative—as developed in the preceding chapter—it would seem that the "pure concept of efficiency," proposed by Gulick as the basic "good" of administrative study, is a mirage. For is not the ultimate question "Efficient *for what*"? Is not efficiency for efficiency's sake meaningless? *Is efficiency not necessarily measured in terms of other values?*

Surely it is impossible—or at least immoral—to posit the desirability of accomplishing all purposes efficiently. For some purposes are execrable. Moreover, the proposal to base the "science of administration" upon efficiency is open to the objection that it provides no real differentia for that science. Accomplishment of the "work in hand" with the least possible margin between potentiality and actuality is an important consideration in practically all human endeavors; it is not less true of farming and fan-dancing than of administration.

We hold that efficiency cannot *itself* be a "value." Rather, it operates in the interstices of a value system; it prescribes relationships (ratios or proportions) among parts of the value system; it receives its "moral content" by syntax, by absorption. Things are not simply "efficient" or "inefficient." They are efficient or inefficient for given purposes, and efficiency for one purpose may mean inefficiency for another. For the purpose of killing a bear, for example, a large-bore rifle is more efficient than a bag of meal, but for the purpose of keeping a bear alive, the reverse is true. If we may again paraphrase Robbins' statement about the data of economics, "There is no quality in administrative organizations and procedures taken out of their relation to men's purposes that can make them efficient."

Color of truth is given this analysis by a consideration of the usages of efficiency. Efficiency, as Dimock has observed, "is a mendicant—it begs the question until the auditor can discover the particular connotations the user has in mind." [33] Various persons obviously mean quite different things by "efficiency." And as above noted, there has been an increasing awareness of the moral referents or framework for efficiency; until prefixed with "social" it becomes a short-hand notation for a *Weltanschauung*. If these considera-

[33] *Op. cit.,* 120.

tions are valid, Gulick's proposal to make efficiency "the fundamental value upon which the science of administration may be erected" must be rejected. The very flimsiest structure cannot be erected upon a reflection.

Conciliation of Normative and Objective Efficiency.—But, it is objected, cannot efficiency be used in a purely descriptive manner to designate ratio or proportion, potentiality or effectiveness? Are not particular "means" efficient in and of themselves, without respect to the "ends" or values that they may happen to serve? Is it not ridiculous to suppose that the efficiency of a calculating machine or of a system of double-entry bookkeeping depends upon the purposes of the operators?

How is one to mediate between the "normative" and the "objective" interpretations of efficiency?—for surely the truth must lie between them. We propose this formula: *the descriptive or objective notion of efficiency is valid and useful, but only within a framework of consciously held values.*

It is clear that "efficiency" as a designation for the ratio between energy or potentiality on the one hand, and effects or results on the other hand is legitimate and useful. But it should also be clear that "effects" or "results" is a normative conception. One— or more—of the terms of the ratio is "loaded" with human purpose. If it were not, indeed, for the element of purpose, it would not occur to anyone to apply the notion of ratio to the relations among any particular phenomena.

Consider: Man observes the workings of nature, and some of them—such as the streamlining of the whale—it occurs to him to designate as efficient. Now the relationship between a whale's contours and the energy he expends is presumably "true" irrespective of men's minds. But when we call this relationship "efficient" we are making a judgment *about* that relationship in terms of our own purposes and experiences. And this judgment is *in our minds,* not "out there." The reading of "efficiency" or "inefficiency" into the phenomena of nature is a manner of anthropomorphism.

Or consider the case, say, of an internal combustion engine. From the viewpoint of persons with ends to accomplish, petroleum oil is a more efficient lubricant than graphite, and graphite more efficient than emery powder. This is man's judgment about the facts; so far as we know, the engine, the oil, the graphite, and the emery powder are neutral on the subject. The efficiency of an engine can be accurately computed—*only after the frame of reference for the calculations is fixed.* "Give me a fulcrum upon which to rest my lever—." [34]

Similarly, so long as the frame of reference is made clear, studies of "efficiency" in public administration are possible and useful. At least computations can be made that will serve many of our purposes. It may not even be necessary for us to agree upon what efficiency is "in essence" in order to take its measure for purposes upon which we agree. Man measures many things—such as time—the nature of which he has not fathomed.

The Idea of a Hierarchy of Purposes

The concept of *a hierarchy of purposes* may be of value in mediating between the normative and the descriptive aspects of efficiency. At least it holds the promise of being a useful "pragmatic" tool in dealing with efficiency.

The proposal can be stated in the form of a series of theses: that efficiency can be measured at various "levels" of human purpose; that on the "lower levels" the purposes of various individuals and groups are much the same, but that there is increasingly important disparity in purposes entertained, values pursued, in the "higher levels"; that the "efficiency" of various instruments and procedures at the lower levels of purpose is likely to be the same or nearly the same for various persons and groups, because the purposes are the same or nearly the same, *i.e.* the frame of reference is constant; but that in the higher levels of human purpose the "efficiency" of various instruments and procedures tends to differ because the purposes differ significantly—the frame of reference is not constant. Human purposes range—to go no lower—from the irrational urge to scratch an itch to the noblest promptings of humanitarianism and religion. The measurement of efficiency must take cognizance of this fact.

In practice, the proposed scheme means that the efficiency of various instruments and procedures of a mechanical and routine nature, those that serve "unimportant" purposes *or that serve ends that are important only in terms of other or higher ends,* will be approximately constant in all organizations; but that the less mechanical and routine the instruments and procedures, and the more important *or more nearly ultimate* the purposes they serve, the less likely is

---

[34] The "relativity" of efficiency in terms, not only of purpose, but also of alternate methods or instruments and of historical change, has not been adequately explored. What finality can be given to a measurement of the efficiency of an administrative device when that measurement takes place in a unique historical context? Is the true efficiency of a tool reduced by the invention of a "better" tool for the same purpose?

their efficiency to be constant. The efficiency of a given typewriter under given operating conditions is the same for all organizations. It is the same for the Eureka Shoe Company as for Field Headquarters of the British Army or for the office staff of the *Daily Worker*. It is the same because the immediate purpose is the same: the production of typewritten words. It is equally clear that the efficiency of a given "span of control" or of a given scheme of centralized purchasing would *not* be the same for these organizations.[35]

Recognition of the hierarchical or pyramidal relationship of the values that men entertain will enable students of administration to make both more accurate and more significant studies in efficiency. Efficiency, it was concluded above, can be measured only in terms of purpose. If one part of the ratio is unknown or obscure, the measurement cannot be accurate. Statement by a student of the "level" upon which he is proceeding, of the frame of reference which he accepts, will enable others to appraise his results and articulate their studies with his.

We suggest in closing that the notion of a "pyramid of values" may be of value in evolving a new philosophy of the relationship of the student of administration to his subject matter. We have observed how the "politics-administration" dichotomy sprang up to provide the basis for this philosophy, how it caused confusion and contradiction, how it has been increasingly rejected as unrealistic. Through the idea of a "pyramid of values," the rigid division between "politics" and "administration" is replaced by an organic interrelation.[36] This concept recognizes as valid what most students of administration have strongly felt: that there is a realm of "science" where "objectivity" is possible and "efficiency" can be measured. On the other hand, it takes cognizance of the fact that, increasingly, as one's frame of reference widens and disagreement about ends becomes important, "science" and "objectivity" are more difficult, judgments of "efficiency" less accurate, more controversial.

---

[35] "Internal" or "circumstantial" proof for these reflections may be found in the literature of public administration: those convinced of the fundamentality or objectivity of efficiency measurments have chosen their examples from the lower "mechanical" levels of administration; those who have sought to reject or enlarge the concept of efficiency have chosen their examples from the "higher" aspects of administration.

[36] An essentially "pyramidal" view is expressed in Gulick's "Politics, Administration, and the New Deal," 169 *Annals* (Sept., 1933), 55–66, 61, in his critique of traditional politics-administration philosophy. The "pyramidal" viewpoint is also given in Ridley and Simon's conclusion that efficiency can be "measured at a number of different levels." Harvey Pinney's essay "Institutionalizing Administrative Controls" also discusses the measurement of efficiency in terms of proceeding "from the objective to the more subjective levels." 38 *Am. Pol. Sci. Rev.* (Feb., 1944), 79–88, 79 ff.

Chapter 11

CONCLUSION: NOTES ON THE PRESENT
TENDENCIES

Students of administration, writes J. M. Gaus, have become "more uncertain in recent years as to the ends, aims and methods which they should advocate." It is difficult to view in their entirety and in perspective the writings on public administration that now pour from the presses. But this is hardly necessary to confirm the truth of Gaus' statement.

The situation at present is this: there is a large core of "orthodox" public administration ideology, but also a considerable measure of doubt and even iconoclasm; an increasing disposition to engage in empirical or functional studies in which theoretical postulates are obscure and perhaps denied, but also a number of foci of theoretical activity of great potential importance; and a number of theoretical problems that should be recognized, clearly stated, and competently treated. The field at present shows much evidence of vigor and growth, and considerable progress in criticism, synthesis, and creative thought can confidently be predicted.[1]

At the heart of "orthodox" ideology is the postulate that true democracy and true efficiency are synonymous, or at least reconcilable. Clustered about this postulate are a number of formulae for effecting this reconciliation. Another important doctrine is the politics-administration formula; the notion that the work of government is divisible into two parts, decision and execution, and that execution (administration) is or can be made a science. "Science,"

---

[1] There have been many evidences of a thirst for philosophy in recent years, and not a few invitations to students of political theory to join in broadening public administration. But any fruitful cross-fertilization will take considerable time and awaits development of a "philosophy for the philosophers." For the "political theorists" have also become objective, scientific; they are now in the position of the art-museum curator of cartoon humor, who "knows all about art, but doesn't know what he likes." Students of administration have generally been unread in the history of political thought, but they have had no doubts about "what they like." Students of theory can offer "sophistication" to students of administration, but they have a long way to go before they can offer much positive assistance with fundamental problems, such as the relationship of administration to democracy, or to science. Cf. Donald Morrison, "Public Administration and the Art of Governance," 5 *Pub. Adm. Rev.* (Winter, 1945), 83–87, 85, on the divorce of "theory" from "administration"—with mutual stultification.

to the orthodox, connotes fact-finding, rejection of theory, and perhaps Pragmatism. The notion that there are "principles," scientifically and ethically valid, that can be uncovered by scientific study, is also still an orthodox tenet. And students of administration remain generally of the opinion that the values and practices of American business can be accepted for governmental administration with only slight reservations.

There is an area of explicit doubt and skepticism about all of these tenets except the first: that true democracy and true efficiency are reconcilable. This is so fundamental that, by definition, it could hardly be denied by an American writer on public administration. But critical thinking has taken place even here, in the form of a broadening or rejection of the original *definitions* of democracy and efficiency. Concerning "politics-administration," doubt has arisen about both the possibility and the desirability of making a sharp separation of power or division of function between the deciding and the executing agencies of government. Thinking about the nature and imperatives of "science" and "principles" becomes increasingly more critical, more subtle. And there are those who would remodel extensively the historical structure—organization and procedures—of American business, as well as that of governmental administration, in the name of Democracy, or for the sake of giving the Expert his proper role.

One of the most obvious features of recent writing on public administration is its large volume and wide scope, together with an increasing tendency to specialized, factual or "empirical" studies. This increasing specialization is perhaps normal and desirable, representing healthy progress in the discipline. Much of the specialization, however, is in the functional aspects of administration, rather than in its institutional aspects. This fact, together with the sheer volume and increasing diversity of institutional study, poses in a very acute form the problem whether there is a study of administration "as such"; at least whether there is a "function of administration," as such, in which training or specialization is possible.

In view of recent tendencies it is pertinent to ask of those who are digging ever deeper into the "stuff" of administration, whose object is to present a section of unvarnished administrative truth or criticism of naive "principles," this question: Have you not gone too far in rejecting "principle" and embracing an uncritical empiricism? In some sectors the pertinent question is whether sophistication has become cynicism, whether in rejecting nineteenth-century concepts of "principles" the purpose or theory that must enlighten

and inform any significant inquiry has not also been denied. Without faith or purpose, individuals or societies stagnate.[2]

The future of administrative theory is dependent, of course, upon
what happens in the world at large, and particularly what happens in
and to these United States. Whether the One World for which we
poured out our treasure of life and goods becomes Two Worlds
and then, one day, No World—this is the First Fact. If new forms
and methods of international—or "world"—cooperation do develop,
administrative thinking will be turned in new directions (although
to date the considerable amount of "international" writings on
administration is generally characterized by a pedestrian, earth-
bound quality[3]). Upon the success of our business civilization in
meeting the extraordinary economic and social stresses of postwar
readjustment depends the course of much future thinking. In one
way or another the development and use of atomic energy will have
effects reaching to the very foundations of administrative thought.
But before its implications can even be projected in imagination it
is necessary for the thinking organism to recover from the shock
of so fundamental and spectacular a fact. Administrative thought
will affect, as well as reflect, the future events. But it will not be
one of the Prime Forces, at least in the near future. The number
of its devotees and the range of its influence, are too limited. It is
only now freeing itself from a strait jacket of its own devising—
the instrumentalist philosophy of the politics-administration formula
—that has limited its breadth and scope.

Whatever the far-reaching implications of world cooperation and
atomic energy may be, the Second Great War's aftermath of chaos
and ill will seems likely to have more important effects upon administrative thinking in the short run. Two observations as to these
effects may be hazarded. The first is that, since crises usually result
in centralization and integration of authority, we may expect a
strengthening of the currents of centralization and integration [4]—

---

[2] "Perhaps our sorest lack is doctrine in the theological sense to govern the flow
of cooperative energies in a free commonwealth." F. Morstein Marx, "The Lawyer's Role in Public Administration," 55 *Yale Law Jour.* (April, 1946), 498–526,
503.

[3] The barrier between politics and administration, though being destroyed in the
domestic field, is almost completely intact in our thinking about international matters. Urgently needed is some hard, creative thinking in the area lying between advanced administrative thought and advanced thinking on the future of world politics,
represented—in my opinion—by E. H. Carr's *Nationalism—And After* (New York:
1945).

[4] See, however, J. M. Gaus, "A Job Analysis of Political Science," 40 *Am. Pol.
Sci. Rev.* (April, 1946), 217–230, 224–225, on possible "decentralizing" effects of
atomic-bomb rivalry. "I found myself . . . turning again to materials on regional

at least in comparison to what might have been the case had the end of the war brought with it "peace" and "normalcy." The second is in some sense the converse of the first: the success of the movement to decentralize and "democratize" administration depends upon the subsidence of threats to the security of America. Whatever force there is in the socialist belief that "you can't build socialism in one country" applies similarly to democracy.

In addition to economic, political, and social events that will influence the future of administrative thought, there are a number of movements and personalities that at present are impinging on administrative thinking and may give it content and direction in the future. Some of these have been discussed above; others lie at present so far from main channels that they have been, at most, only mentioned.

Perhaps most important of the theoretical movements now influencing American administrative study is scientific management. At the level of technique or procedure, borrowing from and liaison with scientific management will undoubtedly continue. Although some doctrines, such as "pure theory of organization," have already affected public administration, how influential other theoretical aspects of scientific management will be remains to be seen. In its "democratic" or "anarchistic" doctrines, conceivably, there is enough force to reconstruct present patterns of administrative thought, at least if conditions become favorable. M. L. Cooke,[5] Ordway Tead,[6] Henri Fayol,[7] Oliver Sheldon,[8] Lyndall Urwick,[9] and Elton Mayo [10]

centers, on the future role of state governments, on state capitals as contrasted with regional centers, on the experience of Great Britain during the war with regional commissioners, and a plexus of problems in political geography, comparative government, and administration."

[5] I refer particularly to his more recent essays. See especially, "Notes on Governmental and Industrial Administration in a Democracy," 3 *Soc. Adv. Man. Jour.* (July–Sept., 1938), 139–143.

[6] Various of his books, but especially, *New Adventures in Democracy* (New York: 1939), and *Democratic Administration* (New York: 1945). *Cf.* "What Is a Democratic Approach to Economic Problems?" 165 *Annals* (Jan., 1933), 101–108; "Is Industrial Self-Government Possible?" 5 *Advanced Management* (Jan.–Mar., 1940), 21–25.

[7] *Industrial and General Administration* (London: 1930), trans. J. A. Coubrough.

[8] *The Philosophy of Management* (London: 1924). This is widely cited, but it does not appear that all the juice is yet squeezed from it.

[9] Urwick's writings are very stimulating, deserve close attention. *Cf. Management of Tomorrow* (London: 1933); "A Republic of Administration," 13 *Jour. Pub. Adm.* (July 1935), 263–271; "Executive Decentralization with Functional Coordination," 13 *Jour. Pub. Adm.* (Oct., 1935), 344–358; "Bureaucracy and Democracy," 14 *Jour. Pub. Adm.* (April, 1936), 134–142; "An Industrial Esperanto," 14 *Bull. Taylor Soc.* (July, 1929), 150–153; "The Problem of Organization: A Study of the Work of Mary Parker Follett," 1 *Bull. Taylor Soc. and Soc. Indust. Engineers* (July, 1935), 163–169.

[10] Particularly, *The Human Problems of an Industrial Civilization* (New York: 1933).

may be mentioned as among the more prominent of those associated with the scientific management movement whose writings may possibly affect the future of public administration—as they have already in some degree. Several of these persons have been influenced by the philosophy of Mary Parker Follett. This is not the place to embark upon a discussion of her theories, but an understanding of some present tendencies must depend upon a reading of her works, as well as those of the more reflective scientific managers.

It is possible—though it appears at present unlikely—that Pragmatic philosophy may play a larger role in the future than in the past. In recent essays by Horace S. Fries,[11] for example, an attempt is made to demonstrate that Pragmatism (of the Dewey variety) is not only the philosophy of science, but the proper vehicle for expanding "democracy" in both scientific management and public administration.

The probability that the recent influx of foreign, especially continental, students of administration will exert a measurable influence over theoretical development has been touched upon above. Of the simple *fact* of influence there can be no doubt, but it is yet too early to state with any certainty what will be its force.

The problem of the place of the expert in a democratic society, particularly the expert in "things-in-general" cannot be regarded as having been satisfactorily treated,[12] and will probably continue to engage the attention of administrative writers. The problem is perhaps too broad to be solved by a few thinkers in a short period of time. The answer should evolve out of experience and the gradual reconstruction of our theory by thinkers in many fields.

Closely related is the problem of providing adequate preparation and a "philosophy" for our administrators. Are training in the mechanics of administration and codes of professional ethics enough? Or should our new Guardian Class be given an education commensurate with their announced responsibilities and perhaps be imbued with a political philosophy? The present gap between the content of our administrative curricula and what we announce to be the

---

[11] "Some Democratic Implications of Science in Scientific Management," 4 *Advanced Management* (Oct.–Dec., 1940), 147–152; "Liberty and Science," 3 *Pub. Adm. Rev.* (Summer, 1943), 268–273. Fries' essays are profound statements of a legitimate viewpoint. But this viewpoint is to me as unsatisfying as the Hindu cosmology—and for the same reason.

[12] In an Introduction to Scudder Klyce's *Universe* (Winchester, Mass., 1921) M. L. Cooke expresses the opinion that Klyce's work provides a philosophical justification for the exercise of power by technical experts. I cannot comment on this, as I am unable to understand Klyce's strange work.

responsibilities of our Administrators is appalling.[13] Presuming that we are in the midst of some sort of "managerial revolution,"[14] can we say that either the problem of our philosophy *about* managers or the proper philosophy *for* managers, has been satisfactorily treated?

The problem of the philosophy that our Administrators entertain is intimately related, in turn, to that of the adequacy of "theory of organization." The question is this: Are students of administration trying to solve the problems of human cooperation on too low a plane? Have they, by the double process of regarding more and more formal data over a wider and wider field of human organization, lost insight, penetration? Is formal analysis of organizations without regard to the purposes that inspire them but a tedious elaboration of the insignificant?

The main tenets of the public administration movement emerged in the decades preceding 1914; they crystallized into a general political theory in the Progressive years. This "orthodox" point of view is by no means an unchallenged faith; but generally, it is still gospel in our schools, at least in undergraduate courses. Perhaps the tenets of orthodoxy still represent the "truth" for our time and our needs. Assuredly, their air of certainty and stability appeals to the emotions in these days of crisis and confusion. But the apparent likelihood of a disintegration of the old outlook and the synthesis of a new

---

[13] Speaking in 1945 to the Washington Chapter of the American Society for Public Administration, Herbert Emmerick listed as first among the administrative lessons of the war the failure of our administrative curricula to produce adequate line administrators, as distinguished from persons trained to do housekeeping and staff work. To the same effect see M. E. Dimock, "Administrative Efficiency within a Democratic Polity," in *New Horizons in Public Administration* (University, Alabama: 1945), a symposium, 21–43, 41–42.

[14] James Burnham's *The Managerial Revolution* (New York: 1941) is perhaps a significant book. It is not, however, within the scope of this essay. In terms of Burnham's treatment, the literature with which this study is concerned would be the ideological trappings of the new ruling group.

The fundamental defect of Burnham's book, the reviewers have emphasized, is that, despite the fact that the argument is set forth as a refutation of orthodox socialism, it is essentially Marxian. Burnham, that is to say, has a Marxian past, and the characteristic vices of that habit of mind are carried over—the neat black and white categorizing, the itch for simplicity, the presumption of omniscience, the proclamation of inevitability. Burnham simply puts new wine in the old Marxian bottles. (In his more recent *The Struggle for the World* (New York: 1947), in fact, he performs the feat of turning the Marxian approach against the Marxists.) For an essentially Marxian refutation of Burnham's "Marxism" see "The Technicians and the New Society," ch. 14 in *Strategy for Democracy* (New York: 1942), J. Donald Kingsley and David W. Petegorsky. This is an interesting essay, discussing the general failure of left-wing movements of all kinds to recognize the need for "management" to achieve their objectives and the means by which a bureaucracy can be made to serve the ends of a "democratic collectivist state."

must be recognized. In any event, if abandonment of the politics-administration formula is taken seriously, if the demands of present world civilization upon public administration are met, administrative thought must establish a working relationship with every major province in the realm of human learning.

SELECTED BIBLIOGRAPHY

The items in this bibliography have been selected because of their unusual importance in tracing the development of American administrative theory. It would be useless to repeat here the hundreds of titles on limited topics cited in the text.

BOOKS, PAMPHLETS, REPORTS

Allen, W. H., *Efficient Democracy* (New York: Dodd, Mead & Co., Inc., 1907).

Anderson, William, and Gaus, J. M., *Research in Public Administration* (Chicago: Public Administration Service, 1945).

Appleby, Paul H., *Big Democracy* (New York: Alfred A. Knopf, 1945).

Beard, Chas. A., *Government Research, Past, Present and Future* (New York: Municipal Administration Service, 1926).

———, *Philosophy, Science and Art of Public Administration* (Address delivered before the annual conference of the Governmental Research Association, Princeton, N. J., Sept. 8, 1939).

———, "The Role of Administration in Government," in *The Work Unit in Federal Administration* (Chicago: Public Administration Service, 1937—a collection of papers), 1–3.

Bruere, H. J., *The New City Government* (New York: D. Appleton & Co., 1912).

Buck, A. E., *The Reorganization of State Governments in the United States* (New York: Published for the National Municipal League by the University of Columbia Press, 1938. See also previous editions).

Caldwell, Lynton K., *The Administrative Theories of Hamilton and Jefferson: Their Contributions to Thought on Public Administration* (Chicago: University of Chicago Press, 1944).

Cleveland, F. A., *Organized Democracy* (New York: Longmans, Green & Co., 1913).

———, *The War—Its Practical Lessons to Democracy* (A paper read before the National Municipal League at a conference held in Detroit, Nov. 22, 1917. Boston? 1917?).

———, and Buck, A. E., *The Budget and Responsible Government* (New York: The Macmillan Co., 1920).

Cooke, M. L., *Our Cities Awake* (Garden City: Doubleday, Page & Co., 1918).

Dimock, M. E., *Modern Politics and Administration* (New York: American Book Co., 1937).

Fairlie, J. A., "Public Administration and Administrative Law," in *Essays on the Law and Practice of Governmental Administration*, C. G. Haines and M. E. Dimock, eds. (Baltimore: The Johns Hopkins Press, 1935), 3–43.

Gaus, J. M., *Reflections on Public Administration* (University, Alabama: University of Alabama Press, 1947).

———, *A Study of Research in Public Administration* (Published in mimeographed form; a study prepared for the Advisory Committee on Public Administration of the Social Science Research Council, 1930).

———, White, L. D., and Dimock, M. E., *The Frontiers of Public Administration* (Chicago: University of Chicago Press, 1936—a series of essays).

Goodnow, F. J., *Politics and Administration* (New York: The Macmillan Co., 1900).

Gulick, Luther, and Urwick, Lyndall, eds., *Papers on the Science of Administration* (New York: Institute of Public Administration, 1937).

Herring, E. P., *Public Administration and the Public Interest* (New York: McGraw-Hill Book Co., Inc., 1936).

Holcombe, A. N., *Government in a Planned Democracy* (New York: W. W. Norton & Co., Inc., 1935).

Leighton, Alexander H., *The Governing of Men: General Principles and Recommendations Based on Experience at a Japanese Relocation Camp* (Princeton: Princeton University Press, 1945).

Meriam, Lewis, and Schmeckebier, Lawrence, *Reorganization of the National Government: What Does It Involve?* (Washington: The Brookings Institution, 1939).

Merriam, Charles E., *The New Democracy and the New Despotism* (New York: McGraw-Hill Book Co., Inc., 1939).

———, *On the Agenda of Democracy* (Cambridge, Mass., Harvard University Press, 1941).

———, *Public and Private Government* (New Haven: Yale University Press for Indiana University, 1944).

Metcalf, Henry C., and Urwick, Lyndall, eds., *Dynamic Administration: The Collected Papers of Mary Parker Follet* (New York: Harper & Bros., 1942).

Millspaugh, A. C., "Democracy and Administrative Organization," in *Essays in Political Science,* J. M. Mathews and James Hart, eds. (Baltimore: The Johns Hopkins Press, 1937), 64–73.

———, *Democracy, Efficiency, Stability: An Appraisal of American Government* (Washington: The Brookings Institution, 1942).

Morstein Marx, F., ed., *Elements of Public Administration* (New York: Prentice-Hall, Inc., 1946).

———, ed., *Public Management in the New Democracy* (New York: Harper & Bros., 1940).

Mosher, W. E., *Adjusting the Sights for Public Administration* (Presidential address delivered at a joint session of the annual conferences of the American Political Science Association and the American Society for Public Administration at Chicago, Ill., Dec. 28, 1940; published in pamphlet form and in part in *Public Management,* Jan., 1941).

National Municipal League, *A Municipal Program* (New York: Published for the National Municipal League by The Macmillan Co., 1900).

New York Bureau of Municipal Research, *The Constitution and Government of the State of New York: An Appraisal* (New York: Bureau of Municipal Research, 1915).

Pfiffner, J. M., *Municipal Administration* (New York: The Ronald Press Co., 1940).

———, *Public Administration* (New York: The Ronald Press Co., 1935). Rev. ed., 1946.

President's Committee on Administrative Management, *Report with Special Studies* (Washington: Government Printing Office, 1937).

Ridley, C. E., and Simon, H. A., *Measuring Municipal Activities* (Chicago: The International City Managers' Association, 1938).

Stone, H. A., Price, D. K., and Stone, K. H., *City Manager Government in the United States* (Chicago: Public Administration Service, 1940).

Walker, Harvey, *Public Administration in the United States* (New York: Farrar & Rinehart, Inc., 1937).

Wallace, Schuyler C., *Federal Departmentalization: A Critique of Theories of Organization* (New York: Columbia University Press, 1941).

White, L. D., "Administration, Public," in 1 *Encyclopedia of the Social Sciences* (1933), 440–449.

——, *The Future of Government in the United States* (Chicago: University of Chicago Press, 1942), containing essays by White, V. O. Key, J. P. Harris, and J. A. Vieg.

——, *Introduction to the Study of Public Administration* (New York: The Macmillan Co., 1939).

——, *et al., New Horizons in Public Administration: A Symposium* (University, Alabama: University of Alabama Press, 1945).

Willoughby, W. F., *Principles of Public Administration* (Washington: The Brookings Institution, 1927).

——, "The Science of Public Administration," in *Essays in Political Science,* J. M. Mathews and James Hart, eds. (Baltimore: The Johns Hopkins Press, 1937), 39–63.

PERIODICALS

Ascher, Charles S., "Organization (Mercator's Projection)," 3 *Public Administration Review* (Autumn, 1943), 360–364.

Barnett, Vincent M., "Modern Constitutional Development: A Challenge to Administration," 4 *Public Administration Review* (Spring, 1944), 159–164.

Beard, Chas. A., "The Place of Administration in Government," 2 *Plan Age* (Dec., 1936), 5–10.

——, "Reconstructing State Government," 4 *New Republic* (Aug. 21, 1915, Supplement), Part II, 1–16.

Brownlow, Louis, "Democracy and Council-Manager Government," 18 *Public Management* (Nov., 1936), 325–328.

Coker, W. F., "Dogmas of Administrative Reform," 16 *American Political Science Review* (Aug., 1922), 399–411.

Dahl, Robert A., "The Science of Public Administration: Three Problems," 7 *Public Administration Review* (Winter, 1947), 1–11.

Dimock, M. E., "The Study of Administration," 31 *American Political Science Review* (Feb., 1937), 28–40.

——, "What Is Public Administration?" 15 *Public Management* (Sept., 1933), 259–262.

Finer, Herman, "Principles as a Guide to Management," 17 *Public Management* (Oct., 1935), 287–289.

Fries, Horace S., "Liberty and Science," 3 *Public Administration Review* (Summer, 1943), 268–273.

Gaus, J. M., "The Present Status of the Study of Public Administration," 25 *American Political Science Review* (Feb., 1931), 120–134.

Gulick, Luther, "Politics, Administration, and the New Deal," 169 *Annals* (Sept., 1933), 55–66.

Hyneman, C. S., "Executive-Administrative Power and Democracy," 2 *Public Administration Review* (Autumn, 1942), 332–338.

Key, V. O., "The Lack of a Budgetary Theory," 34 *American Political Science Review* (Dec., 1940), 1137–1144.

Levitan, David M., "Political Ends and Administrative Means," 3 *Public Administration Review* (Autumn, 1943), 353–359.

Leys, Wayne A. R., "Ethics and Administrative Discretion," 3 *Public Administration Review* (Winter, 1943), 10–23. (By a philosopher who had been told that "administrators need some philosophical insights.")

Merriam, Chas. E., "Public Administration and Political Theory," 5 *Journal of Social Philosophy* (July, 1940), 293–308. (Printed also in 5 *Advanced Management* (July–Sept., 1940), 130–138, under the title "The Development of Theory for Administration.")

Morrison, Donald, "Public Administration and the Art of Governance," 5 *Public Administration Review* (Winter, 1945), 83–87.

Morstein Marx, F., "The Lawyer's Role in Public Administration," 55 *The Yale Law Journal* (April, 1946), 498–526.

Pearson, Norman M., "Fayolism as the Necessary Complement of Taylorism," 39 *American Political Science Review* (Feb., 1945), 68–80.

Simon, Herbert A., "The Proverbs of Administration," 6 *Public Administration Review* (Winter, 1946), 53–67.

Spicer, G. W., "Relation of the Short Ballot to Efficient Government and Popular Control," 11 *Southwestern Political and Social Science Quarterly* (Sept., 1930), 182–192.

Stene, E. O., "An Approach to a Science of Public Administration," 34 *American Political Science Review* (Dec., 1940), 1124–1137.

Vieg, John A., "Democracy and Bureaucracy," 4 *Public Administration Review* (Summer, 1944), 247–252.

Walker, Harvey, "An American Conception of Public Administration," 11 *Journal of Public Administration* (Jan., 1933), 15–19.

Walker, Robert A., "Public Administration: The Universities and the Public Service," 39 *American Political Science Review* (Oct., 1945), 926–933.

Wilson, Woodrow, "The Study of Public Administration," 2 *Political Science Quarterly* (June, 1887), 197–222.

NAME INDEX

SUBJECT INDEX

Secular spirit, as characteristic of modern public administration, 23

Self-consciousness, gift of, as academic contribution to public administration, 26–27

Senate Select Committee to Investigate Executive Agencies of the Government with a View to Co-ordination, 119

Separation of powers, attitude of American reformism toward, 36; and attention by administrative students, 104; attitude toward by reformism and political science, 105ff; Goodnow's treatment, 106–111; classic treatments by public administration, 106ff; appraisal of Goodnow's theories, 111–112; Goodnow's theories, 106–111; Willoughby's theories, 111–114; "orthodox" theory on, 113ff; appraisal of Willoughby's theories, 114; contrary interpretations of in public administration, 115ff; and anomaly of elected chief executive, 115–116; theories of President's Committee on, 117–118; theories of "Brookings" on, 118–120; "legalist" theories of J. M. Landis on, 120–121; rise of recent "heterodox" theories, 121ff; theories of Luther Gulick on, 123–125; new theories, 123ff; as adjustment to actual circumstances, 124–125; and "administrative politics," 125–126; and the role of the chief executive, 126–127; "responsibility" in relation to, 127; and "dogmas of centralization," 131ff (*See also* Politics and administration, Administrators, Functionalism)

"Social efficiency," 196–197

Socialism, in relation to public administration, 70

Society for the Advancement of Management, 55

"Solidarity," social, as aspect of scientific management, 51

Span of control, measurement of efficiency of, 205

"Specialist in generalization," in relation to advance in specialization, 9; in relation to separation of powers, 126 (*See also* "Administrators," "Ruling class")

Specialization, advance of, in relation to rise of public administration, 9–10

Specialization of function, and Division of labor, 104

Spoils system, in relation to constitutional system, 8

State government, related to public administration as a field of study, 24

Taylor Society, compared to Sacred College of the Apostles, 48, cited, 61n

Technocracy, in relation to scientific management, 48

Theory of organization, characterized, 153, 173ff; and rationalism, 173–174; "pragmatic" opposition to, 175

Training movement, setting of, in America, 31; in relation to rise of public administration, 30–31

Tuck School Conference, first, cited, 61n

T.V.A., 149–150

United States Tariff Commission, rationale of, 80

Urbanism, and Good Life for public administration, 66, 73

Urbanization, effect of on rise of public administration, 7

Utilitarianism, compared as a movement to public administration, 22; similarity to public administration in reception of "business," 42; as an aspect of public administration, 71; as movement similar to public administration, 77–78; compared with Positivism, 80; and "social efficiency," 197

Utopias, in relation to the "Good Life," 65

Values, and the idea of principles, 170ff; and scientific method, 181; in economics, 183–184; exclusion from public administration, 188n; as related to economy and efficiency, 200ff

War (*See* First Great War, Second Great War)

"Who should rule?", literature on, characterized, 100–101; inadequate treatment of problem, 101–102

World of Tomorrow Futurama, as illustrating Good Life in public administration, 66

World-View, of scientific management, 52–53